THE NEW POLITICS OF
PORNOGRAPHY

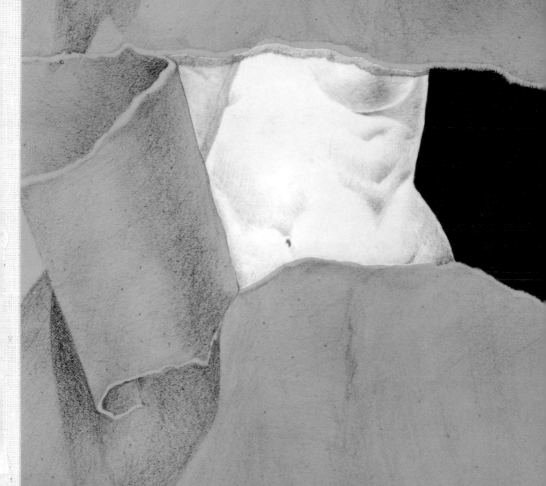

Donald Alexander Downs

THE NEW POLITICS OF
PORNOGRAPHY

THE NEW POLITICS OF
PORNOGRAPHY

Donald Alexander Downs

THE UNIVERSITY OF CHICAGO PRESS

CHICAGO   LONDON

DONALD ALEXANDER DOWNS is associate professor of political science at the University of Wisconsin at Madison. He is the author of *Nazis in Skokie: Freedom, Community, and the First Amendment.*

The University of Chicago Press, Chicago 60637
The University of Chicago Press, Ltd., London
© 1989 by The University of Chicago
All rights reserved. Published 1989
Printed in the United States of America
98 97 96 95 94 93 92 91 90 89   5 4 3 2 1

Library of Congress Cataloging-in-Publication Data

Downs, Donald Alexander.
   The new politics of pornography / Donald A. Downs.
      p.   cm.
   Bibliography: p.
   Includes index.
   1. Obscenity (Law)—United States. 2. Obscenity (Law—Minnesota—Minneapolis. 3. Obscenity (Law)—Indiana—Indianapolis.
4. Pornography—United States. 5. Pornography—Minnesota—Minneapolis. 6. Pornography—Indiana—Indianapolis. I. Title.
KF9444.D69   1989
344.73'0547—dc20
[347.304547]   89-34968
   ISBN 0-226-16162-5 (cloth)   CIP
         0-226-16163-3 (paper)

To my students at the University of Wisconsin. Redirecting
Henry Adams, students can never tell where their influence stops.

Be careful, lest in casting out your devil you cast out the best that is in you.

Nietzsche

CONTENTS

vii

CONTENTS

ACKNOWLEDGMENTS

I would like to thank several people who helped me in this project. First, the staff at the University of Chicago Press who showed noteworthy patience and fortitude in seeing the work through to its conclusion. I am very grateful and hope that the result comes close to justifying their commitment.

I am grateful to the Graduate Research Committee at the University of Wisconsin for providing the financial assistance in 1987 that enabled the project to proceed. I am also grateful to my colleagues at Wisconsin, who have created an environment that is conducive to intellectual production. In particular, Joel Grossman and Richard Champagne have assisted me. Joel has been everything a senior mentor could be, and the patience and worthy contributions that he provided are most appreciated. Rick discussed the pornography issue with me many times, and offered invaluable insights concerning law and politics. Rick has been everything a junior colleague could be.

Finally, I would like to express my gratitude to the many students I have been fortunate enough to teach at the University of Wisconsin, to whom I dedicate this book. My students have constantly renewed my interest and curiosity, redeeming the academic life.

INTRODUCTION

Pornography and Free Speech under Fire

In December 1983, two nationally prominent feminist activists, Catharine MacKinnon and Andrea Dworkin, stood before the largely liberal Minneapolis City Council poised to initiate an extraordinary public hearing on the anti-pornography ordinance they had authored. The measure represented a new approach to the restriction of erotic materials, defining pornography as "the sexually explicit subordination of women, graphically or in words." [1] Treating pornography as "discrimination against women," it was to be administered by the city's Civil Rights Commission rather than by the Criminal Justice Division, the traditional unit of enforcement. This approach departed from the legal treatment of sexual materials that has prevailed for more than a century in the United States. Where previous "obscenity law" focused on the alleged moral harms wrought by certain sexual materials, the new ordinance postulated a social relationship between pornography and the systematic oppression of women. And where obscenity doctrine held back from designating sexually explicit material as obscene if its dominant theme gave it "serious literary, artistic, political, or scientific value," [2] the new ordinance admitted no such delimitation in determining whether a work was pornographic.

The new ordinance also departed from more general First Amendment doctrine, which stipulates that speech cannot be restricted because of its political or social implications. The measure pointed to the political and social meaning of pornography and pornography's role in perpetuating the subordinate status of women in society. Drawing on aspects of contemporary feminist thought, it construed pornography as a form of group libel and argued that pornography should be restricted in order to protect the reputation and image of women. The ordinance also took note of the social and environmental influences on individual choice and action, and pointed to the responsibility of the individual to others.[3] It also drew on recent psychological research, suggesting that certain violent forms of pornography influence the reason and self control of the male consumer and condition him to associate sex with violence. Pornography thus shares the blame for sexual violence with those who actually attempt or commit sexual assault. Accordingly, in one of its most ambitious and important sections, the Minneapolis ordinance provided for civil action against pornography and pornographers if plaintiffs could demonstrate that a specific sexual assault resulted from an attacker's exposure to such material—a provision that would have returned the law governing sexual depictions to legal norms that have been abandoned in the modern era. MacKinnon introduced the ordinance by describing its central tenets:

> As the Committee knows, Andrea Dworkin and I are here today to discuss with you the proposed ordinance which we have drafted together under contract with the City to define pornography as what it is, that is to say as a violation of the Civil Rights of Women. We are proposing for your consideration a statutory scheme that will situate pornography as a central practice in the subordination of women. . . .
> The understanding and the evidence which we will present to you today to support defining pornography as a practice of discrimination on the basis of sex is a new idea . . . In particular we want to show how the concept of pornography conditions and determines the way in which men actually treat women . . . and we will show that it is central to the way in which women remain second-class citizens.[4]

Over the course of the next two days, witnesses from a variety of backgrounds gave impassioned testimony about the harm of pornography, especially to women and children. To MacKinnon, Dworkin, and their followers, the new ordinance heralded a new era of anti-pornography politics and law. Non-traditional feminist views and new academic research on the nature and effects of pornography would now supplement or supplant traditional tenets in the attack on porn. A divided Minneapolis city council passed the ordinance with unusual speed. Charging that it violated the free speech guarantees of the First Amendment, however, Mayor Donald Fraser vetoed it. Conservative Indianapolis then took up the fight and passed a modified version of the ordinance with the support (at least public) of most city leaders. But the local federal judge was less enthusiastic and struck down the Indianapolis version of the ordinance as a violation of the First Amendment.

Despite its constitutional problems, the ordinance gained wide prominence and support, sparking a national debate concerning pornography and related social issues. The ordinance was important for a related reason as well. Efforts to censor sexual materials in previous decades had been dominated by conservative forces, but now radical feminists, usually considered part of the Left, were leading a call for censorship. The new politics of pornography soon forged unusual alliances between the Right and Left in a revivified challenge to the availability of sexually explicit materials.

Campaigns to pass similar ordinances in other cities lost steam when the federal courts ruled against Indianapolis. A version of the ordinance was offered as a referendum in Cambridge, Massachusetts, but was rejected by the voters.[5] After a full year of intense and polarizing debate, the Los Angeles County Board of Supervisors, on June 4, 1985, voted 3–2 against a version of the ordinance supported by MacKinnon and the county commission for women.[6] Contributing to the narrow loss was fear of another legal defeat like the one in Indianapolis. Feminist and conservative groups in Madison, Wisconsin, presented a tighter version of the ordinance (focusing on violence), only to have its two leading supporters on the Dane County Board of Supervisors withdraw it before it reached the full board.[7] Conservatives in Suffolk County, New York, supported a version of the ordinance; there, too, efforts were dropped after the Indianapolis ruling.[8]

In addition to offering a more specific alternative to current obscenity law, the anti-pornography ordinance was intended by its creators and supporters to provide an alternative to generally prevailing assumptions about the meaning of the First Amendment as interpreted by federal courts in recent times. I will elaborate on the modern doctrine of free speech in the next chapter; here, I need only mention three of its key principles. First, the state must exhibit a preference for individual liberty of expression unless the expression poses substantial direct harm to other people or society. Second, the state must maintain neutrality toward speech that involves politics, ideas, or public issues.   xiii

The state must not interfere with the content of such speech that possesses intellectual value. Because "obscenity" has been held to lack intellectual or social value, however, it has been excluded from First Amendment protection and the requirement of state neutrality toward its content. But even while regulating expression that does not possess the requisite social or intellectual value, the state may not engage in "viewpoint discrimination." Expression, whether it fits a protected or unprotected category under the First Amendment, may not be treated differently from other forms of expression in its category, especially if such treatment is predicated on any ideological bias on the part of the state.[9] Third, the public is the ultimate determinant of political values and truth, rather than the state. Public philosophy is to arise through the marketplace of ideas and is not to be imposed by government through the exercise of censorship.[10]

Thus understood, the heart of the modern doctrine of speech has incorporated liberal tenets, at least as interpreted in Ronald Dworkin's definition in his landmark essay, "Liberalism." Dworkin observes that liberals, conservatives, socialists, and others agree that government ought to treat citizens as equals, but these groups differ concerning the *manner* in which equal treatment is to be attained.[11] To conservatives, equal treatment depends on substantive norms of virtue derived from a shared tradition and supported by the state: "the content of equal treatment cannot be independent of some theory about the good for man or the good life, because treating a person as an equal means treating him the way the good or truly wise person would wish to be treated."[12] To socialists, equal treatment is based on abstract principles derived from a political theory of egalitarian community. Both conservatives and socialists believe that the state should advance certain political and moral values and that the form of equality fostered by the state should be framed in relation to these more substantive values. Liberals, according to Dworkin, differ. They maintain that equality and equal treatment by the state require state neutrality and indifference concerning competing notions of the good or the virtuous life:

> The [liberal] theory of equality supposes that political decisions must be, so far as possible, independent of any particular conception of the good life, or what gives value to life. Since the citizens of a society differ in their conceptions, the government does not treat them as equals if it prefers one conception to another, either because the offi-

cials believe that one is intrinsically superior, or because one is held by the more numerous or more powerful group.[13]

This view of liberalism as entailing state neutrality toward individual conceptions of the good life is challenged by competing past and present concepts, and it does not characterize social or political policy in all areas of American life. What it does capture is the essence of the *modern doctrine of speech,* which mandates state neutrality toward the content of speech that has intellectual or social value and forbids discrimination among viewpoints for all types of expression. The state, of course, promotes different substantive moral ends, depending upon which political party or alliance controls it, but the modern doctrine of speech requires that all speech, if it can claim the necessary intellectual value, be equally unrestricted under the law. Accordingly, when I discuss "liberalism" or "liberal doctrine" in my analysis of the new politics and law of pornography, I refer to the type of liberalism that advocates state and legal neutrality concerning the substantive content of belief and values. It is this liberal concept that has been put at risk by the new attacks on pornography.[14]

Major critiques of pornography on both the Left and Right today question not only the validity of obscenity law, which has itself incorporated liberal precepts in recent decades, but also the propriety of the broader liberal precepts embodied in First Amendment doctrine. Vocal conservatives charge that the liberal approach creates a "naked public square" where substantive moral values are subordinated to vacuous concepts of individual autonomy and liberty. They advocate a reunion of liberty and moral virtue.[15] Some contemporary feminists attack the liberal approach to speech as an ideological charade that masks male power and gender inequality. The modern doctrine of speech, they say, assumes an essential equality of social condition that simply does not exist, so it perpetuates the power of the gender favored by the status quo. They seek a new speech policy that will transcend the content neutrality doctrine and take account of unequal social conditions that make the idea of equal treatment a hoax.[16] The pornography debate also reflects currents in contemporary thought that have influenced certain schools of feminist theory. This view construes all social structures—the discourses of law, custom, language itself—as mechanisms of power. Liberal society is as much pervaded by power relationships as any other. These discourses, of which pornography can be taken as

xv

an example, shape those who use them, to such an extent that individual autonomy is an illusion. Liberal societies and their citizens are not so free as they suppose.[17]

In this book I will deal with the theoretical context of the new politics and law of pornography only as necessary in considering the validity of the liberal modern doctrine of speech and the appropriateness of the present legal treatment of sexually explicit materials. I am not concerned with broader questions of social life but rather with the roles of competing political theories as they relate to free speech law and policy.

The new politics of pornography suggests that society is presently reconsidering liberal tenets. At issue is which public philosophy should govern free speech. As a prominent feminist theorist has declared, "In the face of growing political polarization over sexual matters, the liberal position, so welcome (if so tepid) in the '60s, is now collapsing as it encounters conservative opposition in today's political climate. The pornography debate has been playing an important and problematic role in this process, splitting liberalism itself into a number of factions." [18]

The new politics of pornography continues the American tradition of reevaluating and redefining the meaning of freedom and democracy.[19] Such reconsiderations have often contributed to significant social change, as have those sparked by the civil rights and womens' movements. But in anxious times, as we will see in Chapters 1 and 5, non-liberal First Amendment doctrines have failed to protect unpopular speech from repression. Consequently, hard questions must be asked before undertaking any reconsideration of liberal principles relating to free speech and sexual materials.[20] Would unwelcome consequences follow if the basic liberal approach to free speech and sexual materials were dismantled? Would such a change be likely to further or thwart the opportunities for social change and political discourse? Would there still be a viable, principled foundation for free speech adjudication after major restructuring of the First Amendment? To what extent should liberal principles in free speech law (including the law governing sexual materials and expression) be modified or balanced with other values? These are the broader questions that must be addressed as we consider the treatment of sexually explicit materials.

My discussion of the political and legal aspects of the new approach to pornography will reflect three contentions. First, I believe that the new politics of pornography has ventured too far in its rejection of the modern doctrine of speech. Second, because pornography arguably has potential for both benefit and harm, the competing understandings of this elusive form of expression often have been too one-sided to provide a foundation for viable public policy. This critique applies both to absolutist liberals who scorn any censorship and to anti-porn activists who would suppress any material they deem improper. Third, the extreme positions taken during the most prominent episodes of the new attack on pornography have demeaned the quality of public discourse on this issue and have jeopardized the quality of democratic debate in general.

The Political Aspects of the New Politics of Pornography

Activists on all sides in the recent debate over pornography have too often taken emotional, symbolic, and polarizing stands that are not conducive to thoughtful and responsible discussion.[21] Richard Sennett has shown how such intemperate politics can undermine the civil quality of democratic public life.[22] Neither anti-porn activists nor anti-censorship liberals have shown much willingness to understand their opponents' concerns. There has simply been a clash of views holding that pornography is either all bad or completely harmless.

This was certainly the case in the two main controversies described in this book. Political leaders in Minneapolis allowed feminist activists to dictate the terms of debate and drown out dissenting voices during consideration of the anti-pornography ordinance, just as their counterparts in Indianapolis yielded the floor to organized conservative forces. Activists in each instance espoused largely monolithic interpretations of pornography, so public debate assumed an "all or nothing" quality. In permitting themselves to be captured by activists, civic leaders forsook not only their obligation to protect their offices and institutions from undue outside pressure but also their responsibility to approach major reforms of free speech doctrine with caution.[23] This collapse of political leadership augurs poorly for institutional support of free speech when community passions are aroused. Concurrently, the opponents of censorship contributed to polarization by refusing to concede any validity to the concerns addressed by the ordinance. The branches of the American Civil Liberties Union in Minneapolis and Indianapolis reacted vehemently and categorically to the new proposals, denouncing them as assaults on the very foundations of free speech. Although the ordinances did indeed challenge the modern doctrine of speech, my interviews with leaders of the civil liberties unions revealed neither particularly subtle understanding of the measures nor appreciation of the threat felt by their opponents in the face of certain forms of pornography. The Minnesota Civil Liberties Union was particularly intransigent, refusing to support even the mildest of noncensorious regulations that were considered in the aftermath of the debate—zoning of stores selling erotic material, opaque covers for pornographic magazines displayed in public, and the like.[24]

The suppression of discussion thwarted realization of civic virtues that have been claimed for the modern doctrine of speech.[25] In arguing for allowing hate groups to air their controversial views, Lee Bollinger, for instance, suggests that legal (not moral) tolerance of hate groups' speech promotes civic virtues by compelling citizens to restrain the urge to censor the expression of disturbing thought. Self-restraint in the face of threatening ideas, he says, promotes "enlargement" of individuals and their community through an "internal dialectic of tolerance" that, in turn, begets political maturity and responsibility. Legal tolerance works to strengthen public reason in two respects. First, it compels the community to deal with uncomfortable but inescapable social and political situations: the Ku Klux Klan will not go away simply because its parades and pamphlets are kept out of sight. Second, it restrains the all-too-natural impulse to silence the potentially threatening, the strange, or the different, and so accustoms the community to accept its own diversity.[26] In Minneapolis and Indianapolis, the rewards of civil discussion foundered on incivility.

Civility and tolerance do not always preclude censorship, however. A tolerant society need not legally tolerate all forms of expression. Indeed, censorship may promote tolerance, if the message being censored is patently intolerant or dehumanizing and if the censorship does not undermine basic free speech values. For example, restricting expressions of hatred in special instances in which they are targeted at specific racial or religious groups or individuals may enhance tolerance without harming basic First Amendment interests.[27] These expressions may be considered a form of "fighting words"—insults or taunts meant to incite a violent response—or intimidation, which constitute assault as much as speech. And pornography made with the participation of children not only exploits a particularly vulnerable population but is itself a record of the crime of child abuse. The U.S. Supreme Court has unanimously ruled that laws proscribing child pornography are constitutional (see Chapter 1). Other forms of pornography, ones depicting rape or violence directed against vulnerable groups in sexually explicit contexts, might be treated similarly.

But in a mature democratic society proposals of censorship should be approached by government officials and civic leaders with caution and deliberation, especially where serious restructuring of free speech doctrine is at issue, as it was in the anti-pornography controversies. Alas, one-sidedness prevailed in Minneapolis and Indianapolis, despite the private reservations of many about the wisdom of the ordinances under consideration, and despite the fact that the pornography issue is inescapably complex. This suggests that the civil toleration upon which the First Amendment depends is in shorter supply than might have been hoped. The self-restraint that Bollinger describes as necessary for mutual understanding and acceptance of diversity did not appear; rather, both sides took intransigent symbolic positions that required agents from outside the debate to step in and restore the balance required for the functioning of public life.

The Legal Policy Issue

Because pornography involves the complex phenomena of sexuality and sexual representation, dealing with the resulting legal questions requires willingness to compromise and the need to balance competing legitimate claims. Pornography is neither all bad nor all good; like many other things, it is a bit of both.

The new critics of pornography would not agree. They associate certain forms of sexual representation, particularly those involving violence and force, with direct and indirect harms to women and to society as a whole. While the traditional critique of pornography focused on moral issues, the new critiques are largely gender-related: they point to harms to women who are coerced into making pornography; harms to victims of sex crimes that, they charge, are inspired by pornography; and the broader harm to society that follows from the powerful influence of repeated displays of negative images of women.[28] Beginning in the 1970s, a radical second wave of feminism attempted to link pornography to the systematic oppression or disadvantaging of women. Pornography, in this view, reflects and causes the subordination of women by eroticizing power and domination.[29] The public interest thus may be served either by adopting a new restrictive approach to certain sexual materials or by deliberalizing obscenity law and vigorously enforcing it.

The legal treatment of sexual materials has long been marked by ambivalence and compromise, and with good reason. Different forms of pornography raise both questions of free expression and concerns about the abuse of sexuality. The meaning and connotation of sex have remained mysterious throughout history, and will likely remain so. The mystery and power of sexuality do not yield to easy resolutions.

Accordingly, a sense of the normative quality of sexuality is perhaps natural for human beings, as communities strive to give human form to what is at least partially an animalistic appetite. Whether sexual conventions are formed by society or reflect a numinous quality inherent in the sexual impulse, this aspect of human experience remains undeniably central—and highly charged.[30]

Western societies have oscillated between periods of relative sexual openness and periods of repression, between liberty and restraint. Different societies have drawn the line between permitted and prohibited (and obscene and non-obscene) in different locations, but all have drawn a line somewhere.[31] Recent decades have been remarkable both for their freedom of discussion about sexual matters and for the availability of sexually explicit materials. One student of this trend has declared, "Before now [the 1970s and 1980s], sexual libertinism has been confined to narrow elite circles, often around a court. Its dissemination among a population at large, as has occurred in the last 20 years, is a phenomenon unique in the history of developed societies."[32] But the sexual dialectic now confronts this much publicized libertinism with a counter-reaction that focuses on the alleged problems that unrestricted pornography and sexuality can spawn.

So society's concerns about pornography may be construed as part of the cycle of changing attitudes about sexuality. The recent feminist interpretation of pornography has added a new argument to the cycle. Despite the weight of disapprobation, however, evidence of pornography's effects is mixed and hardly one-sided. Certain forms of pornography are arguably beneficial to some individuals and to society in general, for reasons I will explore in Chapter 5. Pornography's harms and benefits are not easy to disentangle.

Pornography's frequent admixture with art magnifies the difficulty. Since its inception in the eighteenth century, modern "pornography" has often been held to contain artistic or intellectual value. The numerous prosecutions of literature with sexual content from the mid-nineteenth century until recent decades attest to this connection, as witness the cases against *Madame Bovary, Fanny Hill, Ulysses,* and the like. Further, pornographic art has been the subject of modernist intellectual inquiry, especially in the field of depth psychology, which often emphasizes the sexual wellsprings of personality. Recent experimental writing and criticism have added their explorations. Some naturalistic novels and forms of art have been interpreted as portraying the animalistic aspect of human sexuality and its conflict with social norms.[33]

In a related vein, philosophical naturalism looks to scientific principles to explain all phenomena. In this view, the actual perceptions or passions (sometimes unconscious) of individuals, rather than transcendent ideals, are all that can be known of reality. This "emotivist" theory of knowledge may not be conducive to a virtuous society, but it is an aspect of modern life with which we must reckon even if we do not accept its tenets or implications.[34]

Thus First Amendment values are often at stake when society and government seek to control pornography. While such "pornographic knowledge" has many detractors, it merits First Amendment consideration just as does other controversial intellectual expression. The Minnesota anti-pornography ordinance was problematic, among other reasons, because it could readily have been used to restrict sexual material that possessed literary or intellectual merit.

As was demonstrated in the literary prosecutions mentioned above, the psychological complexity of sexuality and its representation cannot be accommodated by morally simplistic or absolutist social policy. Sexuality reaches into the depths of human experience. Tabooed thoughts and impulses conflict with more socially approved norms in a dynamic, and sometimes fruitful, tension. Indeed, many of the satisfactions of civilized life may ultimately be rooted in the so-called primitive desires, which must be tempered and redirected toward more culturally acceptable objects (desire with a human face).[35] The struggles that issue from these tensions seem to define our very being, forming the stuff of religion, moral philosophy, literature, and psychology. Good and bad—or, psychologically, the healthy and unhealthy—often coexist in everyday life and experience. In Jung's analysis, our conscious selves coexist with our rejected or undeveloped qualities and it is futile, even destructive, to deny the properties of our "Shadow" that dwells within.[36] Health and wholeness entail achieving a balance between the forces of the shadow and those of conscious rationality.

Consequently, while society attempts to maintain a normative model of sexuality, it must also maintain some measure of tolerance toward alternative sexual expressions, at least as far as they involve consenting adults.[37] Sex is (among other things) an exploration of the dynamic tensions of human experience. Recognition of this fact counsels tolerance toward consensual adult sexual activity as well as society's right to draw a normative line somewhere. As in any area of social policy dealing with mental and emotional states, lines cannot be drawn with the precision we demand in less highly charged domains of knowledge and life.

Now, tolerance is especially appropriate in confronting forms of evidence and representation that reveal to us the ambiguities of our knowledge and codes of behavior. Material that deals in an intellectual or artistic manner with the sexual aspect of individuals and society teaches us something about the tensions within our natures and within our culture. Certain forms of pornography give expression to the conflicts and joys inherent in sexuality and therefore comprise a form of knowledge. As John Milton wrote in *Areopagitica,* "Good and evil we know in the field of this world grow up together almost inseparably; and the knowledge of good is . . . involved and interwoven with the knowledge of evil." [38] In this light, it is as overreaching to suppress sexual expression in order to abolish moral temptations or to avoid the power conflicts in gender relationships as it is to abandon all restraint and so affront the deep sense of reticence toward sexual matters felt by many people. Neither indifference to nor exaggeration of the conflicts that arise from sexuality are helpful when attempting to resolve the pornography dilemma.

Society must seek a policy that accommodates tolerance and moral ambiguity while it acknowledges reasonable demands for sexual restraint and norms. In doing so it acknowledges the tensions, breadth, and possibilities of human nature while also recognizing the community's need for order and mutual respect. As ethologist Mary Midgley comments, "What is evil must in some way be part of our nature, since what stands right outside it could be no temptation to us, would even be beyond our power. It has to be something possible for us, something for which we are equipped and to which we are drawn—but outrageous, damaging to the proper arrangement of the whole [of the cultural and human order]. If it prevails, it does so at a monstrous price, destroying what is more central." [39] Midgley's perspective is most apposite to thinking about sexuality, as well as its representation, pornography; for these phenomena possess the potential for constructive growth as well as corruption. But pornography has a greater claim on tolerance than does sexual action. Representation is more limited and less immediate than action, and certain forms of pornography may have something to teach us about ourselves and our social condition. When pornographic depictions move beyond the plausibly educational or the politically relevant to degrade persons or to provide a model for violence, however, they begin to be cause for serious social concern.

In summary, pornography cannot be categorized as all good or all bad. Pornography comes in many forms, conveys different messages, and, depending on the situation, has a range of effects. This point applies to those who wish to censor pornography as well as to zealous libertarians who refuse to acknowledge the potential harms of pornography. Absolutism must be avoided on either side of the pornography debate in favor of sensitivity to the need for civil compromises. In Max Weber's terms, the absolutist ethic of ultimate ends must yield in this particular area of public policy to the ethic of responsibility, which acknowledges the limits of moral absolutism.[40] This approach is consistent with some strands of recent constitutional scholarship, which have rejected one-sided interpretations of the Constitution in favor of pluralistic approaches.[41]

The Format of the Book

The argument that follows reflects the two-fold approach just outlined. In Chapter 1, I will examine the legal and political context of the new politics of pornography and demonstrate how it challenges the liberal doctrine of freedom and speech. I will also discuss obscenity doctrine—the traditional, essentially conservative approach to the control of sexual material—and how it has been modified in the modern era by liberal principles.

In the next three chapters, I will focus on the law and politics of the anti-pornography ordinance that vaulted to national attention in Minneapolis and Indianapolis in late 1983 and 1984. The ordinance, with its novel civil-rights orientation, constituted the most significant aspect of the anti-pornography movement of the 1980s. The ordinance encapsulated the critiques of recent speech doctrine launched by the new politics of pornography, and witnessed interesting and unusual alliances between radical feminists and conservatives in favor of censorship.

The ordinance also gained the respect of some intellectuals who had previously opposed censorship of sexual materials, thus weakening the long-standing broad consensus supporting the liberal doctrine of free expression. Chapter 2 looks at the legal and theoretical aspects of the ordinance in Minneapolis and Chapter 3 covers the politics of the conflict in that city. Chapter 4 discusses the politics and law of the ordinance as it was presented in Indianapolis. In neither city did political leaders seem to act with sufficient deliberation in the face of pressures exerted by anti-porn activists. Attention to the implications of the ordinances for free speech was too scant to be meaningful.

In addition to tracing the progress of the ordinance, these chapters refer to other aspects of the new politics of pornography, including the work of the 1986 U.S. Attorney General's Commission on Pornography. The commission's *Final Report* synthesized the viewpoints of the most prominent anti-pornography activists, and concluded that a tidal wave of pornography was threatening American society. Although its members were predominantly conservative, the commission took account of much of the new radical feminist argument against pornography; it also highlighted new academic research indicating that some pornography could cause significant harm.

In Chapter 5, I address the legal issue of what to do about pornography. This chapter is devoted to legal analysis of the anti-pornography ordinance in relation to developing obscenity doctrine. It considers the feasibility of new restrictions on the availability of pornographic (as distinct from obscene) material and discusses the desirability of maintaining liberal principles as the basis of general First Amendment doctrine. In concluding, I reject the search for a single perspective on the legal treatment of sexual materials. I acknowledge conservative and feminist concern in regard to violent and degrading sexual materials, representations that may lead viewers to consider such practices as acceptable. I endorse maintaining social control over this extreme form of sexual depiction if it also meets the Supreme Court's test for obscenity. In other cases, I advocate legal tolerance and endorse preserving the liberal core of general First Amendment law for expression that may possess intellectual value.

O N E

THE NEW POLITICS OF PORNOGRAPHY AND THE CHALLENGE TO THE MODERN DOCTRINE OF FREE SPEECH AND OBSCENITY

There has never been a society—until our own—in which all representations were available equally to any observer at any time. . . . Our society has been unique in regarding increased license, sexual or otherwise, as a gain.

Walter Kendrick, *The Secret Museum.*

[Sexual libertinism's] dissemination among a population at large, as has occurred in the last 20 years, is a phenomenon unique in the history of developed societies.

It may well not last much longer, in view of the deepening moral tangle about abortion . . . the rising tide of anti-pornographic feminism, and the steady expansion of 'moral majoritarian' prudery and demands for sexual control. . . . What is certain is that [the recent trends of sexual liberation] do not seem to be increasing the sum of human happiness, as was anticipated when the sexual revolution began in the 1960s. Sexual liberation is forging its own new chains.

Lawrence Stone, "Sex in the West."

The Tale of Two Commissions

Anti-pornography movements have been part of the American landscape since the 1870s, but the 1980s have spawned new arguments and alliances that have altered the terms of debate. National commissions in Britain, Canada, and the United States have reassessed the pornography issue in recent years, coming to differing conclusions.[1] The 1986 Attorney General's Commission on Pornography in the United States examined numerous studies and took testimony in six cities. In its *Final Report,* the commission called for legal restrictions

1

on "violent" and "degrading" types of obscene pornography that it considered to have harmful effects on individuals and society.[2] The commission did not recommend broadening the legal definition of obscenity or extending censorship beyond obscenity; rather, it urged more vigilant enforcement of obscenity laws and much more aggressive regulation short of censorship of certain forms of pornography that it considered harmful but not legally obscene.

The *Final Report* was a synthesis of the competing perspectives in the politics of pornography of the 1980s. First, the commission meticulously presented experimental studies on the effects of exposure to various types of pornography. Second, it drew on the feminist theory of pornography, although it couched its views in largely conservative language. It even used the logic of the anti-pornography ordinance in the most important part of its report—in the chapter "The Question of Harm." Here the commission concluded that "degrading" but nonviolent pornography, which it claimed comprised most of the pornography available, causes substantial harm through its influence on attitudes and the status of women in society.[3] Nevertheless, the commission did not endorse a new legal approach to censorship or regulation and showed respect for liberal concerns.

The 1986 commission's positions turned the tables on the previous national commission recommendations. The 1970 Commission on Obscenity and Pornography recommended by a vote of 12 to 5 eliminating all legal restrictions on use by consenting adults of sexually explicit books, magazines, pictures, and films. This view was congruent with the basic liberal view of sexuality and sexual depictions: that unless sexual or pornographic acts directly harm others, they should be tolerated as matters of individual choice and taste. Absent direct harm, the meaning of sexuality and pornography lie in "the eye of the beholder." President Nixon was not pleased, but intellectuals and liberals applauded this posture.[4]

Differences between the commissions might be attributed to their compositions. A dominant liberal faction controlled the 1970 group whereas the 1986 force was made up of conservative members, most with records of finding harmful effects in pornography; critics charged that the 1986 commission was stacked.[5] But the differences transcending membership composition had changed. Broader social and political forces had arisen by the 1980s that challenged the liberal stance of the 1970 report. The 1986 commission's restrictive recommendations were greeted with interest in at least some mainstream legal circles.[6]

2   Before we consider these political and legal forces, however, we

should look more closely at the concepts of modern free speech and obscenity, as these are the doctrines under attack in the new politics of pornography. I will examine the history and development of obscenity doctrine in order to illustrate the tensions that have bedeviled this area of law from its inception.

The Modern Doctrine of Speech

No single theory holds absolute sway over modern First Amendment doctrine because speech is a complex phenomenon that defies reduction to a single value.[7] But modern doctrine is weighted in a liberal individualistic direction, especially in the domain of politically oriented speech. According to Robert Post, liberal individualism "has unquestionably become the great tradition of First Amendment thought" despite the continued presence of other cultural values.[8] Over much of the twentieth century the U.S. Supreme Court has moved away from the more traditional idea that only socially valuable thought and rational speech deserve constitutional protection to the principle that individuals and groups merit the right of free speech unless they threaten society or others with direct, imminent harm. The Supreme Court adopted this approach in reaction to the social and political upheavals of the 1960s, recognizing that traditional majoritarian notions of social value were giving way to cultural and value pluralism.[9]

Before this period, the Court allowed restriction of speech in two basic situations: on grounds of danger to society or lack of redeeming social value. That is, censorship or punishment was allowed if the speech advocated unlawful action or posed a "clear and present danger" to society. Under this approach, a great deal of unpopular speech was punished, for the Court applied the danger test in a loose, unprotective fashion. A mere "bad tendency" to cause harm was enough to constitute the requisite "danger."[10] Then, to deal with other forms of controversial speech, the Court constructed a "two-level" test. In *Chaplinsky v. New Hampshire* in 1942, the Court capsulated this approach stating that forms of expression such as obscenity, lewd and offensive speech, libel, and fighting words (words likely to trigger a hostile reaction) were not protected by the First Amendment even if they pose no "clear and present danger" because "such utterances are no essential part of any exposition of ideas, and are of such slight social value as a step to truth that any benefit that may be derived from them is clearly outweighed by the social interest in order and morality."[11] Categories of speech mentioned in *Chaplinsky* thus received less constitutional protection than speech that was recognized as having

3

social value. Government action against the latter would call for a higher level of judicial scrutiny and protection.

During the 1960s and 70s, the Supreme Court altered this approach in a liberal fashion. First, the Court tightened the danger test in a series of cases culminating in *Brandenburg v. Ohio,* a case involving the right of a Klan group to advocate racial strife. The Court held that advocacy of violence or other unlawful action is protected by the First Amendment unless it directly incites *imminent* unlawful action that significantly harms society.[12] The mere possibility of harm from speech ("bad tendency") would no longer justify abridgement; the state had to demonstrate the imminence of danger. Second, the Court issued a series of decisions that refashioned *Chaplinsky*'s two-level approach in a liberal direction by establishing much more constitutional protection for libel, lewd and offensive expression, and obscenity.[13] The two-level approach was not abandoned, so certain forms of speech remained unprotected; but the reach of each of the unprotected categories was significantly narrowed, and the Court harbored doubts about the efficacy and legitimacy of the two-level logic. As a result of these decisions, extremist and offensive expression—hate group speech, obscenity, profanity, and the like—became more prevalent in the public sphere. But this result was, perhaps, the necessary by-product of an unprecedented widening of the public forum to include dissenting voices. The civil rights movement, the women's movement, and the anti-Vietnam War movement all flourished in the public forum in the 1960s and 70s under the aegis of this approach.[14]

The liberal approach holds that the best way to achieve political and social justice is through an open marketplace of ideas. Thus, this approach to First Amendment doctrine emphasizes procedure more than substance. It is concerned to maintain an open public process rather than to encourage certain outcomes.[15] The principle of legal tolerance plays a major role in this theory: individuals and society must tolerate disagreeable speech unless it is clearly dangerous, part of criminal action, or conspicuously without social value. In this respect, First Amendment jurisprudence is more consistently liberal than many other areas of constitutional law. For example, despite present pressures to the contrary, today's First Amendment law of libel is very liberal, especially concerning the libel of public officials. Such libel is compensable only if made with "actual malice." Unlike other areas of tort law, constitutional libel law has resisted the movement toward a fiduciary ethic, one which emphasizes protection from harm rather than liberty of action. [16] In addition, the Supreme Court has steadfastly rejected laws designed to apply affirmative action principles to the realm of speech. It has refused to sanction designs to equalize the market place of ideas by restricting speech or spending on speech by wealthy persons or corporations.[17] And the federal courts struck down the Indianapolis anti-pornography ordinance, which attempted to equalize the marketplace of sexual ideas by censoring pornography.[18] In Isaiah Berlin's terms, the First Amendment is concerned with "negative liberty," or freedom from restraints, rather than with "positive liberty," which entails particular conceptions of the good life or social empowerment.[19]

In addition to the marketplace of ideas and legal tolerance, four other, related assumptions undergird the modern doctrine governing protected speech.

1. The modern doctrine of speech assumes that the individual citizen is autonomous and responsible, qualities defined in a classic Millian, anti-paternalistic sense.[20] Speakers are not held responsible for illegal actions taken in response to their speech, unless the speech incites immediate lawlessness (*Brandenburg*). The Minneapolis/Indianapolis anti-pornography ordinance went counter to the presumption of individual responsibility by implicating pornography and its makers in the crimes committed by its users.

2. The modern doctrine takes a limited notion of equality, defined as equal treatment under the law and equal opportunity to compete in the public forum or marketplace of ideas. This notion of equality entails *state neutrality* in allocating the speech right.[21]

3. The modern doctrine's concept of citizenship and right applies to the individual rather than a class or group. The modern First Amendment certainly accommodates the formation of groups, but it construes individuals as the basic units of rights and groups as vehicles for individuals. It also treats groups in a neutral manner; thus, laws impinging on free speech may not seek to equalize the power of competing groups by engaging in an affirmative action that favors the weaker group over the stronger.[22]

4. The doctrine makes a basic, if imperfect and inexact, distinction between speech and action. Speech is protected unless it constitutes unlawful or tortious action or is directly tied to unlawful action, such as libel, incitement, solicitation, conspiracy or the like.

The anti-pornography ordinance contested each of these assumptions.

Three constitutional doctrines sustain these First Amendment and liberal principles: neutrality as to content; no discrimination as to viewpoint; and demonstration of direct harms. The content neutrality doctrine holds that the state may not abridge speech because of its content unless the speech falls within one of the limited categories of unprotected speech established by the Supreme Court in *Chaplinsky*. If one of *Chaplinsky*'s exceptions does not apply, government must remain neutral in its treatment of speech. Of course, government has not been and should not be absolutely neutral in all its functions, but where speech and the marketplace of ideas are concerned, the doctrine of speech now holds government especially obligated to remain neutral toward any particular viewpoint. As we have seen, in recent decades the Supreme Court has narrowed *Chaplinsky*'s categories in a liberal direction. In 1982, however, the Court added child pornography to the exclusion list in *New York v. Ferber*, a case to be discussed more fully below.[23]

Except for obscenity, a concept which derives from traditional morality and therefore represents a compromise between liberalism and conservatism, exceptions from the obligation to remain neutral cover expression presumed to inflict *direct* (or immediate) and *substantial harms* on individuals or distinguishable social interests. As Mill and Charles Fried have argued, the "harm principle" is central to the liberal doctrine of individualism because it protects liberty until the state finds specific, demonstrable, and sufficiently substantial harm resulting from it: the principle creates breathing space for action and expression, as it were.[24] The harm principle is part of the movement from a traditional, communitarian theory of freedom to an individualist conception of legal right and responsibility. While this liberal principle has never been given constitutional recognition in areas outside of speech (many so-called victimless crimes have been criminalized for decades without violating the protection given by the Fifth and Fourteenth Amendments), it does pertain to speech that qualifies for First Amendment protection. This is an important point, *for it means that a demonstration of merely consequent harm is not necessarily sufficient to justify restriction of expression. The level of harm must be significant and it must be imminent.* Indeed, the very concept of a right implies that it must be honored even though it is associated with some harm. Rights are special entitlements that require an exceptional showing of harm before they may be subject to restriction.[25] In regard to free speech, this approach focuses on the rights of the speaker, which can be limited only when the speaker directly harms the rights or opportunities of others. Harm to the collective image of a group or to individuals identified with a group are not acknowledged as legally meaningful.

To be sure, the Supreme Court upheld a conviction for group libel in 1952 in *Beauharnais v. Illinois;* a white man had published and distributed anti-black pamphlets in Chicago. In the last decade, however, lower federal courts have consistently rejected laws based on group libel logic as incongruent with the modern doctrine of speech. The famous Skokie litigation of 1978, in which federal courts ruled that a Nazi group's planned demonstration in a village of holocaust survivors was protected by the First Amendment, epitomized this rejection of *Beauharnais.*[26] The new anti-pornography activists, as we will see, espouse concepts of harm that repudiate this liberal approach and resurrect the logic of *Beauharnais.*

Finally, the anti-discrimination principle, forbidding discrimination among viewpoints, originated in equal protection jurisprudence and is logically related to the content neutrality principle and to the more comprehensive neutral principles tenet. In this regard, judgments of speech based on content are presumptively discriminatory. At a minimum, the state may not play favorites and allow some forms of expression within protected categories but not others. It may limit expression that represents one of the established categories of exception in *Chaplinsky,* yet even here it must treat all exceptions alike. Criticizing this approach, Owen Fiss presents an alternative group advantaging principle that MacKinnon has drawn on in building her feminist legal theory. Fiss observes that "the anti-discrimination principle embodies a very limited conception of equality, one that is highly individualistic and confined to assessing the rationality of means." [27] The principle is based on the relation between the state and citizens conceived according to neutral principles as equal before the law; all parties within a particular legal classification must receive equal treatment. The principle takes no overt account of unequal social conditions resulting from gender or race. The anti-pornography ordinance attempted to supplant this approach with a more substantive notion of equality consistent with a more progressive form of liberalism or, perhaps, with a more radical political theory. It would have given constitutional recognition to a distinction between pro-female and anti-female viewpoint in sexual material.[28]

As we saw in the Introduction, the modern doctrine of speech is ultimately premised on the liberal theory of state neutrality toward ideas and values held by citizens. Before turning to consider obscenity doctrine, we should note that earlier notions of liberalism may have differed from this one. In the nineteenth and early twentieth centuries, for example, Americans construed liberty to be related to more substantive notions of moral duty. They spoke of "ordered liberty," not "liberty" in isolation from its responsible exercise and the maintenance of social order.[29] And the founders of modern liberal thought, such as Bentham, Mill and Dewey, favored individual freedom but also believed that the state should promote well-being and happiness.[30] There is a tradition of pragmatic liberalism that differs from the value-neutral liberalism espoused by Ronald Dworkin. Pragmatic liberalism rejects state neutrality toward individual choice and action and accepts a role for the state in promoting the good life.[31] There are as well progressive forms of liberalism that have arisen in recent decades and downplay neutrally equal treatment of citizens by the state. "Affirmative action," for example, calls for limited and temporary abandonment of strict state neutrality in the treatment of citizens if unequal treatment of certain disadvantaged groups is necessary to redress past wrongs or to give citizens with fewer resources the ability to compete on equal terms in the marketplace of social goods. Such affirmative action may be reconcilable with pragmatic or progressive liberalism, as it is intended to promote the conditions that make the good life and true equality available to all citizens.

Similarly, the anti-pornography ordinance could be interpreted as a form of pragmatic liberal affirmative action. It would have restricted pornography on several grounds: because pornography might lead to sexual violence; because it influences men's attitudes toward women as a group; and because it has a long-range impact on the political and social status of women, being not conducive to a truly equal society. Restriction on such grounds is compatible only with a progressive interpretation of liberalism, we have seen. The ordinance was in conflict with the modern doctrine of speech because it defined pornography in political, ideational terms and did not require the finding of direct harm before imposing restrictions.

Obscenity Doctrine: *Sedley* to *Hicklin*

Although it has had to make significant accommodation to liberalism in recent decades, obscenity doctrine historically has been moored in conservative logic. The conservative understanding of sexuality and sexual depiction is wary of the corruptive aspects of sexual interest and desire. It holds that sexual desire should be restrained by rationality, interpersonal commitment, and responsibility. Pornography is seen as bad because it encourages impersonal desire and recreational sex. The tensions and ambiguities between conservatism and liberalism in this area have persisted through thirty years of constitutional obscenity adjudication by the U.S. Supreme Court. The introduction of feminist arguments could help to resolve the conundrum—or complicate it all the more. We will examine the conservative theory of sexuality and sexual depictions more fully in Chapter 4.

Before turning to the development of obscenity doctrine, let us define the most important terms of our inquiry. Although *obscenity* and *pornography* were used interchangeably until recent times, they are not synonymous. *Obscene* pertains to those things considered disgusting, offensive, filthy, foul, repulsive. It also entails making public that which society deems should be hidden (the Latin root *obscaenus* means "ill-omened" or "adverse"; also *obscaena,* or "not for stage").[32] The concept of the obscene is not limited to sexual matters, although obscenity law in America does confine it to sexually explicit depictions. The Supreme Court, for example, has held that depictions of violence per se are not obscene.[33] In essence, obscenity doctrine attempts to distinguish wholesome (socially acceptable) from unwholesome (unacceptable) forms of sexuality and sexual depictions, or those depictions appropriate for public view ("scene") from those which are not ("obscene"). Obscenity doctrine is normative in nature.

Pornography has a different meaning. It "derives from the Greek words for harlot and writing" and pertains to depictions of "sexual lewdness or erotic behavior."[34] Pornography is often sexually explicit, but it need not be obscene, for its presentation of sexual matters need not be "unwholesome" or "prurient." Thus, the historical definition of pornography is generally broader than obscenity, although conservatives have often construed the two as largely synonymous, considering virtually all sexual depictions to be suspect. Yet such suspicion is not confined to the Right; the Minneapolis ordinance's definition of pornography covered much more ground than the present legal definition of obscenity.

Sexual depictions have existed in virtually every society for which we have historical records. The modern meanings of *pornography* and *obscenity* in the West, however, derive from the mid-eighteenth to mid-nineteenth centuries, following upon the discovery of the remains of Pompeii in the early eighteenth century. As excavators unearthed these remains, they discovered artifacts and documents that revealed

9

to them "a moral laxity far more extreme than even the bitterest satires of Juvenal had suggested."[35] This discovery challenged the contemporary norms of sexual probity even as it piqued artistic and sexual interest.

Obscenity law doctrine antedated the eruption of modern "pornography," but before the seventeenth century sexual works in both the East and the West—including very explicit and bawdy ones—were tolerated unless authorities deemed them impious (blasphemous) or dangerous to established authority (heretical).[36] Nevertheless, virtually all societies restricted the display of sex and enforced public norms of shame and modesty. "There has never been a society—until our own—in which all representations were available equally to any observer at any time."[37]

With the rise of Puritanism and capitalism, modern standards of sexual morality began to develop—ironically in reaction to the spirit of revolt expressed in these movements. The first known case involving the enforcement of public morality distinct from heresy or blasphemy was *King v. Sedley*, decided in 1663. In *Sedley* the state prosecuted a man for a variety of acts: getting drunk, uttering a profane speech from the balcony of a tavern, removing his clothes, pouring urine on the taunting crowd below, causing a riot. Sedley was convicted not merely for breach of peace but for the unprecedentedly distinct offense of *offending public morality*, thus tentatively laying the legal and theoretical foundation for modern obscenity law.[38]

Sexual literature in the later seventeenth and eighteenth centuries continued to challenge the moral and political order, suggesting the possible political dimensions of pornography. English translations of foreign pornography also appeared, providing occasions for English courts to slowly develop the logic of *Sedley*. But prosecutions for obscenity per se remained the exception rather than the rule in eighteenth-century England.[39] Even at the beginning of the nineteenth century, "it remained the case that in most of the world there was greater tolerance for sexually explicit writing, printing, and drawing than there would be fifty years later."[40] Only when social mores began to change in reaction to the expansion of the pornography market and the entrenchment of Victorian morality in the nineteenth century were there regular prosecutions for obscenity and did Parliament act to supplement the common law with legislation. With the rise of private groups dedicated to fighting pornography and sexual vice—especially the Society for the Suppression of Vice in England—the official war against pornography was born. From the early 1800s to 1850, the society instigated 159 criminal obscenity prosecutions and won convictions in 154![41]

The nineteenth century also witnessed the development of realism in the novel as part of the broader social criticism directed against the bourgeoise order; sensational novels mixing sex with violence and the first sexual biographies and bibliographies also appeared. Urbanization, technological innovations, and growth in literacy created a new type of amorphous reading public that "liked its amusements strong, and it responded to them with infantile, brutal immediacy." [42] A large underground market for pornography also arose in the nineteenth century. It was fed by a type of pornography with few artistic pretensions, written simply to arouse sexual excitement. It exhibited "a deadly absence of all human context, and feeling, and differentiation . . . the separation of lust from love, which Sigmund Freud was not the first to stigmatize as pathological, is complete." [43]

Despite an acceleration of obscenity prosecutions in the nineteenth century, no official definition of obscenity existed until 1868, when the Queen's Bench established one in the famous case *Regina v Hicklin*. Magistrates had ordered the destruction of 252 copies of an anti-Roman Catholic pamphlet written by an Anglican named Henry Scott; this work, *The Confessional Unmasked,* obscenely depicted imagined events in the confessional. In the appeal, Lord Chief Justice Alexander Cockburn created a very conservative legal test that was to reign for decades in England and the United States: "Whether the tendency of the matter charged as obscene is to deprave and corrupt those whose minds are open to such immoral influences, and into whose hands a publication of this sort may fall." [44]

Hicklin's authoritative judicial definition of obscenity "made it clear in England, for the first time, that publications might be prohibited as 'obscene' solely because of their sexual content, and not because of their attack upon the government or upon religious institutions." [45] Its logic favored the moral interest of society rather than liberty of expression. The intent and motive of the author were irrelevant as long as the work was itself obscene; a work was regarded obscene if the effect of even isolated passages on the most susceptible persons was deemed corruptive—an early version of the "bad tendency" test. This conservative approach prevailed for almost one hundred years in England and formed the basis of American law until the *Ulysses* case in 1933. Along with the *Madame Bovary* trial in France in 1857, the *Hicklin* decision signaled "the emergence of the obscenity problem into the full glare of public controversy. 'Pornography' as the world would learn to

11

understand it, is a public term, native to the courtroom." [46] After *Hicklin*, the major battles in the war over pornography shifted to the United States.

Obscenity Law in America: *Roth* to *Miller*

Very little obscenity prosecution took place in the United States until after the Civil War, although Congress did pass the first federal obscenity statute as part of the customs law in 1842. The impetus, as in England, came with importation of foreign material and with the growth of private anti-smut organizations. In 1872, Anthony Comstock formed what would become the New York Society for the Suppression of Vice, leading Congress to broaden the 1865 federal mail act to prohibit the mailing of obscene materials. This act—dubbed the "Comstock Act"—made Comstock a special agent to the post office with virtual *carte blanche* authority to enforce the law. In Comstock's apocalyptic vision, America stood face to face with filth and the devil: "Satan lays the snare, and children are his victims. His traps, like all others, are baited to allure the human soul." [47]

By the time of Comstock's death in 1915, the war against pornography was thriving. Comstock's agents, sometimes in alliance with progressive forces, had succeeded in driving the porn market underground, where it would remain until the 1950s. As part of this effort, prosecutors in the first decades of the twentieth century commenced actions against works that exhibited both sexual ideas and literary or artistic merit. Although judges often made ad hoc exceptions for "classics," prosecutors won convictions based on the *Hicklin* test against works such as *Lady Chatterly's Lover, An American Tragedy,* and Radclyffe Hall's *The Well of Loneliness* as late as 1930. [48]

In 1933 and 1934 the first significant liberal change in the judicial treatment of obscenity took place when federal district and appeal courts held that James Joyce's *Ulysses* was not obscene despite the presence of pornographic passages. [49] Judge Woolsey of the district court rejected the *Hicklin* test in favor of a more libertarian standard: *whether the author had "pornographic intent," and if not, whether the effect of the work as a whole on the average reader was to "stir the sex impulses or to lead to sexually impure or lustful thoughts."* The effect of isolated passages on a susceptible reader no longer sufficed to make a work obscene.

Most courts quickly adopted the *Ulysses* test. Although obscenity prosecutions of serious books continued to swell, courts began to discern enough literary merit to render works nonobscene. [50] The courts held to this course despite the anti-porn and moral uplift efforts that followed the Second World War. However, blacklists of even high-level writing issued by private organizations such as the National Organization for Decent Literature had their chilling effect on publishers and distributors. "It was not until the early 1960s, when the Supreme Court began actively to scrutinize the contents of material found to be obscene, that attempted prosecutions of unquestionably serious works largely withered, and that most of the legal battles concerned the kinds of material commonly taken to be pornographic."[51] Furthermore, no court addressed the constitutional implications of obscenity laws until the later 1950s; until then, cases simply dealt with statutory meanings of obscenity.

Though the Supreme Court had an opportunity to deal with the First Amendment implications of obscenity law in 1948, it did not do so until 1957, in *Roth v. U.S.*[52] Sixty-five-year-old Samuel Roth had been convicted of mailing obscene sexual advertisements, a sex magazine called *Good Times,* and a book entitled *American Aphrodite.* The Court (per Justice Brennan) assumed that the material was obscene, so the sole issue in the case was whether obscenity as a category of expression fell within the realm of First Amendment protection. The Court pointed out that Western society had universally considered obscenity socially worthless:

> All ideas having even the slightest redeeming social importance—unorthodox ideas, controversial issues, even ideas hateful to the prevailing climate of opinion—have the full protection of the guarantees [of the First Amendment], unless excludable because they encroach upon the limited area of more important interests. But implicit in the history of the first amendment is the rejection of obscenity as utterly without redeeming social importance.[53]

The Court also relied on the logic of *Chaplinsky v. New Hampshire*'s two-level approach and *Beauharnais v. Illinois,* the 1952 group libel case.

After affirming that the First Amendment does not protect obscenity, the Court had to determine just what obscenity is. In the second part of the decision, Brennan stressed that obscenity is narrower than pornography or sexual material in general. It "is material which deals with sex in a manner appealing to prurient interest," or "impure" sexual desires.[54] In constructing its test for obscenity, the Court also addressed the questions of community standards, the overall nature of

13

the work, and the type of person to whom it appealed. *Roth*'s definitive test accepted the quasi-liberal logic of *Ulysses* and its progeny: "whether to the average person, applying contemporary community standards, the dominant theme of the material as a whole appeals to the prurient interest." This test made official the constitutional rejection of the *Hicklin* test.[55] *Roth*'s definition of obscenity contained the following elements: 1. obscenity appeals to the prurient interest in sex; 2. it has no serious literary, artistic, political, or social value; and 3. it is offensive to the average person under contemporary community standards.[56]

In its attempt to balance liberal and conservative values and to clarify the status of obscenity, *Roth* raised many questions that would have to be dealt with in the future. First, it was not clear whether the redeeming value of a challenged work had to be substantial or only minimal. Second, the decision used two potentially conflicting explanations of what "prurient interest" means: "having a tendency to excite lustful thoughts," and a "shameful and morbid interest in sex."[57] The latter meaning emphasizes psychologically unhealthy sexual appeal, whereas the former does not. In addition, the Court did not specify the geographic boundaries of the community standards nor say whether the standards had to be enduring ones or might be more ephemeral. Nor did the Court address the tension between the definition of obscenity and the protection of the First Amendment: a conflict could arise between a work's potential prurient effects on the community and the merits of the work apart from these effects.[58] Finally, all the key terms of the entire edifice—prurient interest, average person, community standards, social value and so on—were fraught with a vagueness and uncertainty that still haunt obscenity law.

Despite *Roth*'s seeming sanctions of crackdowns on obscenity, the decade following witnessed an unprecedented increase in the availability of pornographic materials and concomitant Supreme Court liberalization of obscenity standards. "Books that no one had dared bring to trial before were discovered not to be 'utterly' worthless."[59] In 1959 the Court ruled that the state may not censor a movie simply because the movie seems to approve of (or advocate) sexual immorality; the film had to be obscene in fact. In 1961, the Court ruled that the state could not eliminate the prosecution's burden to prove scienter (knowledge of the content of the material) in an obscenity prosecution of a bookseller.[60] The latter ruling, however, did not affect *Roth*'s holding that scienter was not required in the prosecution of an author, as distinct from a vendor.

In 1962, the Court took a significant liberal step in *Manual Enterprises v. Day*, a case involving a post office declaration that three homosexual magazines were obscene. Justice Harlan stated that for the material to be obscene, the appeal to the prurient interest must be made in a "patently offensive" manner; that is, it must go well beyond what the Court would later call "customary limits of candor" in depicting or describing sex.[61] This requirement bestowed First Amendment protection upon material that could be prurient under *Roth*, even if the material lacked meaningful intellectual value. Then in 1964 the Court further modified the obscenity test in *Jacobellis v. Ohio*, a case concerning the exhibition of the French film *Les Amants* ("The Lovers"). Justice Brennan took *Roth*'s rationale for excluding obscenity from First Amendment protection—that it is "utterly without redeeming social importance"—and applied it to *the test* for obscenity (the second part of *Roth*). As a result, the presence of virtually any idea "or any other form of social importance" would salvage constitutional protection for a sexual work.[62] This approach inverted nineteenth century logic: whereas works with small amounts of obscenity were once ruled obscene even if their dominant themes were not obscene, under *Jacobellis* material otherwise obscene could be saved by the presence of even minimally valuable material.

In 1966 the Court combined recent standards to form a new obscenity test. In *Memoirs v. Massachusetts*, the state court had argued that *Roth* did not protect John Cleland's 1748 pornographic novel *Fanny Hill* because it had only minimal social value. In rejecting this interpretation, Justice Brennan promulgated a new three part test:

> (a) the dominant theme of the material taken as a whole appeals to the prurient interest in sex; (b) the material is patently offensive because it affronts contemporary community standards relating to the description or representation of sexual matters; and (c) the material is *utterly* without redeeming social value.[63]

Not surprisingly, Justice Brennan detected that *Fanny Hill* was not "*utterly* without redeeming social value," especially given the historical interest surrounding it.

The *Memoir* test shifted the emphasis in this and subsequent cases to the presence or absence of even minimal social value, whereas *Roth* had focused on the presence of prurient appeal. Each prong of the three-part test had to be met, so the minimal social value prong became decisive in most cases.

15

Memoirs pushed the Court along the path to concluding that only "hard-core" pornography, material well beyond the limits of candor, could be designated obscene.[64] In response, Grove Press and others began publishing more pornographic classics, including the works of Sade; the anonymous sexual biography *My Secret Life; The Pearl,* an anthology of Victorian pornography; and Frank Harris's *My Life and Loves.* The *Fanny Hill* case was a turning point:

> As at Pompeii, once excavation was begun it had to continue, no matter what horrors the past might yield up. The same impulse seemed to operate in modern fiction, as novels like Hubert Selby's *Last Exit to Brooklyn* and Pauline Reage's *Story of O* pushed hard against the outer limits of community tolerance. Whatever one might think of these books, old or new, they were no longer "obscenity"; that had been pared down to the hard core—'worthless trash,' as Rembar [the defense lawyer] called it at the *Fanny Hill* trial.[65]

From 1967 to 1971, a divided Court sputtered along the liberal path, issuing *per curiam* reversals in thirty-one cases—the so-called *Redrup* reversals.[66] Meanwhile, the availability of pornographic material mushroomed. Eventually the two markets, mass and underground, that had coexisted on different planes until the middle of 1960s would merge. Lower courts followed the Supreme Court's example and declined to convict except in the most extreme cases, which dealt with hard-core materials. As a result, obscenity regulation dwindled to a minimum, and American society witnessed "a consequent proliferation of the open availability of quite explicit materials."[67] Material available by the mid-1970s contained sexual explicitness that was unimaginable as recently as 1968. Highly explicit mass-marketed films, such as *Deep Throat, Behind the Green Door,* and *The Devil in Miss Jones,* and magazines like *Hustler* are among the most prominent examples.[68] In addition, pornography became arguably more violent in content (see next section). Because the question of the value of sexual literature was settled by 1970, "there was nowhere else to turn but toward the hard core. Like the ancient detritus of Pompeii, modern trash had been lurking in darkness all along, waiting for the light of day."[69]

In 1969, in *Stanley v. Georgia,* the Warren Court trod within one step of the ultimate liberal position by overturning a state conviction for the knowing possession of obscenity. Police had found obscene material in Stanley's home while conducting a lawful search for evidence of bookmaking. The Court stated, "The right to receive information and ideas, regardless of their social worth, is fundamental to our free society," and the state's power to control obscenity "simply does not extend to mere possession by the individual in the privacy of his own home."[70] *Stanley's* privacy right swept only one logical step away from the right to produce and sell obscenity to consenting adults for their private use. But even as liberals gathered to conduct an unmournful "requiem for *Roth*," the newly annointed Burger Court ostensibly retreated from the liberal implications of *Stanley*.[71]

In 1973, in *Miller v. California,* a case dealing with a conviction for sending five unsolicited obscene brochures through the mails, the more conservative Burger Court abruptly abandoned the *Memoirs* approach, forged a majority position for the first time since *Roth*, and came up with a new obscenity test that seemed to elevate social standards of value:

> (a) whether "the average person, applying contemporary community standards" would find that the work, taken as a whole, appeals to the prurient interest; (b) whether the work depicts or describes, in a patently offensive way, sexual conduct specifically defined by the applicable state law; (c) whether the work, taken as a whole, lacks serious literary, artistic, political, or scientific value.[72]

Miller's major change lay in altering the social value prong of the obscenity test. Value must now be "serious," rather than merely minimal as in *Memoirs*. The determination of value, however, was intended to be more a question of law for the judge than a question of fact for the jury, in order to maintain constitutional control over state action.[73]

Miller's patent offense test was a compromise, however, since Justice Burger stated that only hard-core materials could be designated patently offensive. Thus, *Miller* did not, in fact, differ from *Memoirs* as much as it may have appeared. Material is hard-core if it "goes substantially beyond customary limits of candor in description or representation of such matters."[74] In the end, the patent offense test is the crucial test, and it boils down to hard-core pornography.

Burger presented some "plain examples" of hard-core depictions that a state could proscribe for giving patent offense: "(a) patently offensive representations or descriptions of ultimate sexual acts, normal or perverted, actual or simulated," or "(b) patently offensive representations or descriptions of masturbation, execratory functions, and lewd exhibition of the genitals." In subsequent years, the Court allowed states to create further examples.[75] Sexual material need not portray actual sexual activity in order to be hard-core. Such depictions as "photographs which focus on, exaggerate, or emphasize the genitalia or 'erogenous zones,'" or even "suggestive poses or lewdly intertwined bodies, even in the absence of actual sexual activity" and "excess of detail" in portrayals have been found by state courts to be hardcore in the years succeeding *Miller*. And while depictions of heterosexual intercourse may be obscene, "most hard core pornography emphasizes various other sexual practices, such as homosexuality, bestiality, flagellation, sado-masochism, fellatio, cunnilingus, and the like."[76]

Since *Miller*, courts have become progressively more proficient in separating the obscene from the non-obscene according to the hard core/non-hard core distinction. As a result, a significant area of sexual representation is relatively secure from prosecution. *Playboy* is virtually beyond attack and the somewhat more explicit *Penthouse* has been found to lack serious value only twice by federal courts. "Materials found not to be obscene under *Miller* frequently depict nudity without explicit sexual activity or merely contain some sexually explicit language."[77]

Finally, a majority of the Court addressed the question of scope in relation to standards for the first time in *Miller*, rejecting national standards in favor of community standards to be determined by juries. States may adopt local, state, or national-based standards of patent offense and prurience, subject to judicial scrutiny, the hard-core delimitation, and the value standard.[78]

Conservatives hoped that *Miller* would stimulate greater prosecution and stem the rising tide of pornography. It did not do so for several reasons.

Miller's Aftermath and the Failure of Implementation

Most of the cases after *Miller* have reinforced liberal delimitations of obscenity doctrine, in particular the hard-core standard. The process began in *Jenkins v. Georgia,* a 1974 case dealing with the film *Carnal Knowledge.* Justice Rehnquist proclaimed that "nudity alone is not enough to make material legally obscene under the *Miller* standard." Such poses may be somewhat prurient, but they are not "unhealthy."[79] Further, the Court ruled that trial courts' findings of prurient appeal and patent offensiveness should be more closely scrutinized by appeals courts, even though these standards were meant to be questions of fact, which are normally left in the hands of juries at the trial level, rather than law. In sum, *Jenkins* made it "clear that determinations of obscenity were not primarily matters of local discretion" but rather determinations to be limited by national constitutional standards.[80]

But in *Young v. American Mini Theatres* (1976), the Court in its first pornography zoning decision upheld a Detroit law that regulated the locations and number of theatres that showed sexually explicit movies, even though not all the films fit the technical *Miller* definition of obscenity. The plurality decision justified this marginal intrusion on First Amendment values by adopting a novel argument and balancing test that would be drawn on by legal advocates of the anti-pornography ordinance in the Indianapolis litigation: non-obscene sexually explicit materials possess only minimal value, so limiting access to them, as opposed to prohibiting them outright, does not injure the First Amendment.[81] In 1981 the Court appeared to limit the *American Mini Theatre* precedent by striking down an ordinance that forbade all "live entertainment," including non-obscene nude dancing. The Court reasoned that nude dancing deserved some First Amendment protection and that the total ban on it distinguished the case from the Detroit zoning regulation.[82] In 1986, however, the Court upheld a very broad and restrictive zoning law that included sex videos and cable television along with porn shops, based on the city interest in protecting neighborhoods from the "secondary effects" of crime and economic deterioration that were said to accompany the establishment of pornographic businesses. This case, *Renton v. Playtime Theatres, Inc.*, could signal greater judicial deference to zoning schemes involving regulation rather than prohibition.[83] Although it is too early to tell, greater constitutional tolerance of zoning in the wake of *Renton* could provide one feasible compromise in the pornography conundrum.[84]

In 1982, as we have seen, the Court unanimously ruled, in *New York v. Ferber*, that child pornography is not protected by the First Amendment and that the state may punish its distribution even if it is not obscene. The Court stressed the reasonableness of the state's conclusion that mental, emotional, and physiological harm resulted to children used in making such material, that the social value of child pornography is minimal, and that the market must be eliminated in order to protect children.[85]

Next, a 1985 case attempted to clarify the nature of prurient interest, left dangling by *Roth*. A 1982 Washington state law declared lewd publications and films a moral nuisance if they constituted a major part of an enterprise's business. The state defined "lewd" in terms of the *Miller* obscenity test; yet it defined prurience as "that which incites lasciviousness or lust." The Supreme Court ruled that this definition reached material that aroused both normal ("lust") and abnormal ("lascivious") sexual responses, and that neither *Roth* nor *Miller* allowed material directed at normal sexual responses to be regarded obscene.[86] This case reinforced *Miller's* delimitation of obscenity to the hard-core.

Finally, in *Pope v. Illinois,* decided in 1987, the Court (per Justice White) held that the jury must determine whether alleged obscene material lacked serious value on the basis of what a "reasonable person" would determine, not simply according to whatever community standards happen to prevail.[87] This seemingly more objective approach to the question of value (*Miller's* third prong) is an extension of the nationalization of standards in *Jenkins*, as the reasonable man is to represent the nation as a whole and not just the local community. Although the dissenters and one concurring justice considered the reasonable man test to be utterly vague, the Court appears to have desired to tighten the standards protecting speech by moving away from the community standards logic.

Despite the Court's adherence to *Miller,* the availability of pornography has continued to grow. "Since 1973 . . . the nature and extent of pornography in the United States has changed dramatically. The materials that are available today are more sexually explicit and portray more violence than those available before 1970. The production, distribution and sale of pornography has become a large, well-organized and highly profitable industry."[88] Furthermore, the few studies available show that the number of prosecutions and appeals of obscenity convictions nationwide have declined rather than increased since *Miller,* at least until the mid-1980s.[89] The 1986 Attorney General's commission appears to have encouraged greater enforcement efforts in some localities, according to press reports, but this effect may not persist.

Why then has there not been greater carrythrough on *Miller?* Several reasons have been offered:

1. Low priority has been given to obscenity cases by prosecutors because of the scarcity of resources, prosecutors' unfavorable attitudes, and greater concern for other crimes.

2. Relative public tolerance of freedom of choice in this area reinforces similar attitudes on the parts of juries and judges.

3. Confusion over the meaning of key parts of the *Miller* test—"prurience," "serious value," "patently offensive," "community stan-

dards"—make prosecutors reluctant to prosecute and juries reluctant to convict, especially given the need to find guilt "beyond a reasonable doubt." Complex laws and judicial instructions confuse juries, making them less inclined to convict, and few laws are more confusing and complex than obscenity laws.[90]

4. The vagueries of political pressure.

5. Under-complaining by the public to the police, under-investigation by police, and under-sentencing by judges.[91]

6. Attorneys involved in obscenity cases pointed out another reason: many jury members are sexually aroused by the material presented and are therefore loathe to declare it obscene on the grounds that it appeals to unhealthy, abnormal ("prurient") interests![92]

7. Finally, pornographers are seasoned litigants who manipulate the factors mentioned above and consider court battles a part of doing business. Prosecutors have won many battles but often lose the war.

Enforcement problems must bedevil any complex law that attempts to reconcile subtle and conflicting values and interests and which is, in certain respects, divided against itself.

The divisions begin with attitudes toward the thing itself. Pornography has negative connotations and few public defenders; yet while sexual materials may be harmful in certain respects, they may also be beneficial or expressive of inner needs. If despite its stigma, pornography serves important personal and social needs, it is unlikely that it can be eradicated or even seriously restricted.[93] I will discuss the psychological and functional aspects of pornography in Chapter 5.

We will see below that some cities have managed to stem the pornographic tide to some extent; and more strenuous prosecution may ultimately bear fruit if the Supreme Court becomes more conservative because of Reagan and Bush appointments. Nevertheless, the equivocation we have observed in the foregoing overview of obscenity doctrine reflects genuine and tenacious social ambiguity. Effective enforcement will come only if society achieves a strong operating consensus on the harms of certain types of pornographic materials.

In summary, obscenity doctrine has taken an ambivalent course in the last fifty years. The irony of *Roth* was that its conservative doctrine was announced at precisely the time in American history when the law of free speech and civil liberty was setting out on a liberal path. Obscenity law after *Roth* has been characterized by precarious attempts to reconcile conservative obscenity doctrine with the liberal trends of other First Amendment adjudication and constitutional law. Novel feminist arguments have complicated the situation all the more, even though the courts struck down the first version of feminist anti-pornography legislation. This is only one of the broader social and political forces that have recently altered the pornography debate, however. Let us now turn to a closer look at these extra-legal factors.

Pornography and Society:
Changes in Distribution and Perception

Not only have the new politics and law of pornography cast the tenuous compromise forged by *Miller* into question, pornography itself has undergone significant change since the 1970 commission on obscenity surveyed the field. The porn market, growing for over a hundred years, exploded in the 1970s, turning pornography into a multi-billion dollar industry. Advances in technology made printed porn easier and cheaper to produce and put new forms within the reach of virtually everyone—home videos, cable porn, and telephone porn.[94] While the 1970 commission could state "with complete confidence that an estimate of $2.5 billion sales grossly exaggerates the size of the 'smut' industry in the United States under any reasonable definition of the term," this figure would be a clear understatement by 1980. This explosion also confounded the commission's prediction that increasing exposure to porn would eventuate in boredom and indifference.[95]

The content of pornography may have changed in a disconcerting fashion as well, at least in the eyes of many citizens. While no systematic survey of the content of hard-core or violent pornography was available in 1970, later studies found significant amounts of violent, more graphic, and abusive images in such widely marketed material as *Playboy* and *Penthouse*. In addition, one researcher found that the average number of rape depictions in hard-core paperback books doubled from 1968 to 1974. Two other researchers who studied images on the covers of over seventeen hundred heterosexual magazines between 1970 and 1981 noted a similar change: while simple portrayals of single nude women predominated in 1970, "Bondage and domination imagery increased very markedly since 1970 and in 1981 constituted 17.2% of the magazine covers, second in frequency only to the depiction of couples in sexual activity." [96]

Such studies support the claims of anti-porn activists that new quantities of violent and explicit images have been unleashed upon society. But more recent evidence garnered in reaction to these studies suggests that their conclusions may be exaggerated, at least in regard to the amount of violent material as a percentage of all pornography. No surveys have come close to covering all available material, and ones conducted in the 1980s suggest that the percentage of violence may have tapered off after the mid-1970s. For example, one study of *Playboy* depictions found that the level of violence in 1983 was below the level surveyed in 1977; and another has shown that X-rated videos from 1979 to 1983 showed more "egalitarian" and "mutual" sex depictions than did adult films shown in theatres—thereby suggesting, perhaps, that the content of sheer pornography is adapting to new, less sinister, social inclinations.[97] Nonetheless, violence, where shown, is likely to be much more graphic than in the past. And, even as a small percentage of available porn, the sheer amount of violence and hard-core material is certainly much greater now than before the 1960s. The simple *awareness* of this increased availability and conspicuousness, which has sparked closer scrutiny and opposition, may be the most important factor, beyond the actual content, influencing current social attitudes toward pornography.[98]

At the same time, new scientific research in the 1970s and 80s began demonstrating that pornography might be harmful. Interestingly, the 1970 commission triggered a new era in research: "Prior to the appearance of the commission's summary report in 1970, knowledge about the effects of explicit erotic stimuli was severely limited. . . . In general, the behavioural effects under investigation . . . involved only selective affective, evaluative, and imaginative responses. . . . With the publication of the commission's work, this tentative trickle of research was suddenly augmented by the opening of a floodgate. Over the past few years, such research has steadily grown into one of the mainstream concerns of social, personality, and clinical psychologists." [99] The work of the 1970 commission was limited in several ways: (1) the sexually explicit materials studied contained little of the violence that is available today; (2) only one of the commission's studies addressed the effect of pornography on men's attitudes; and (3) none of the studies dealt with the long-term cumulative effects of pornography.[100]

Recent academic studies have indicated that some forms of pornography may be socially harmful. The more careful of these researchers emphasize that their findings are most reliable in suggesting the harmful effects of violent pornography; the jury is still out on degrading but non-violent pornography, and no strong correlations have yet been demonstrated between harmful effects and non-degrading and non-violent sexually explicit materials.[101] Furthermore, critics point out that the new experiments on the effects of pornography are subject to inherent limitations that make extrapolation from the laboratory situation problematic. These limitations include: (1) the studies show

23

correlation, not causation; (2) the samples are too small to support conclusive generalizations; (3) the studies do not sufficiently weigh positive effects with negative effects; (4) the studies do not show that every subject is affected negatively or dangerously; (5) the duration of the effects has not been established; and (6) the laboratory setting, regardless of sample size, is unreliable as a basis for extrapolation to society.[102] Researcher Daniel Linz maintains that no research will be conclusive until a longitudinal study is conducted that measures the comparative exposures of young males to media images of sex, and then tracks their attitudes and actions into manhood; such a difficult study is unlikely to be attempted.[103]

Nonetheless, studies do exist that suggest that pornography, especially the violent kind, is potentially more harmful that the conclusions of the 1970 commission would indicate. And the new research offers scientific and intellectual legitimacy to anti-pornography arguments. Nor have anti-porn activists on both the Right and the feminist Left been reluctant to stretch the implications of this research for their own partisan purposes.[104] Non-liberals have begun to deploy this significant body of research to discredit the liberal position of the 1970 commission on obscenity. This trend is analogous to the growth of scientific data on the consequences of pollution and the causes of disease. Greater knowledge of effects brings about demand for greater regulation.[105]

It should be noted that public opinion concerning pornography, if somewhat equivocal, is essentially negative. The public disfavors sexually explicit material but also frowns upon censorship except in more extreme cases: it endorses less censorious measures of control for less explicit and violent material. In effect, citizens balance the competing values of sexual morality and freedom, reflecting a reasonable awareness of the clash of values in this area of public policy. Polls have indicated that a majority of the public disapproves of photographs and movies of sexual activity more strongly than it disapproves of depictions in books, agrees that pornography influences aggression and negative attitudes toward women, and believes that pornography causes moral decay. A Gallup poll in *Newsweek* in March 1985 found the following attitudes toward restrictions in varying circumstances:

1. Magazines that show nudity: 21% for banning; 52% for no public display; 26% for no restriction

2. Magazines that show adults having sexual relations: 47% for banning; 40% for no public display; 12% for no restriction

3. Magazines that show sexual violence: 73% for banning; 20% for no public display; 6% for no restrictions

4. Theatres showing X-rated films: 40% for banning; 37% for no public display; 20% for no restrictions

5. Theatres showing films with sexual violence: 68% for banning; 21% for no public display; 9% for no restrictions.[106]

The findings of the 1970 commission were similar. Although that commission found less overall public concern about sexuality explicit material, a majority of its sample did favor some restriction of material found to be harmful. The major difference between 1970 and 1985 was the degree of public concern.[107]

Another study indicates that community leaders and legal elites—especially the latter—are more tolerant of freedom of choice in this area than is the mass public, a finding consistent with studies that show greater elite support of other civil liberties.[108] The politics of the anti-pornography ordinance is an exception that tests the rule, however; in Minneapolis and Indianapolis the political elite lined up in support of the measure. No broad public demand accompanied the ordinance's emergence, though special interest groups joined the political processes that led to enactment.

The Political Environment

Along with the factors just discussed, important political and cultural changes altered the face of American politics in the 1970s, preparing the stage for the new politics of pornography and its challenge to the modern doctrine of free expression. First, the political and social upheavals of 1968 and after provoked a reaction. James Q. Wilson portrayed Ronald Reagan's candidacy in 1980 as part of a larger "moral regeneration" in the wake of alleged self indulgence, narcissism, and sundering of tradition. He compared this movement to other periods of moral renewal in American history and concluded that the Reagan revival was potentially a fourth historical episode of the "Great Awakening" variety. Others have interpreted the 1970s more psychologically, arguing that the decline of social cohesion and tradition begat uncertainties and fears that worked their way into politics.[109] From this perspective, movements in the 1980s against assorted evils such as pornography, drugs, liquor, smoking, and other allegedly victimless crimes are largely symbolic movements driven by deeper underlying causes, including anxieties over social change and the search for more secure psychological boundaries.[110]

25

The search for boundaries also may incline individuals to grasp at absolutes and certitude in the face of complexity and uncertainty. Sexual issues are prime candidates for this talismanic quest because sex is central to personality, mysteriously powerful, and inherently complex. Psychological and sociological theories have been pressed into service to explain Rightist anti-pornography movements in the past, as well as other forms of Rightist protest against modernism. These theories are instructive and will be used as appropriate in this book. Yet care must be taken lest they be used to explain away valid moral and social argument. We may note in this regard that researchers have not applied the psychological model as vigorously to the Left. But the Left, or a part of it, has now entered the politics of pornography and is probably not exempt from influence by the inner forces that theorists have attempted to explicate on the Right.

The 1970s also witnessed the political appearance of two key groups that have exerted a significant effect on the politics of pornography: the New Right and the radical feminist Left. Although the election of Richard Nixon in 1968 foreshadowed the rise of conservatism, few observers foresaw the rise of these groups to national prominence.[111] But anti-pornography movements in the 1960s already portended the emergence of new conservative forces. According to Zurcher and Kirkpatrick, "A momentum was observed to be sweeping the nation—a momentum of righteous individuals who were no longer going to stand by passively while all they respected and valued was challenged by individuals and events urging or stimulating dangerous alternatives. Those comments hinted at the dynamics which some months later would be illustrative of the awakening of the 'silent majority.'"[112]

In the politics of pornography, conservatives espoused normative standards regulating sexual desire and depictions. They believe that sexual desire should be expressed within a framework of rationality and interpersonal commitment. More broadly, the Right urges a revival of religious and communal values in the face of what it construes to be moral and social decay caused by liberal laxity. According to Walter Dean Burnham, "The proliferation of atomistic hedonism comes to be seen as subverting the foundations of the social order and of Christianity itself. It is therefore not surprising that religious sects of all sorts have proliferated in recent years, that evangelical Protestant denominations in particular have had major growth, and that the political Moral Majority has emerged as a reactionary-revitalization cultural movement."[113]

Of course, contemporary conservative anti-pornography politics has ancestral roots. After modern pornography emerged in the eighteenth century, the first major attempts to restrict it for moral reasons in America and Europe arose in the nineteenth century. These movements were generated largely by conservative political action groups like Anthony Comstock's New York Society for the Suppression of Vice. But Comstock and his followers also allied themselves with "the emergent group of Progressivist social hygienists who were intent on applying the laws of modern science to control sexual appetites" and other forms of "filth." [114] A similar alliance of conservatives and progressives also formed in the moral crusades against prostitution and sexual diseases in England in the late nineteenth century; critics have charged that the alliance enabled conservative men to coopt emergent feminism. [115] Censorship based on notions of sexual hygienics returned in America during and after the First World War, but by the 1930s and 1940s liberalization of obscenity law was underway, culminating in the mushrooming of pornography and obscenity in the later 1960s and the 1970s.

This explosion in the scope and nature of pornography helped to energize the initially under-reported resurgence of conservative activism in the 1960s and 1970s. Most of the activists of this period were white, middle-aged people with strong religious affiliations. Like Comstock, some viewed pornography as an apocalyptic, religious, and moral symptom of social and moral decline:

> The use of pornographic material was associated, causally
> or correlatively, with venereal disease, drug use, sex crimes
> of all sorts, the failure of marriages, juvenile delinquency,
> failure in school, loss of religion, disrespect for authority,
> parent-child difficulties, arson, theft, purse-snatching,
> mugging and murder. At the highest level of abstraction,
> pornography was seen as causally related to the general
> decline of basic values in American society. [116]

The political emergence of the New Right and evangelicalism in the 1970s reinvigorated the conservative anti-pornography movement and contributed to building a more formidable national movement in the 1980s. [117] Groups already in existence, such as Citizens for Decency Through Law (CDL, founded in 1957 by Charles H. Keating, Jr., a dissenting member of the 1970 Commission on Obscenity and Pornography) and Morality in Media (founded in New York in 1962) enjoyed significant growth in the 1970s and 1980s. [118] Other conservative groups have sprouted in the 1980s, including Morality in America (established in 1984), the National Federation for Decency (established recently by the Rev. Don Wildmon, a major mover and shaker in the conservative, religiously inspired anti-pornography movement; Wildmon is militantly conservative and very political), and the National Consultation of Pornography (established by Dr. Jerry Kirk of Cincinnati, Wildmon, and other leading anti-porn activists in 1983 to serve as an umbrella organization for several prominent conservative groups).[119]

"Networking" and activism by groups such as CDL have burgeoned since the late 1970s and have helped to restrict pornography in some areas despite the general pattern of increased availability. With CDL's help, Fort Wayne, Indiana, managed to eliminate most pornographic establishments through vigorous private and public actions from 1982 to 1984.[120] In 1982 in Cincinnati, Dr. Jerry Kirk allied himself and his church following with CDL and formed Citizens Concerned for Community Values (CCCV). CCCV engaged in mass picketing and protests against pornographic establishments and pushed for vigorous prosecution of obscenity laws. By 1985, Cincinnati could declare itself the "Anti-Porn Capital of America."[121] Similar local efforts have succeeded in limiting pornography in many other towns, including Atlanta, Pittsburgh, Phoenix and Columbia, S.C.[122] More recently, efforts to restrict access to pornography by means of zoning have proliferated, especially since the Supreme Court's *Renton* decision opened the door to widespread dispersal zoning in order to protect the quality of neighborhoods.

Another group of traditionalists that became active in the 1980s is the National Consultation on Obscenity, Pornography, and Indecency. The consultation first convened in 1983 and is now a national focus of anti-pornography forces. It holds an annual meeting in Cincinnati that draws largely conservative activists, religious groups, police, and government officials to discuss and organize attacks on pornography. Groups at the 1984 meeting at Cincinnati included Morality in Media, CCCV, CDL, the National Federation for Decency, the National Obscenity Law Center, and the National Christian Association. The gathering heard vigorous calls to activism and sometimes apocalyptic denunciations of the liberal forces alleged to be subverting America. It concluded with a strong "Resolution on Pornography and Obscenity" and "Call to National Righteousness," which asked for affirmation of "holy living as taught in the Scriptures," "societal standards of righteousness," and "family, church, and community values."[123]

28

Although the contemporary women's movement had been growing for a number of years, it did not erupt as a formidable political force until the 1970s: "The feminist movement could not emerge until . . . there was a constituency which believed that women should have the same opportunity as men, that women were denied these options because of discrimination, and that the government is responsible for eliminating discriminatory practices." [124]

Feminism is a complicated movement that defies monolithic treatment; it has undergone development and factionalization in the last fifteen years similar to those besetting the larger body politic. Feminists are far from united on the meaning of pornography and the issue of censorship. [125] Among the many forms of feminism are "liberal feminism," which emphasizes equal civil rights and holds that "an individual woman should be able to determine her social role with as great freedom as a man"; Marxist feminism; "radical feminism," which sees the family as a unit of control over women and society as a patriarchical construction of domination; "lesbian separatism"; and "socialist feminism," which rejects some aspects of classical Marxism as untenable and views some tenets of radical feminism as "ahistorical, antidialectical, and utopian." Non-liberal forms of Leftist feminism differ from liberal feminism "in believing that women are first and foremost members of a group or class, not individuals who are female." [126] For example, the "socially based" radical feminism of Catharine MacKinnon and Andrea Dworkin emphasizes the social and historical domination of women as a group: in MacKinnon's words, the theory "treats women as a social group, not in individualist, naturalist, idealist, moralist, voluntarist, or harmonist terms." [127]

Historically, liberalism and feminism have gone hand in hand. "Since at least the mid-nineteenth century, the fight for women's rights has been largely fought under the banner of liberalism. The ethical principles of people like John Stuart Mill formed the moral justification for these struggles, and many of these individuals were themselves committed to the cause of women's equality." [128] Yet the feminists who link inequality with pornography believe that it is time to reconsider this association. Against their critics, who assert that "mistrust of civil liberties reveals a lack of historical perspective . . . feminism and civil liberties are inextricable," [129] the more radical feminist position counters that rules associated with civil liberty are not in fact equal or neutral. Supposedly neutral rules reinforce the values and biases of those in power—who are males—so such rules simply disguise or obscure social inequality. Liberalism is a form of false consciousness because there is no substantive equality and freedom for women.[130] Mac-Kinnon expressed this view in a speech at Harvard Law School:

> The liberal view is that abstract categories—speech or equality—define systems. Every time you strengthen free speech in one place, you strengthen it elsewhere. . . . What I will be exploring is the way in which substantive systems, made up of real people with real social labels attached, are also systems. You can reverse racism abstractly, but white supremacy is unfudgeably substantive. Sexism can be an equal abstraction, but male supremacy says who is where. . . .

In MacKinnon's view, the problem with the liberal principle of neutrality is its "equation of substantive powerlessness with substantive power and calling treating these the same, 'equality.'" Distrusting free speech, since freedom to speak is inextricably linked with power, MacKinnon essentially advocates a form of "progressive censorship"—censorship of dominant conservative or reactionary ideas in order that progressive concepts can be heard and acted upon. This is similar to the position that Herbert Marcuse made famous in a 1969 article.[131]

The first feminist organization in America dedicated to eliminating pornography came into existence as recently as 1976, when Women against Violence was founded in San Francisco.[132] It is revealing that even in 1979, a *University of Pittsburgh Law Review* symposium on free speech that also dealt with obscenity and pornography did not include the feminist interpretation of pornography to any significant extent, although one anti-pornography writer did touch on this approach while making a largely conservative argument.[133] Since the late 1970s, however, feminist anti-porn organizations have proliferated, including Women against Pornography (New York), Women against Violence against Women (Los Angeles), and the Pornography Resource Center (Minneapolis). Not surprisingly, the 1979 Williams Committee in England—whose liberal conclusions, like those of the 1970 American commission, were disavowed by its government—encountered no feminist views during its hearings. The first feminist attacks on sex shops took place only as the committee met, but they mushroomed soon after the report was written. According to commissioner A. W. B. Simpson, the only *original* or *creative* objections to the commission's report were feminist; conservative critiques, on the other hand, offered "no new ideas."[134]

The modern feminist movement has consisted of at least two main branches: an older branch, which is more liberal, legally-oriented, and organizational (exemplified by the National Organization for Women), and a more recent movement, which is more mass-based, experimental, and activist.[135] The anti-pornography feminist movement belongs more to the latter, so it is not surprising that the Minneapolis and national branches of NOW were not in the forefront of those dealing with the ordinance.

The rise of feminist and conservative critiques has accompanied the crumbling of the national intellectual consensus concerning civil liberty policy and the role of the state. The traditional consensus governing civil rights policy, which is different from but related to the liberal doctrine of free expression, emphasized individual rights over group or social rights and state neutrality in enforcement of civil rights policy.[136] But this consensus dissolved in the social changes of the 1960s and 1970s. According to Burnham, "Since then, of course, the content of "liberalism" has undergone very profound changes. In particular, racial, minority, and social issues are very much more important to political conflicts within the Democratic party than they were then." [137]

Conflicts over the meaning of civil rights and civil rights policy were sparked by multiplying group claims (feminist–traditional women, black–feminist, black–Jewish, homosexual–heterosexual, and so forth) in connection with affirmative action and other issues. Indeed, conflict may be inevitable when controversial issues move from general affirmation of principle to actual implementation of policy.[138] Controversies over Supreme Court decisions concerning "privacy" (especially abortion), affirmative action, busing, the death penalty, and prayer in schools reflected the lack of social consensus on the substantive content of civil liberty. The "rootless" Burger Court's striking inability to formulate a coherent approach to these matters probably was due less to the factions on the Court than to the want of consensus in society on the substantive content of civil liberty.[139]

Contemporary debate over pornography has taken place in this controversial environment, which has increased the complexity. Feminist arguments against pornography have offered new Leftist justifications for censorship; conservative arguments have grown in sophistication, drawing on new research, feminist argument, and other sources. Before the late 1970s, most writers on the issue of obscenity and pornography described the debate as a simple dichotomy: the forces of reaction versus the forces of freedom. D. F. Barber's widely cited 1972 work, *Pornography and Society*, depicts the battle in typical fashion: 31

> Each and every case, in its own way, has been a head-on
> clash between the desire to impose a standard of sexual
> behavior on society at large and the need to challenge the
> status quo. As such, the debate about pornography, in all
> its multifarious guises, is a dialogue about morality.

Barber also portrays the conflict using terms such as "The Establishment v The Alternative Society" and "the two armies"; he declares
that hard-core pornography is "rare," "swiftly destroyed," "unde-
fended and undiscussed." [140]

Most serious works on pornography before 1980 deal with relatively benign forms, mainly artistic. This buttresses the liberal position
by making censorship appear unnecessary and neurotic. Barber, for
example, declares, "It is difficult sometimes not to sympathize with
those who see the whole argument as an expression of an essentially
puritan anxiety neurosis about sex." The leading defense lawyer in Indianapolis echoed Barber's viewpoint: men who attack pornography
are "uncomfortable with or afraid of their own sexuality." [141] Doubt is
cast on such benign depictions of the nature of pornography and its
politics, however, when opponents point to the at least ostensible
spread of violent, hard-core material and raise non-traditional arguments about pornography's effects.

Conclusion

The new debate over pornography is part of a broader controversy
concerning the nature of liberty and freedom in society. The liberal
core of the First Amendment has been affirmed in the court decisions
of the last twenty years, even in the erstwhile conservative domain of
obscenity law. But many critics now question whether the First
Amendment, in its application to sexual materials (or even beyond),
should be reinterpreted in a manner more consistent with other, less
liberal, areas of law and with non-liberal social values, whether progressive or traditional.

We have seen how conservatives and some radical feminists present
serious alternatives to liberal models of justice, free speech, and pornography. Their critiques are fortified by suggestive new research. Although modern obscenity law has striven to balance, however precariously, liberal and conservative values, many conservatives are now
pressing to redirect obscenity law in a conservative direction, while
many feminists seek to establish a new context for regulating sexual
depictions. Activists on both Left and Right question the status quo.

In the next three chapters I will look more closely at the politics and law of pornography, giving special attention to the politics of the anti-pornography ordinance in Minneapolis and Indianapolis. This examination reveals the political and legal aspects of new attacks on pornography and raises urgent questions regarding pornography policy. Do the politics and law of pornography require us to maintain or reform the law governing sexual depictions? What does the new politics of pornography suggest about the social and institutional status of free speech and tolerance in the United States?

THE MINNEAPOLIS ORDINANCE AND THE FEMINIST THEORY OF PORNOGRAPHY AND SEXUALITY

> Pornography no longer describes only the sexual activities be-
> tween prostitutes and their customers. Sexual liberation has
> brought into the home many of the bizarre sexual activities that
> men have demanded of prostitutes. Pornography depicts not just
> what one can do with a whore but with one's lover, one's wife,
> and even one's daughter. Through pornography, time-honored
> distinctions of society are now blurring and the gap is quickly
> closing between love and violence, madonnas and whores.
>
> Kathleen Barry, *Female Sexual Slavery*

In this chapter I examine the nature of the anti-pornography ordinance
and the theory out of which it developed. I devote particular attention
to Andrea Dworkin's and Catharine MacKinnon's theories of pornography, as they were the authors of the ordinance, but I will also discuss
related ideas, for the ordinance synthesized the views of many feminist
theorists. An understanding of the theory underlying the ordinance is
needed to grasp the significance of events in Minneapolis and to deal
adequately with policy issues posed by the new politics of pornography. The politics of the ordinance in Minneapolis will be examined in
the next chapter.

MacKinnon, Dworkin, and Radical Feminist Theory

A number of factors prepared the way for the anti-pornography ordinance—the ongoing development of feminist theory, special background circumstances in Minneapolis, and the actions of the Minneapolis City Council—but they were brought together by the ability
34   and perspicacity of its authors. Dworkin and MacKinnon fashioned

the ordinance in a class they taught at the University of Minnesota Law School in Minneapolis in fall 1983. Although I will often criticize them in the pages that follow, Dworkin and MacKinnon certainly deserve credit for what they accomplished. They transformed feminist pornography theory into a legal reality; they acted to seize the opportunity presented them by the Minneapolis City Council; and they catapulted the pornography debate to national attention. Support for the ordinance arose within the small circle of Dworkin and MacKinnon's class on pornography at the law school and spread outward to encompass part of the council, the city, and, eventually, the nation. It made a powerful impression—positive or negative—on virtually everyone who encountered it.

Catharine Mackinnon is a "social" radical feminist whose prolific writings on pornography and feminist issues grew out of her earlier work on sexual harassment and related concerns.[1] The other side of the team, Andrea Dworkin, provided the rhetorical, psychological, and theoretical underpinnings of the ordinance. Dworkin is also a prolific author; her work on pornography has attained canonical status in the radical movement.[2] Paul Brest and Ann Vandenberg, whose article on the politics of the Minneapolis ordinance will be cited frequently in the next chapter, describe the duo:

> MacKinnon and Dworkin have powerful and charismatic styles that complement each other. MacKinnon is the consummate critic. Severe in appearance and manner, she writes and speaks in intense, structured phrases with emphatic cadences to make her points. Dworkin expresses herself in an expansive, flowing style. Although her writing is angry and polemical, in person she exudes a galvanizing generosity of spirit and optimism.[3]

In discussing Dworkin and MacKinnon's theories, I will quote them at some length so that their ideas may speak for themselves.

Feminism and Pornography

Feminists hold various views on pornography and free speech. While many supported the ordinance, others were ambivalent or opposed. Nonetheless, it is possible to identify points of agreement in the feminist critique of pornography as it emerged in the late 1970s and the 1980s. The following sketch is not intended as an exhaustive portrait of the feminist interpretation of pornography but as a summary of its central tenets.

The feminist critique of pornography rejects both the moralism of the conservative position and the freedom of choice of liberalism. According to one feminist, "what distinguishes the feminist anti-pornography movement from traditional religious-moralist concerns is the argument that what is objectionable about pornography is not the sexually explicit nature of the material. Feminists argue that pornography has little to do with sex, and everything to do with power." [4] The feminist theory of pornography is derived from the feminist theory of sexuality: pornography reflects and reinforces the subordinating structure of male sexuality and power. More radical feminists construe male sexuality as predominantly, even totally, subordinating; less radical feminists draw distinctions between humanistic (egalitarian) and non-humanistic male sexuality, as well as violent and nonviolent erotic variations. Consequently, feminists differ over the possibility of achieving equal sexual relations—the more radical the theory, the less sanguine the assessment. According to Andrea Dworkin, for example, "Terror issues from the male, illuminates his essential nature and his basic purpose." [5]

The concept of equality is the key to the feminist theory of sexual depictions. Eric Hoffman observes, "Feminists distinguished between liberating, egalitarian images and degrading images; images within the first category are erotic, whereas images within the second category are pornographic." Obscenity doctrine focuses on the prurient effect of obscenity on the (usually male) reader; but the feminist interpretation of "pornography" is more relational and political, focusing on the effects of pornography on *women* as objects of desire. Pornography objectifies, degrades, and brutalizes women in the name of sexual stimulation or entertainment for men. Pornography (distinguished from erotica, which is more egalitarian) dehumanizes women as a group by depicting them in demeaning ways; women "are manipulated and are thereby robbed of their subjectivity and their capacity to define reality in their own terms." [6] Pornography socially constructs women's subjectivity in a manner which makes them objects of male pleasure and power and strips them of their own autonomy. Thus, pornography is an ingredient in the pervasive patriarchical silencing of women's voices and beings. According to a radical feminist in Minneapolis who played a role in the politics of the ordinance, "In very real and direct ways, pornography functions successfully to silence women's speech." [7]

This critique parallels the conservative critique of pornography, which also stresses pornography's depersonalizing effects, but it focuses on the effects of pornography on women rather than on the moral virtue of men. Its more radical versions construe the anti-humanistic implications of pornography as typical of male nature and male-oriented society rather than atypical. MacKinnon, Dworkin, and other radical feminists, for example, have come close to rejecting the distinction between erotica and pornography because they believe that egalitarian sex is virtually an impossibility in a system permeated by male domination. Accordingly, all forms of pornography are equally suspect and implicated in sexual domination: "Pornography is the theory, and rape the practice," Robin Morgan charges in a famous tract.[8]

Because of these critical understandings, this feminist position recommends restriction of pornography at the least. Although some feminists approve of traditional restrictions of pornography by means of obscenity law, zoning, nuisance laws, and the like, most prominent anti-pornography feminists see these as insufficient compromises and illegitimate moralism.[9] Further, some feminists assert that the individualistic basis of the modern liberal doctrine of speech is an expression of male interests and values: first, only men possess true autonomy in a patriarchical system, so a system of law built on this norm serves only men; and second, the abstract notions of individualism and autonomy supporting the modern doctrine of speech are an ideological smoke screen. These notions are either expressions of the abstracting, individuating quality of the male mentality, or they are ways of obfuscating the reality of domination that makes male autonomy possible and female autonomy impossible.[10] Hence, using traditional methods to control pornography is like employing the fox to guard the chicken house.

MacKinnon, Dworkin, and Pornography.

MacKinnon's understanding of pornography, like Dworkin's, is radical, rooted in her interpretation of sexuality and gender. Rather than being deviant, violent pornography and sexuality express the underlying violent reality of male power. In this view, any distinctions between "erotica" and "degradation" and "violence" misconstrue reality. Pornography exemplifies a sexuality that is the most important cause of the subordination of women as a group. MacKinnon professes:

> sexuality itself is no longer unimplicated in women's
> second-class status. Sexual violence can no longer be cate-
> gorized away as violence not sex. . . . What is sex except
> that which is felt as sexual? When acts of dominance and

37

submission, up to and including acts of violence, are experienced as sexually arousing, as sex itself, that is what they
are. The mutual exclusivity of sex and violence is preserved in the face of this evidence by immunizing as "sex"
whatever causes a sexual response and by stigmatizing
questioning it as repressive. . . . Violence is sex when it is
practiced as sex. . . . Sexuality appears as the interactive
dynamic of gender as an inequality. . . . Gender emerges as
the congealed form of the sexualization of inequality between men and women. Sexual abuse . . . is a terror so
perfectly motivated and systematically concerted that it
never need be intentionally organized—an arrangement
that, as long as it lasted, would seal the immortality of any
totalitarianism.[11]

Pornography eroticizes violence and subordination of women. It is
the literal expression of male sexual domination. As such, pornography is more than simply a form of expression distinct from action: it is
intricately and inextricably bound up with the subordination of
women. According to MacKinnon:

In Andrea's work, expression is not just talk. Pornography
not only teaches the reality of male dominance. It is one
way its reality is imposed as well as experienced. It is a
way of seeing and using women. Male power makes authoritative a way of seeing and treating women, so that
when a man looks at a pornographic picture—pornographic meaning that the woman is defined to be acted
upon, a sexual object, a sexual thing—the viewing is an
act, an act of male supremacy.[12]

If sexuality and pornography are thus central in the systemic social
subordination of women, remedial action must reach beyond obscenity law. Obscenity law is wrong on several counts. It incorrectly assumes that male sexuality is fundamentally moral; and it obfuscates
reality by focusing on the abstract issue of morality, whereas the key
problems with pornography are concrete and political. MacKinnon
declares:

Obscenity law is concerned with morality, specifically
morals from the male point of view, meaning the standpoint of male domination. The feminist critique of pornography is a politics, specifically politics from women's
point of view, meaning the standpoint of the subordination
of women to men. Morality here means good and evil;

politics means power and powerlessness. Obscenity is a moral idea; pornography is a political practice. Obscenity is abstract; pornography is concrete. . . .

Contrast this view with the feminine analysis of Andrea Dworkin, in which sexuality itself is a social construct, gendered to the ground. Male dominance here is not an artificial overlay upon an underlying inalterable substratum of uncorrupted essential sexual being. Sexuality free of male dominance will require *change,* not reconceptualization, transcendence, or excavation. Pornography is not imagery in some relation to a reality elsewhere constructed. It is not a distortion, reflection, projection, expression, fantasy, representation, or symbol either. It is sexual reality.[13]

Because male sexuality and pornography are implicated in the subordination of women, the harms they cause are more wide-ranging and systemic than can be comprehended by the modern speech doctrines of individual meaning and direct harm. Most directly, women are coerced and harmed in the very making of pornography. Liberal doctrine would be concerned here if individual women were coerced into making pornography or physically harmed in making it, as obvious direct harm and lack of autonomy would be present. But MacKinnon and Dworkin's understanding of harm even at this level goes beyond liberal assumptions. They assume coercion in virtually all instances of women's participation in making pornography because the general subordination of women in society creates systemic pressure in each case. It is illusory to presume voluntariness on the part of women who enter into relations, business or otherwise, with men. Subordination is so deeply embedded in the system that any individual action is tainted by the subordinating elements of the whole society. This is especially the case when the context is erotic as in the making of pornography, because the erotic context is the most acute locus of gender domination.

Consequently, MacKinnon, like many radical feminist critics, maintains that pornography is harmful *in itself,* not only because it may trigger specific sexual violence or harmful attitudes (the "direct harm" looked for by liberal principles); pornography also constitutes an ideological instrument of male domination that generates and reinforces subordination and discrimination against women in a broader systemic sense. Thus, while pornography may have different meanings for different individuals in society, individual experiences that vary from

39

the norm of domination ultimately cancel each other out when the social whole is considered.[14] Reality and language partake in fundamentally social, power-based (and universal, categorical) meanings. Individualism and the individual construction of meaning is illusory, since the individual is shaped by history and society. This understanding links MacKinnon's theory with Marxism and Structuralism.[15]

This approach rejects the modern speech doctrine's direct harms principle in favor of a notion of systemic harm, analogous to the "institutional" or "societal" violence perpetrated against poor people or minorities.[16] Accordingly, the alleged kidnapping of Linda Marciano to force her to play "Linda Lovelace" in the pornographic movie *Deep Throat* is not atypical but archetypal, an example of pornography's essential functioning in an unequal society.[17]

This systemic understanding of pornography construes harm and cause and effect differently than does the modern doctrine of free speech, which assumes the legitimacy of the marketplace of ideas: under the sway of liberal doctrine, where harm is not immediate and no emergency prevails, "the remedy to be applied is more speech, not enforced silence." [18] Dworkin and MacKinnon disavow this individualistic and analytical approach, which focuses on individual entities in isolation from the whole, and, concomitantly, the speech/action dichotomy that underpins free speech jurisprudence. MacKinnon elaborates this critique in reflecting on Linda Marciano:

> From thinking further about Linda's relation to the film
> (*Deep Throat*) in the context of Andrea's analysis, I
> learned that the social preconditions, the presumptions,
> that underlie the First Amendment do not apply to
> women. The First Amendment essentially presumes some
> level of social equality among people and hence essentially
> equal social access to the means of expression. In the con-
> text of inequality between the sexes, we cannot presume
> that that is accurate. The First Amendment also presumes
> that for the mind to be free to fulfill itself, speech must be
> free and open. Andrea's work shows that pornography
> contributes to enslaving women's minds and bodies. As a
> social process and as a form of "speech" pornography
> amounts to terrorism and promotes not freedom but si-
> lence. Rather, it promotes freedom for men and enslave-
> ment and silence for women. . . .
>
> Pornography terrorizes women into silence. Pornogra-
> phy is therefore not in the interest of our speech. . . . First
> Amendment logic, like nearly all legal reasoning, has diffi-

culty grasping harm that is not linearly caused in the
"John hit Mary" sense. The idea is that words or pictures
can be harmful only if they produce harm in a form that is
considered an action. . . . The trouble with this individu-
ated, atomistic, linear, isolated, tortlike—in a word, posi-
tivistic—conception of injury is that the way pornography
targets and defines women for abuse and discrimination
does not work like this. It does hurt individuals, not as individuals in a one-at-a-time sense, but as members of the
group "women." [19]

The 1986 Attorney General's Commission also used a broader conception of harm than is espoused by the modern doctrine of speech.
But the concept of "multiple causation" utilized by the commission—
that the presence of pornography increases the total incidence of sexual violence in society, although pornography is not the only cause and
particular uses or expressions of pornography do not always have this
effect—was not intended to be a constitutional standard; it was a tool
of empirical analysis, not a legal test.[20] Nor was it as wide-ranging in
its scope as the theory of harm that we are considering.

Andrea Dworkin's theory of pornography is similar to MacKinnon's
but more visionary. Like MacKinnon, Dworkin renounces the modern
speech doctrine's speech/action distinction and the accompanying direct harms principle. Dworkin's understanding of reality is holistic and
synthetic, holding that facts, individuals, or actions cannot be understood apart from their relation to the larger whole. In Dworkin's inter-
connected universe, pornography leads to violent male sexuality because "everything leads to everything else."[21] From this perspective,
individual depictions of subordination that are seemingly isolated in
meaning, according to liberal individualism's analytic mode of understanding, actually bear an integrated meaning. This meaning is that in
patriarchical societies all women are conceived as whores and objects
of male pleasure:

The word pornography does not have any other meaning
than the one cited here, the graphic depiction of the lowest
whores. Whores exist to serve men sexually; whores exist
only in a framework of male sexual domination. . . . The
pornography itself is objective and real and central to the
male sexual system. The valuation of women's sexuality in
pornography is objective and real because women are so
regarded and so valued. The force depicted in pornography is objective and real because force is so used against

41

women. . . . As Kate Millet wrote, women's sexuality is reduced to the one essential: "cunt . . . our essence, our offense."[22]

Like MacKinnon's, Dworkin's theory of pornography disputes the speech/action distinction: pornography, in itself, is *an act* that is inescapably linked to the general disempowerment of women and other acts against women. Cindy Jenefsky, a perceptive student of Dworkin, points out, "the originality of this new conception is that pornography is not just a depiction of harm, but . . . *consists* of harm to women."[23] In Dworkin's logic, pornography is not deviant but rather an *epiphany*. Pornography explosively discloses the truth about women's enslavement to men.

As Jenefsky observes, Dworkin's understanding of porn is supported by her more general rhetorical strategy of synecdoche. Synecdoche is a "concrete universal," or the part that reflects the whole. Kenneth Burke defines *synecdoche* as "part for the whole, whole for the part, sign for the thing signified. . . . The 'noblest synecdoche,' the perfect paradigm or prototype for all lesser usages, is found in metaphysical doctrines proclaiming the identity of 'microcosm' and 'macrocosm.' "[24] For Dworkin, pornography (especially violent pornography) is the microcosm that reflects the macrocosm of partiarchal society. Like MacKinnon's, this understanding distrusts individuality and individual meaning and points to universal and social meaning. Unlike MacKinnon's, however, Dworkin's theory of sexuality seems both biologically and socially based. Men's natures are functions of essentialist biological forces ("terror issues from the male, illuminates his very essence") as well as of the will to political power against women.[25]

Comprehension of the synecdochal meaning of pornography, according to Jenefsky, erupts into consciousness. It is a sudden realization or "fantastic insight" that "does not appear slowly, accumulatively; it arrives with a sudden urgency that instantaneously illuminates previously invisible relationships with objects."[26] We will see in the next chapter that this sense of sudden breakthrough did indeed characterize the ordinance for many of its enthusiasts.

We may note that Dworkin's rhetorical logic, like that of some other radical feminists, reflects gnostic tenets. Gnostic philosophy predicates a "true" self impatiently hiding behind the veil of socialization and appearance, awaiting liberation. The way to self-realization is to strip away the veil of false consciousness and free the authentic self imprisoned within. Radical theories of revolutions in consciousness (among which, radical feminism is now prominent) are based on this transformation from "false" to "true" self.[27]

Interestingly, the so-called gnostic theory of pornography, epitomized by the perverse sexual theory of Sade, preached a similar transformation; its tenets are, ironically, not far removed from the transformation theories of Dworkin and her followers. "One important branch of Gnosticism tries to achieve [liberation of the hidden self] by shattering social rules, psychic organizations, and even natural law, through sex ... the libertine is the savior of the universe for both beings and for the Godhead itself. Sex is an especially appropriate technique for freeing the entangled divine sparks because the Gnostic supreme God is essentially sexual."[28]

In an earlier work (1974) Dworkin, espousing similar views, actually advocated the total abolition of sexual taboos, including the most central, in classic gnostic (and utopian) terms: "The destruction of the incest taboo is essential to the development of cooperative human community based on the free-flow of natural androgynous eroticism. . . . The object is cultural transformation. The object is the development of a new kind of human being and a new kind of human community. All of us who have ever tried to right a wrong recognize that *truly nothing short of everything will really do.*"[29] Dworkin seems to have abandoned her belief in the liberating potential of unbridled sexuality. But her theories of pornography and consciousness raising through fantastic insight still embrace a gnostic-like belief in the total transformation of personality through the proper understanding of sex, and the concomitant rejection of the entire preceding historical process. This understanding raises problems for democratic theory and practice which I will discuss below.

The Content of the Minneapolis Ordinance.

The Minneapolis ordinance created a non-criminal, civil-rights approach to the restriction of pornography. It covered a much larger field than traditional law, as it dealt with pornography rather than obscenity. In many respects, the ordinance's key provisions reversed the assumptions, tenets, and tendencies of modern free speech and obscenity law outlined in Chapter 1. It defined pornography in a social feminist fashion, addressing the problem of the powerlessness of women as a class: as discrimination against women. Enforcement was to be handled by the city's civil rights and affirmative action office. To be subject to civil action, pornographic material would have to satisfy three criteria: it must be sexually explicit; it must subordinate women;

43

and it must subordinate through at least one of nine means. In sum, the original Ordinance crafted in Minneapolis defined pornography as "the sexually explicit subordination of women, graphically or in words," that also includes one or more of the following nine depictions:

(i) women are presented as sexual objects, things, or commodities; or

(ii) women are presented as objects who enjoy pain or humiliation; or

(iii) women are presented as sexual objects who experience sexual pleasure in being raped; or

(iv) women are presented as sexual objects tied up or cut up or mutilated or bruised or physically hurt; or

(v) women are presented in postures of sexual submission or sexual servility, including by inviting penetration; or

(vi) women's body parts—including but not limited to vaginas, breasts, and buttocks—are exhibited, such that women are reduced to those parts; or

(vii) women are presented as whores by nature; or

(viii) women are presented being penetrated by objects or animals; or

(ix) women are presented in scenarios of degradation, injury, torture, shown as filthy or inferior, bleeding, bruised, or hurt in a context that makes these conditions sexual.[30]

According to an advocate of the ordinance, the definition "thus excludes erotica premised on sexual equality, or sex education materials. It excludes material which does contain scenes of sexual degradation, but not in a manner which subordinates women."[31] But the notion of subordination is vague and broad enough to cover a wide amount of material presently protected by First Amendment law.[32] Indeed, the ordinance was intentionally based on viewpoint discrimination, which raises a red flag under the First Amendment. Sections i, ii, v, vi, and vii were especially vague and political, as they dealt more with insinuations of inequality and general subordination than with clear depictions of physical abuse.

By abandoning the notions of immoral or prurient sexual arousal that is the key to obscenity doctrine, the ordinance was tantamount to an effort to reconstitute the law dealing with sexual depictions or a call for a new restriction of free speech. Furthermore, the ordinance omitted a provision in which the absence of "scienter"—knowledge of the nature and contents of the material—would be a defense to civil liability for publishers, retailers, or distributors. This omission further distinguished the ordinance from obscenity law, for the Supreme Court requires scienter in obscenity prosecutions of vendors.[33] The ordinance also differed from obscenity law by permitting restriction through civil process of works on the basis of even a single isolated passage. The Supreme Court had rejected this approach in *Roth* in 1957, as had the U. S. Appeals Court in *Ulysses* in 1934. This feature of the ordinance disclosed its supporters' lack of concern for the artful potential of some pornography. Finally, the ordinance's understanding of harm was predicated on the radical feminist approach rather than the direct harm standard of the modern doctrine of speech. This was most pronounced in the provisions for "trafficking" and "assault," which I will discuss presently.

In regard to civil action, the ordinance provided four separate actionable claims dealing with distinct injuries or harms. First, women "coerced" into pornographic performances were entitled (empowered) to bring civil actions for damages against the makers, sellers, exhibitors, or distributors of the pornography and to suppress the products.[34] To initiate this action, the woman must prove that the material is pornographic according to the ordinance's definition. "She must then show that her performance was coerced, fraudulently induced, or brought about by intimidation."[35] Once coercion has been shown, the burden is on the pornographer to rebut. The allowable terms of rebuttal established by the ordinance reflect the radical feminist theory of systemic powerlessness and the concomitant presumptive lack of genuine female volition and consent in a sexual context. According to a feminist who helped draft the ordinance, "Proof of coercion is rebuttable only by a showing that the woman in fact *meaningfully* consented to the performance."[36] The coercion section of the ordinance listed thirteen defenses or rebuttals that would not suffice to negate the presumption of coercion, including: "that the person is a woman," "that the person has attained the age of majority," "that the person actually consented to a use of the performance that is changed into pornography," "that the person showed no resistance or appeared to cooperate actively in the photographic sessions or in the sexual events that produced the pornography," "that the person signed a contract, or made statements affirming a willingness to cooperate in the production of pornography."[37]

The coercion section attempted to address the issue of direct, nonconsentual harm perpetrated against women in the actual making of pornography and to introduce critical feminist precepts concerning women's special vulnerability in the making of pornography. Because women as a group lack power in society—especially in contexts laden with sexual meaning—the traditional assumption that adults voluntarily consent to their actions is questioned. Consequently, the rebuttal of the presumption of coercion is required to be "meaningful." "The assumptions that the law of the first amendment makes about adults— that adults are autonomous, self-defining, freely-acting, *equal* individuals—are exactly those qualities which pornography systematically denies and undermines for women," MacKinnon has remarked in addressing this action.[38]

The second actionable situation concerns "assault or physical attack due to pornography." If a woman (or any person) can show that the material is pornographic under the law, and that a causal relationship exists between a specific assault and specific pornography, she may bring an action for damages against "the perpetrator, the maker(s), distributor(s), seller(s), and/or exhibitor(s)" and an action to obtain an injunction "against the specific pornography's further exhibition, distribution, or sale." The assault provision was designed to provide action against pornography—inspired harm to women.[39] It embodied the feminist understanding of systemic causal harm and rejection of the liberal doctrine of individual responsibility discussed in Chapter 1. While the liberal doctrine assigns responsibility for consequences to those who act on speech rather than to the speaker (except in limited circumstances), the ordinance's logic would hold both speakers and actors responsible. Thus, action could be brought against a broadcaster or pornographer if an abnormal person committed a sexual crime in imitation of a pornographic scene.[40]

Randall Tigue—a lawyer for the Minnesota Civil Liberties Union and for the Alexander family, the leading pornographic businesspeople in Minneapolis—is correct in pointing out that this logic amounts to a return to the *Hicklin* case of 1868. "In fact, section (o) [the assault provision] of the MacKinnon/Dworkin ordinance is far more restrictive of first amendment rights than the statutes in *Hicklin*. Under section (o), any person sexually assaulted by someone who is inspired by a passage from a book to commit the assault would have a civil cause of action. . . . That single act could result in damages being assessed against the distributor, author, publisher, or retailer of the book. . . . The reaction of the most degenerate reader or viewer in society could determine what the remainder of the population would be permitted to read."[41] The sweeping nature of the assault provision, in the context of the exceptionally vague and broad definition of pornography, results in a truly expansive regulatory potential for the ordinance. A person could be held civilly liable for sexual assault on the basis of a very subjective close call concerning the pornographic content of the material at issue.

The third action leading to liability under the ordinance was for "forcing pornography on a person." Under this provision, any person "who has pornography forced on him/her in any place of employment, in education, in a home, or in any public place has a cause of action against the perpetrator and/or institution."[42] This action covers a privacy right similar to traditional First Amendment doctrine that protects "captive audiences" from unwanted exposure to ideas or expression. But the ordinance would presumably have included the unwanted use of pornography by husbands or male lovers in the privacy of the bedroom.[43] Again, the expansiveness of the definition of pornography threatened to make this provision exceptionally intrusive.

The fourth and final action established by the ordinance covered "discrimination by trafficking in pornography." The "production, sale, exhibition, or distribution of pornography is discrimination against women by means of trafficking in pornography." The trafficking provision stated that "any woman has a cause of action hereunder as a woman acting against the subordination of women," even women who have not themselves been harmed by an act of coercion, forcing, or assault. As Baldwin states, "This provision is aimed at the harm to women posed by the availability of pornography in and of itself."[44]

The trafficking action was extremely ambitious for several reasons. First, it was premised on an understanding of discrimination that is very expansive, congruent with Dworkin's synecdochal theory of action and meaning. Gender discrimination is conventionally conceived as an intentional decision or action (which can, of course, involve speech) that treats women less favorably than men for invidious reasons. A decision to hire men rather than women simply because one does not want women around would qualify, but writing a book favoring sexism would not, even if it might beget sexist thoughts and subsequent actions. Again, advocacy of a position is held to a different standard of liability than action by someone on the basis of that advocacy.[45] By making the sheer existence of pornography actionable as a discriminatory act, the ordinance embodied Dworkin and MacKinnon's absolute conflation of speech and action.

47

Second, the trafficking section put into practice the more diffuse notion of harm discussed above and tied it to the concept of group libel. MacKinnon has said, "So far, opposition to our ordinance centers on the trafficking provision. This means that it is difficult to comprehend a group injury in a liberal culture—that what it means to be a woman is defined by this and that it is an injury for all women, even if not for all women equally." [46]

Third, it turned individual women into enforcers of the civil law, for any woman who encountered what the ordinance defined to be pornography could initiate action. In the other provisions, only those women directly harmed by specific, relatively narrowly defined acts of forcing, coercing, and assaulting could initiate actions. The trafficking provision created a roving citizens' mass surveillance force, which would act on the basis of a very broad and vague definition of pornography. [47]

Administration of the Ordinance

Before we look at events surrounding the politics of the ordinance, we should discuss the administrative features of the measure. The ordinance gave plaintiffs two choices of forum in which to initiate actions and claims. The main route would be use of the existing administrative procedures provided by the city's Civil Rights Commission. Under this choice, a person who believes that he or she has been discriminated against may file a complaint with the director of the Minneapolis Civil Rights Commission, who then may investigate within six months to determine if probable cause exists to support the allegations. If probable cause is found, the director will try to reconcile the parties. [48] If this attempt fails, the case is referred to the full Civil Rights Commission, which within thirty days assigns a special hearing committee (consisting of three commission members, one of whom must be a lawyer) to analyze the complaint. [49] This hearing would be open to the public, according to the Minnesota Administrative Procedures Act. (The ordinance's advocates hoped to turn these hearings into public events that would politicize the pornography issue and provide public empowerment of women.) If the committee decides that discrimination took place, it issues an order requiring the respondent to cease the discriminatory act or acts; it may also take any other steps necessary to implement the goals of the Minneapolis Civil Rights Law. [50] The anti-pornography ordinance added another provision to this existing scheme, authorizing the hearing committee or the court to remove offending pornography or issue an injunction against its future sale. [51]

48

The second route provided by the ordinance was direct civil action in court in cases in which the Civil Rights Commission either fails to hold a hearing on the complaint or dismisses the complaint for lack of evidence of significance. This route is not authorized if a reconciliation is brought about, however. This provision was not likely to stand because municipalities in Minnesota may not create subject matter jurisdiction in district courts for private causes of action.[52]

The administrative features of the ordinance were also ambitious in relation to modern First Amendment doctrine governing prior restraints on expression.[53] Many of the ordinance's supporters claimed that the civil process was non-censorious and non-punitive because it did not amount to prior restraint or apply criminal sanctions. But the ordinance's administrative processes clearly would have led to the prohibition of material presently protected by the First Amendment. Use of the prior restraint doctrine as the exclusive test of constitutionality was another example (like the implicit reliance on the logic of *Hicklin*) of how supporters of the ordinance invoked free speech jurisprudence which had long been either abandoned or supplemented with standards more protective of speech.

The civil process created by the ordinance was closely related to the Ordinance's substantive elements. The promulgators and supporters of the ordinance intended to create a forum in which women's complaints against pornography could be heard and which would facilitate wide-ranging surveillance of offending material. The administrative mechanism would empower women by providing a public forum for previously disempowered women to speak out publicly against pornography; it would allow women to become active public agents of surveillance. As Charlee Hoyt, the Minneapolis council member who led the fight for the ordinance, proclaimed, "the Ordinance empowers women to take an action against an instrument that maintains women in a subordinate status ... not government, police, Big Brother, but the citizens themselves. The key is empowerment, giving them the law as an instrument to bring actions, civil rights actions ... to use the government to give power to make rights real."[54] Naomi Scheman agreed, and specifically linked the public hearing forums established by the ordinance to the empowerment of women as public agents:

> I think that what the Ordinance proposed was radically
> different from obscenity ordinances, not only by how it
> describes what's wrong, but in what it allows to happen.
> That it is civil as opposed to criminal, that it empowers the

49

people who are being harmed by it to seek civil redress. But it allows a range of responses within the civil approach. And it would continue the kind of place of speech that the hearings [on the passage of the ordinance] allowed in the hearing room. That would be the kind of speech that would go on in the civil rights courts hearing this. That is, it would institutionalize a place for that kind of speech.[55]

From this perspective, the process and substance of the ordinance were meant to actuate what Herbert Marcuse called "progressive censorship"—censorship in the name of progressive causes. Because the normal marketplace of ideas is characterized by male domination and the concurrent silencing of women's voices, equal gender justice could not be achieved without the countervailing power or counter-censorship offered by the ordinance.

Conclusion

The Minneapolis ordinance's authors and advocates attempted a major revision of both general First Amendment law and law governing pornographic materials. Its tenets were drawn from a particular strand of radical feminist theory that stresses the links between pornography and the social and sexual domination of men over women.[56] A key aspect of the ordinance was the exceptional breadth of its definition of pornography, which had the potential to extend considerably beyond the law of obscenity.

The serious challenge to present First Amendment law presented by the ordinance should not automatically disqualify it, however. Present First Amendment law may indeed be problematic or defective. We will not be in a position to judge the ordinance until we have explored the validity of the modern doctrine of speech and obscenity law in Chapter 5.

Nevertheless, because the ordinance seriously challenged the modern doctrine of speech, it would have been politically responsible for civic leaders to deliberate it with caution. But this did not happen in Minneapolis or, later, in Indianapolis. Let us now look at the politics of the ordinance in Minneapolis.

T H R E E

THE POLITICS OF THE
MINNEAPOLIS ORDINANCE

All Government—indeed, every human benefit and enjoyment,
every virtue and every prudent act—is founded on compromise.
. . .

Edmund Burke.

Practical politics consists in ignoring facts.

Henry Adams.

Nothing short of everything will really do.
Andrea Dworkin, *Woman Hating.*

The major forces behind the ordinance in Minneapolis were anti-
pornography feminists, a few city council members, and neighborhood groups with a variety of perspectives. Aside from those on the
council, conservatives were largely absent among the forces that
fought for the ordinance because the speed with which the proposal
erupted "caught them off guard." [1] And their input was not desired.
The council reportedly asked a prominent local evangelist to cancel his
plan to testify for the ordinance at the public hearings "because they
didn't want his political spectrum identified as a supporter." [2] Feminists in Minneapolis, as in the nation, were divided; but the voices of
anti-pornography feminists drowned the criticisms of feminists
against censorship.

Despite its unusual features, the ordinance encountered very little
resistance at the council level in Minneapolis, at least during the passage of the first version in December 1983. After it was vetoed by
Mayor Donald Fraser, the council passed a second, less ambitious, ver-

51

sion in July 1984; Fraser vetoed it also. However, the political process leading to the second passage was more democratic and deliberative than the first. During the second effort, the mayor established a special Task Force on Pornography to obtain the input of political and public leaders. The task force overcame the one-sidedness that had marked the first stage of the issue.

The lack of political consensus that typifies Minneapolis politics actually characterized the politics of the ordinance. Rather than build consensus, however, supporters deployed unusual strategies that subverted normal pluralism. The city government's response was largely irresponsible, as I have indicated. Before looking at the process in detail, let us consider the background of the pornography issue in Minneapolis. Despite the importance of national developments in the controversy, factors specific to Minneapolis played major roles. Antipornography forces were politicized by their frustrations over past failures. So they pounced on this new approach that promised sweeping reforms.

The Road to the Ordinance

Minneapolis is a liberal city of unusual cultural and intellectual sophistication for its size. It has also been called "unusual among cities its size for the degree of fragmentation in political institutions and practices that it exhibited."[3] Although some recent mayors have wielded substantial influence in city politics, the mayor's office in Minneapolis is less powerful than in many other cities. A shifting cluster of power bases operates in the stead of a true power center (decidedly unlike the political structure of Indianapolis). Perhaps the most important political body in Minneapolis is the thirteen-member city council. Elections were non-partisan until 1973, and even today city council politics is based more on interest group and personal ties than on party affiliation.[4] Decentralization and fragmentation have generated a particular style of political decision-making: a politics that seeks to build operative consensus out of the clash of interests. There are two possible results. First, if competing groups have stakes in an issue, stalemate ensues unless leaders painstakingly forge agreement; and second, single issue groups in alliance with political allies can prevail in the absence of resistance or counter-mobilization. Thus, a Minneapolis reporter once observed, the real source of power in Minneapolis politics is "small, well-organized groups in coalition."[5]

In the 1960s and 1970s, Minneapolis suffered many of the urban problems that beset other cities. Higher divorce rates, outmigration and declining birth rates contributed to lowering the city's population from 521,718 in 1950 to 370,951 in 1980.[6] In addition, the crime rate escalated, and race riots broke out in 1966 and 1967. "The riots in Minneapolis evoked anger and fear among citizens that were probably disproportionate to the disturbances. The system of consensual politics and liberal social order seemed to have broken down."[7] In reaction to the riots, Mayor Arthur Naftalin established the Minneapolis Civil Rights Commission in 1967 and the Human Relations Commission in 1968. The Civil Rights Commission was to become an important actor in civil rights policymaking, although it was virtually excluded from the debate over the anti-pornography ordinance. The Human Relations Commission was intended to deal with broader relations among the races. Its first head was Ron Edwards, a controversial militant who later became president of the Minneapolis Urban League, and an angry dissenter to the Ordinance. Edwards won confirmation from a divided city council only after well-organized groups rose to his defense.[8]

During this period, like many other urban areas, Minneapolis experienced the growth of sex businesses, including prostitution and pornography. The pornography business in Minneapolis (and Minnesota) has been dominated by the Alexander family since the 1960s.[9]

These developments created opportunities for new types of politicians. Charles Stenvig, who held the Minneapolis mayorship from 1969 to 1973 and from 1975 to 1977, turned these developments to his advantage by waging symbolic politics. Like Nixon and Agnew at the national level, Stenvig "shifted ground to a moralistic opposition to 'deviance,' which included homosexuality, prostitution, and pornography."[10] Stenvig politicized the Minneapolis vice squad and initiated the city's first major crackdowns on pornography. In the 1970s, the local press was replete with accounts of the problem of pornography in Minneapolis, of the Alexanders' power and influence, and of vice raids on Alexander bookstores and movie houses which eventuated in prosecutions.[11] Yet Stenvig's efforts were no more successful than those of many other anti-vice leaders in recent history: court decisions often thwarted vice squad efforts. In 1973, two county district court judges declared Minneapolis' pornography ordinance vague, and the next year the state supreme court issued a new definition of obscenity in light of *Miller v. California*. A week later, a county district court judge threw out 140 pending obscenity cases, halting obscenity prosecution for over a year.[12] Although the Alexanders were prosecuted in a few cases and forced to shut down some theatres in others,

53

they always managed to carry on through the usual methods adopted by serious pornographers—using aliases on ownership forms, disappearing when served notice to supply evidence to grand juries or courts, temporarily closing theatres or moving obscene movies out of town before legal action is taken against them, and using expert legal aid. The last was often supplied to the Alexanders by the Minnesota Civil Liberties Union. Indeed, at the time of the ordinance battle, the MCLU was housed in a building owned by the Alexanders and, according to some people I talked to, it was not charged rent. I was also told that a leading MCLU attorney served as the Alexanders' private counsel for legal matters.[13]

The rise of pornography and the disintegration of the liberal consensus in Minneapolis set the stage for another development that would influence the politics of the ordinance: the emergence of neighborhood groups. Neighborhood groups and their allies among local politicians composed one of at least four interest groups prominent in the debate over pornography; the others can be broadly designated as conservatives, feminists, and civil libertarians.[14]

Neighborhood groups burgeoned nationwide in the 1960s and 1970s in response to urban changes that threatened the established characters of their areas. Growth of the groups was encouraged by the requirement of citizen participation in the renewal and development programs that were bringing federal funds to the cities.[15] In Minneapolis, neighborhood associations sprang up in the mid-1970s, further fragmenting the political structure. At the time of the ordinance controversy, the major group in town was the Neighborhood Pornography Task Force, consisting of representatives of three neighborhoods bordering the Chicago/Lake Street area most affected by pornography establishments.

The neighborhood activists saw the smut business as contributing to declining property values, greater crime, and deterioration in the tone of life. One of them, Liz Anderson, told me, "A number of us decided bookstores were a blight on the neighborhood. So we'd browse in the stores (they called us the 'afternoon bridge clubs') and embarrass the patrons." Her group also employed tactics such as taking pictures of patrons as they left stores, picketing, and demonstrating. "We were careful to take no position on the content of the material, but rather to focus on neighborhood blight. Our position was that they don't belong in our neighborhood. Someone else's, okay. We needed to rehabilitate the neighborhood." Before long, neighborhood groups became more politicized and started pressuring the city council to pass regulatory measures such as zoning and licensing.[16]

Eventually, some neighborhood activists began to look at the content of the pornography itself, especially as they perceived it becoming progressively more violent and degrading. Liz Anderson remarked, "I came to a point where I couldn't ignore the content. I had to take a position on the content. You can only give tours for so long, and look at the materials before they start to impact you. I changed and started to say, 'Wait a minute! Not only is this stuff not okay in my neighborhood, but it's not okay, period. . . . It's not okay to sell materials that show the rape of the young virgin [who] all of a sudden turns into a nymphomaniac.'"[17] Neighborhood groups split into two groups: those who emphasized the quality of the environment and those who also emphasized the degradation of women. Anderson's position, which other neighborhood activists shared, would later form a bridge between neighborhood groups and feminists who supported the ordinance.

The first major council response to neighborhood pressure came in 1977, when a zoning ordinance was passed designed to reverse neighborhood blight. The ordinance prohibited adult bookstores, theatres, and massage parlors from operating within five hundred feet of residential districts, churches, or educational buildings.[18] The ordinance, which gave stores three to four years to comply, followed the Supreme Court's decision in *Young v. American Mini-Theatres, Inc.*, which sanctioned zoning of non-obscene pornography for the first time.[19] Liz Anderson's association was encouraged by the ordinance and "naively thought it would do some good." It did not, because the federal district court declared it unconstitutional in 1982 in a case involving the Alexander brothers, *Alexander v. City of Minneapolis*. The court ruled that the ordinance went beyond mere location restrictions and unduly limited public access to the material—a common problem in zoning efforts.[20] According to one observer, "It was this frustration by local residents of Minneapolis over the inability to find an effective means of restricting pornography which provided the backdrop for the emergence of yet another alternative in banning pornography."[21]

In summer 1983, a new idea arose. Naomi Scheman, a philosophy professor and feminist theorist at the University of Minnesota, delivered a talk to the neighborhood association as a lightning storm flashed outside a large picture window. Anderson remembers that Scheman brought "fresh blood" to the issue and was "not limited by the burnout we felt. She said, 'let's get creative and try some new things.'" [22] At this meeting Scheman entreated the association to adopt a broader feminist perspective. Members of the association were impressed but did not yet embrace a radical feminist interpretation of pornography. A while later, some association members had lunch with some city council members and told them about the new feminist approach to pornography. "A few of the women council members said 'Ha! I never thought of that. What should we do?'" [23]

The council soon asked the City Attorney's Office and the City Planning Department to attempt to rewrite and restructure the zoning ordinance. In preparing for a hearing before the council on this reconsideration, Scheman suggested to the Neighborhood Task Force that it contact two feminist authors and activists who were teaching a course on pornography at the University of Minnesota Law School: Catharine MacKinnon, at the time a visiting professor of law at the school, and Andrea Dworkin. The task force invited MacKinnon and Dworkin to the hearing, which was set for October 18, 1983. MacKinnon and Dworkin obliged, and an extraordinary chapter in the history of the politics of pornography was ready to erupt.

At this time, Anderson's organization, the Powderhorn Neighborhood Association, and the Central Neighborhood Improvement Association formed a joint pornography task force. This group held a different type of demonstration in front of a bookstore—one focusing on the women's rights question. "This time we're trying to be innovative," the president of the Powderhorn Association told the press. "This zoning [ordinance] is a bunch of malarky and gets nowhere. So we're going to approach it from the standpoint that pornography is really violence against women." [24]

The Emergence of the Ordinance

As we have seen, the ordinance was born in Dworkin and MacKinnon's law school class on pornography, which they designed to "bring pornography secrecy into the open, study it, and explore how women are victimized by it." The class had a transforming effect on many of its students (fifty-six women and four men) and on the wider law school community. One class member told the press, "I feel so overcome that it's hard to enter into daily normal conversations." Another remarked, "In a sense, it colors my relationships with the people I care about." Within weeks, debate about pornography raged in the student paper and in the halls, and professors felt pressure to avoid their usual jokes about sex in class.[25] The class also served as a springboard for public action.[26] Although the class was closed to outsiders, council member Steve Cramer did attend one session and observed MacKinnon's effect on the class. Cramer was eventually a supporter of a compromise approach to pornography and co-head of the task force set up by Mayor Fraser, so his comments are those of a moderate sympathizer:

> You could feel the adulation kind of flowing down to her. . . . She was this majestic figure. It was an interesting dynamic. And at that time I was trying to learn about this thing (I'd just been elected to the council), and that sort of set me off. It was an odd feel to the situation. It's almost a cultish kind of situation. . . . She's very definitely a charismatic leader. She and her arguments are very compelling. And she has enough charisma that an hour after the conversation, I said "Wait a minute, that doesn't make sense"—but this response never really clicked with that cadre.[27]

The ordinance's official career began at the October 18 hearing on zoning. MacKinnon and Dworkin attended, as did another crucial actor, veteran council member Charlee Hoyt, a member of the zoning commission. Like Beulah Coughenour, the council member who sponsored the ordinance in Indianapolis, Hoyt is a Republican who voted for Ronald Reagan. But unlike Coughenour, Hoyt long had been a feminist activist. When the idea of the ordinance "struck" her as it did many converts, she pounced on it with a conviction matching that of Dworkin and MacKinnon. I heard different reasons for Hoyt's intense support of the ordinance—her growing discontent with sex and gender injustices, her desire to sponsor a major pathbreaking measure before leaving office, and her desire for the limelight (she left in 1986 and the issue did indeed generate tremendous publicity). In her interview with me, Hoyt declared:

> It empowers women to take an action against an instrument that maintains women in a subordinate status—not government, police, Big Brother, but the citizens themselves. Secondly, I feel that with more recent research, there are things that add to the perception of women that make it harder for them to break out of their subordinate status. [The situation is] similar to segregated schools. The problem is that pornography constantly reinforces in men the notion that women's role is to be dominated by men.[28]

57

Hoyt was pivotal in the enactment of the ordinance. During the initial drive to passage, she opened her office and all its resources to Dworkin, MacKinnon, and their followers. William Prock, a major participant in the issue in the Civil Rights Office, offered a typical observation:

> Hoyt was absolutely a key figure. She shepherded it
> through the council. It was an issue she held very close to
> herself. [Councilman Van] White ran the hearings, but she
> orchestrated them. . . . She made her office available to
> them [activists] twenty-four hours a day. She used her own
> portion of the council budget to allow them to copy—a
> tremendous amount of copying went on. She spearheaded
> the drive to contract with Dworkin and MacKinnon. She
> participated in the marches and vigils. She kept a perpet-
> ual candle in her office.[29]

After some discussion about zoning at the October 18 meeting, Dworkin and MacKinnon stood and dramatically altered the terms of the debate. They suggested that the council and commission were looking at the wrong thing. Pornography was actually a women's issue and zoning had failed because it did not utilize the feminist logic. Dworkin charged that the zoning approach merely reinforced existing class inequities: "This concentration on property indicates to me that property matters and property values matter but that women don't and that city councils frequently don't want real estate values to be hurt, but they ignore the fact that women are being hurt."[30] MacKinnon then presented her statement, indicating that she and Dworkin had fashioned a strategy:

> I suggest that you consider that pornography, as it subor-
> dinates women to men, is a form of discrimination on the
> basis of sex. You already have an ordinance against sex-
> based discrimination in this city. You have the jurisdiction
> to make laws against forms of discrimination. I suggest
> that you hold a public hearing on pornography to which
> you invite scholars whose studies now meet the First
> Amendment tests of even some of the most staunch skep-
> tics as to the relationship between pornography and hate
> literature and violence toward women. The harm of por-
> nography can also be documented by women who have
> been coerced into pornographic performances. You can
> hear testimony of women on whom sex has been forced
> who know that it comes from pornography that has been

consumed by men who force that sex on us, including husbands, bosses, and strangers. We could also talk with prostitutes in this city . . . to address the connection from their
standpoint between how they got into prostitution . . . and
the existence of pornography.[31]

MacKinnon's suggestion for pathbreaking, orchestrated hearings leading to a civil rights ordinance was eventually carried out. She and
Dworkin were eager to build a public record documenting the harms
of pornography in order to legitimate their new approach. For the first
time in an officially sanctioned forum, women's voices would break
the silence of victimization and speak out. "Looking at the world from
this point of view," MacKinnon later declared, "a whole shadow
world of previously invisible abuse [would be] discerned."[32]

MacKinnon's presentation before the city council illustrates her
ability to take charge of a situation and to structure the discourse. She
skillfully associated her proposals with the purposes of the council:
"*You* could hear testimony," "*We* could also talk, . . ." She established
the reasonableness of her suggestions by citing local precedent: "You
already have an ordinance. . . ." and by mentioning scholarly and legal
support for her approach—although she almost certainly overstated
the degree of support existing at the time.

This presentation made an immediate impact on Charlee Hoyt.
"That's the first time I had ever heard of MacKinnon," she remembers;
the whole thing just "came out of the blue." But she was fascinated by
the new approach, finding it "mind-boggling" and "absolutely fantastic." She sent her aide into the audience to set up a private meeting with
the two women in her office.[33]

Dworkin and MacKinnon's argument stunned others in the audience as well. According to one witness:

> All of a sudden they introduced this civil rights concept
> that took us all by surprise. We had invited them to attend,
> but we didn't know what they were going to say. *And that
> concept stopped the hearing!* We went "By George! First
> they tell us to look at this as a woman's concept, then they
> throw in this whole new concept!" It was at this point that
> Charlee Hoyt and some of the other council members said
> "By George, this is really interesting!"[34]

Another feminist activist in Minneapolis had a similar observation:
"You know, we were caught off guard. . . . For me it was a *sudden
realization.*"[35] This effect was not limited to Minneapolis as news of

the city's action spread. Kathleen Nichols, a member of the Dane County Board of Supervisors who pushed for a modified version of the ordinance in Madison, Wisconsin, in 1984 (her version, like Indianapolis's, underscored violence and lack of consent in sexual relations), was struck by the ordinance's premises when she first heard about it on a television news show in late 1983:

> For me it was an *epiphany*. I was just sitting up watching the ten o'clock news in bed. [The story of the ordinance in Minneapolis came on.] I said, "Wait a minute! *This is the answer to my intellectual problems. I was just absolutely struck*. . . . I'm laying in bed—then I sit up just like the mummy and say *"Honey, that's it! That's what I can do!* That's what I can do on women's issues that I couldn't ever do before I was in office, because that's my intellectual answer, and I have the role to do this." *Bam!*[36]

Nichols later was less enthusiastic, coming to disagree strongly with Dworkin and MacKinnon's political tactics and treatment of opposition.

One reason for the ordinance's profound effect was the way it bridged two concerns that previously had been separate: women's civil rights and distress about pornography. Most feminists, including Nichols, have reservations about traditional forms of censorship, not the least because such laws have been enforced by conservatives in the name of traditional values.[37] The ordinance enabled them to attack pornography on progressive feminist and civil libertarian grounds, thereby resolving the intellectual and strategic dilemma. The ordinance managed to turn the logic of civil rights away from its traditional support of pornographic expression. For the first time *censorship* would be a means of *furthering* civil rights. Feminist supporters of the ordinance would parallel the critique of pornography with the critique of racism.[38]

Those who were wary of making common cause with supporters of the traditional social order refused to join the crusade, leading to a rift that still exists in the ranks of feminism.[39] While, according to Brest and Vandenberg, "Many women and men were profoundly affected by the anti-pornography campaigns—'transformed' would not be too strong," the views of those transformed were too often also polarized.[40] Feminist theorist Ann Snitow has remarked that the anti-pornography movement "requires that we oversimplify, that we hypothesize a monolithic enemy, a timeless, universal, male sexual

brutality. When we create a 'them,' we perform a sort of ritual of puri-
fication: There are no differences among men or women. . . . All are
collapsed into a false unity, the brotherhood of oppressors, the sister-
hood of the victims." [41] In Minneapolis, women and feminists who harbored reservations about the ordinance found themselves assigned to
the enemy's camp or accused of being victims of "false consciousness."

After the meeting on zoning, Hoyt, Dworkin, and MacKinnon met
on and off for the next two weeks until Hoyt decided to sponsor the
new approach. Hoyt and some close allies on the council then hired
MacKinnon and Dworkin as consultants to draft an amendment to the
Minneapolis Civil Rights Ordinance. MacKinnon and Dworkin presented their draft to the city council on November 23, 1983. According to one observer, "MacKinnon and Dworkin drafted the ordinance
virtually overnight." [42]

The Passage of the Ordinance and Its Aftermath

When the Government Operations Committee held public hearings on
the amendment on December 12 and 13, Hoyt played the major role,
although the committee was officially headed by her ally, Van White,
the representative from the near northside black community.[43] Experts
and women identified as victims of pornography testified before a
spellbound audience. The hearings set the tone of the debate and
helped persuade more council members to side with the ordinance.
According to the *Minneapolis Star and Tribune*, the room "was noisy
with clapping, hissing, cheering, and booing." Supporters acclaimed
the hearings as "the first time women amassed such a volume of testimony to be heard in a traditional public forum." [44] I discuss the hearings in detail below.

Based on the hearings, the Government Operations Committee reported the amendments favorably on December 22 by a 5–0 vote. On
December 30, the full council passed the amendment by a narrow 7–6
vote. During the week before the vote, activists exerted enormous, perhaps unprecedented, pressure on the council—particularly on Jackie
Slater, a nun who originally opposed the ordinance. She switched to
deliver the swing vote in favor.[45] The council acted despite pleas by
Mayor Fraser, the city Civil Rights Office, the Library Board, and the
City Attorney's Office to delay the vote to provide time to study the
ordinance's constitutional implications.[46] Indeed, because of pressures
from activists, the usual procedure for enacting civil rights laws was
abandoned and council members "were asked to vote on the ordinance with little sense of whether it conformed to the Constitution." [47]   61

The fact that five council members would leave office in January influenced the decision to hurry the vote, as Hoyt, White, and their allies feared that the ordinance might not be approved by the incoming new members.

On January 5, 1984, despite candle light vigils outside city hall and his home, Mayor Fraser vetoed the ordinance, saying that it jeopardized free speech because its definition of pornography was too vague and broad. He declared that further work was needed to tailor the ordinance to First Amendment standards.[48] Fraser's caution on the issue contrasted starkly with the activists' single mindedness. In the mayor's view, there were important issues other than the threat of pornography.

It should be noted that Fraser was a certified progressive liberal. As a former congressman from the Minneapolis area, he co-chaired the famous 1970 Fraser-McGovern Commission on Democratic Party structural reform and delegate selection. This commission's recommendations led to democratizing procedural reforms in the party which culminated in the nomination of George McGovern for president in 1972.[49] Yet the progressive liberal Fraser blocked the "progressive censorship" espoused by the ordinance, revealing the manner in which the Ordinance "split liberalism itself into a number of factions." The equally liberal Harvard law professor, Laurence Tribe, disagreed with the veto. Although in his famous treatise on constitutional law, Tribe had questioned excluding obscenity from First Amendment protection, he wrote Mayor Fraser a letter beseeching him to uphold the ordinance and let the courts decide its constitutionality. After the veto, Tribe wrote to the city council, declaring that "this veto is an abuse of the fundamental structure of our system of government. . . . Hiding behind the First Amendment in the face of this novel measure, whose supposed invalidity follows surely from no clear precedent, the Mayor has usurped the judicial function." Fraser and many other Minneapolis officials considered Tribe's gesture inappropriate and ignored it.[50]

On January 13, the newly constituted council voted on a veto override. Nine votes were needed to override Fraser's veto; the 8–5 vote against override fell four short. On the same day, the ordinance was reintroduced in slightly modified form, mainly clarifying wording changes.

In January, Mayor Fraser created the Task Force on Pornography to study the constitutional aspects of the ordinance as well as other regulatory approaches. The task force was an *ad hoc* group consisting of three council members, including Hoyt and Cramer, two members of the Civil Rights Commission, and one each from the Library Board, the City Arts Council, and the mayor's office.[51] The task force set the second phase of the issue in motion, and was intended to reinstitute the search for consensus that normally prevailed in Minneapolis. MacKinnon and Dworkin were still involved but they had also moved on to other arenas. The weakening of their participation despite, contentious returns to Minneapolis for key votes, helped promote compromise. But many activists saw the more moderate approach as a betrayal of their cause. In reaction, they opened the Pornography Resource Center on Lake Street to provide an alternative, more radical analysis.[52]

The task force met sixteen times—about once a week, more often toward the end of its span; it issued its recommendations on May 1, 1984. Its meetings were open to the public but drew significantly less attendance than had the ordinance hearings.[53] The task force's hearings sought a balance of viewpoints, and they were run by the task force itself rather than by activists. Early sessions dealt with social science research on pornography. In contrast to the ordinance hearings, no one recommended censoring pornography. In later sessions, the task force dealt with constitutional and policy issues.

The task force report divided pornography's harms into two categories: "location-related," which dealt with environmental and residential effects, and "content-related," which dealt with "behaviors, communications and perceptions associated with messages conveyed by materials."[54] In seeking a consensus, the task force ruled out Dworkin and MacKinnon's original ordinance and endorsed a modified, less radical version. The task force stipulated that remedies must "address the harms pornography fosters in a direct and effective way, be a balance between preventing those harms and freedom of speech, be financially feasible, and satisfy the concerns and fears of the public."[55]

The report recommended adopting a public nuisance law, a new zoning law, and an opaque covers law requiring wrappers for pornographic magazines on public display; and it called for revising the city's criminal law to incorporate the standards of *Miller v. California*. In addition, it recommended adopting a revised civil rights ordinance that altered the Dworkin-MacKinnon ordinance by substituting "person" for "women" in the definition of pornography and by changing the definition of "sexually explicit" to conform to *Miller*. Most significantly, the task force recommended that the definition of pornography refer to the "sexually explicit subordination of persons" and narrowed it to graphic depictions of violence.[56] In addition, the task force recommended dropping the crucial trafficking provision of the original ordinance. Co-Chair Steve Cramer justified the recommendations, saying "The best course for Minneapolis lies between the extreme viewpoints." Charlee Hoyt, however, berated the task force for "taking a big eraser and wiping out all the women who testified and the women who wrote it." Andrea Dworkin, back from New York to mobilize support for the original Ordinance in the impending new Council vote in mid-May, concurred: "They're making a mess out of it," she cried. "This city doesn't give a damn about women." [57]

In reaction, MacKinnon and Dworkin crafted their own revision of the ordinance. They retained the original broad orientation but made some concessions to political reality, perhaps fearing that the original version now had no chance. They kept the trafficking provision but made two changes of note: the revision exempted "isolated passages" from trafficking actions; and, like the task force version, it tightened the definition of pornography to emphasize violent depictions, although it did not limit it to violent depictions. [58]

The Government Operations Committee then considered these three sets of measures—a version of the original ordinance, the task force recommendations, and the revised ordinance—beginning in early June 1984. In late June, the committee accepted most of the task force's recommendations but rejected its civil rights proposal in favor of Dworkin and MacKinnon's revised version. A few days later, the Civil Rights Commission announced its opposition to this provision, maintaining that it would compel the commission to act as a censor and dilute enforcement of other civil rights measures "to the detriment of existing protected classes." [59]

Activists mounted a new series of demonstrations in support of the Dworkin-MacKinnon measure. The demonstrations were intense and often hostile, depicting non-supporters as enemies or traitors to women's causes. [60] Then in mid-July, a young woman set herself on fire at Shinder's Read-More Bookstore in town. "Sexism has shattered my life," she wrote in a letter addressed to city officials. "Because of this, I have chosen to take my life and to destroy the persons who have destroyed me." Her stunning action was for activists a "condensation symbol"—one that encapsulates the emotional and psychological meaning of an issue or event. [61] Emotions were highly charged; the young woman lay in critical condition in a hospital as the vote took place. In the meantime, the Minnesota Civil Liberties Union reviled the task force proposals (as well as its work overall) in testimony before the council, declaring that they sacrificed First Amendment principles.[62] The MCLU would agree to no restrictions whatsoever on sexually-oriented materials and made light of concerns about the more violent material.

In the end, the city council passed MacKinnon and Dworkin's modified ordinance 7–6. At this meeting, police arrested twenty-four women for disrupting the council's proceedings.[63] Once again Mayor Fraser exercised his veto, giving the same reasons as in January. On July 27, the council failed 7–5 to override the veto. As this vote was taken, "About thirty women stood in the audience, crying, wailing, moaning, or singing."[64] Yet not all was loss for the anti-pornographers. When it enacted the amended ordinance, the council also passed a resolution declaring that it would reenact the vetoed ordinance if the federal courts upheld the Indianapolis version, which was then pending. The Mayor did not veto this enactment.[65] Furthermore, on July 2 the council passed an obscenity ordinance update with an opaque cover requirement: pornographic and sexual magazines on display in public places would be wrapped to protect minors and unwilling viewers. The U.S. Court of Appeals upheld this law in 1985.[66]

That, in brief, is the history of the Minneapolis anti-pornography ordinance. Let us now look more closely at the most significant aspects of the politics and decision-making process.

The Politics of the Anti-Pornography Ordinance: The Problem of Irresponsibility

The ordinance was a major, untested, and potentially serious departure from the modern doctrine of speech; its presentation was marked by questionable tactics employed by its supporters. Given this situation, a responsible legislative response would have blended openness with caution and deliberation. This approach would have been consistent with the ethic of responsibility, which I discussed in the Introduction, and its demand for respect of competing legitimate values. The complexity of the issues surrounding pornography especially calls for this approach. Indeed, it would have been typical of Minneapolis, which normally practices consensus politics.[67] But the search for consensus broke down in the politics of the ordinance, at least during the passage of the first version. Not only was the ordinance passed with exceptional speed but the method of passage was unusual, especially for an amendment to Minneapolis's civil rights laws. According to participants on both sides of the issue and administrative personnel who took no official position, previous amendments to civil rights law had gone through laborious deliberations that involved the city council, the Civil Rights Commission, the City Attorney's Office, and others. This time around, however, the Civil Rights Commission and the City Attorney's Office—the agencies that would have primary responsibility for enforcing the ordinance—were excluded in important respects from the deliberations, and dissenters on the council were given short shrift. Other procedural irregularities also appear to have occurred; some key observers claimed that the ordinance process deviated from all usual legislative procedures, not just those concerning civil rights. The city council allowed itself to be captured by single-minded activists in a manner that was either extraordinary for Minneapolis or simply irresponsible in a more general political sense. The forces in favor of the anti-pornography ordinance were able to disempower dissenting (and even potentially dissenting) feminist, libertarian, and skeptical viewpoints. They railroaded the ordinance through to passage.

To be sure, the legislative process in America is notoriously beset by special interests and pressure groups, so it would be naive to criticize the process at Minneapolis simply for failing to be balanced and deliberate. And the widespread American practice of judicial review naturally encourages legislatures to take constitutional risks, trusting the courts to protect them and society from the consequences of their popular but dubious actions.[68] Nevertheless, Minneapolis political leaders may fairly be charged with acting irresponsibly in the politics of the ordinance, at least in the important first round of consideration. Many knowledgeable leaders expressed strong reservations about the lack of deliberation, the one-sidedness, and the surreal sense of moral emergency that prevailed. These are precisely the qualities that the politically mature and tolerant society aspires to tame.[69]

This high-handed treatment of a measure that could seriously affect free speech law is particularly questionable because free speech is among the most essential civil liberties. "Freedom of thought and speech" is "the matrix, the indispensable condition, of nearly every other form of freedom," Justice Cardozo once proclaimed.[70] To be sure, support for the ordinance did not in itself signal a lack of respect for free speech. While free speech is necessary to democracy, its extent and delimitation are open to debate and development. The First Amendment has never been absolute in its protection of various types of expression, despite the protestations of absolutists like the American Civil Liberties Union. I will argue in Chapter 5 that there is a conservative and feminist case for limited censorship of the more violent forms of obscenity.

But major modifications of free speech law like the ordinance should be approached with caution and care. The history of First Amendment politics and adjudication is rife with instances of legislative, administrative, and judicial irresponsibility towards free speech values.[71] Without responsible leadership, the larger society does not always exhibit the political maturity envisioned by the modern doctrine of free speech. To those bent on reform, free speech may seem only an impediment to the realization of their desires. Minneapolis and Indianapolis have earned reputations for responsible decisionmaking and supporting civil liberties. But in the politics of the Ordinance, established restraints broke down. Perhaps the most curious aspect of the ordinance episode is the way established political leaders were swept up in the talismanic magic of the moment, which promised the elimination of an evil from society. Let us now look at this process in Minneapolis.

The State of Moral Emergency

The high political and emotional drama of the campaign for the ordinance surrounded the events with a surrealistic atmosphere. For many, the politics brought a transformation of consciousness and political epiphany that revealed the inner meaning of pornography and women's status:

> Indeed, much of the battle over the ordinance was over language, symbols, and the control of discourse. . . . Naming was an important point of their [the authors' and sponsors'] strategy. Establishing the distinction between "obscenity" and "pornography" was, of course, central. Less crucial, but nonetheless passionately defended, was the claim that the ordinance did not "ban" expression, because it did not call for censorship prior to publication or distribution. . . . A zoning ordinance *permits* pornography and thus makes the city complicit in the harms it causes. Pornography *silences* women. It does not just cause violence, but is *violating*. Pornography is not expression depicting the subordination of women, but it is the *practice of subordination* itself. These transformations of language were rooted in a critical view of existing institutions.[72]

In this regard, the ordinance was a culmination of a decade of more of feminist theorizing. Many feminists have stressed the importance of exposing and naming oppressive phenomena that were once invisible

67

or underestimated, such as rape, wife battering, and sexual harass-ment. The more radical advocates of renaming have attempted to lay the foundation for a new order of society and the mind.[73]

The politics also had psychological and therapeutic dimensions. By allowing those who felt themselves victims of pornography to come out of their silence and into the public realm of discourse and politics, the process made harms visible and provided a means for women to confront their plights and inform others; one of the functions of polit-ical language is to seize the selective attention of public conscious-ness.[74] Andrea Dworkin's concepts often burst on their hearers as a "fantastic insight," which entail an "inductive leap," an almost reli-gious breakthrough of the complacency of consciousness.[75] This psy-chological aspect of the ordinance's politics resembles the Skokie free speech controversy of the late 1970s, in which holocaust survivors or-ganized to resist a Nazi party demonstration in their community. This act required the survivors to come out of the shadows of their previous silence in Skokie and publically confront the psychologically destruc-tive persecutions of their pasts. Pornography assaults womens' dignity in a manner similar to Nazi speech in Skokie; both forms of assault must be countered by salubrious collective action. Accordingly, MacKinnon has called pornography a "Skokie-type injury" and law-yer Mary Eberts has averred that "pornography is our Skokie." [76]

But Skokie differed from Minneapolis in one important respect: the Skokie confrontation did indeed present a "clear and present danger" to the community. No such danger confronted the Minneapolis City Council and the ordinance activists—but they acted as if it did. Min-neapolis confronted no dangerous onslaught of pornography which suddenly threatened the status of women (indeed, if Andrea Dworkin is right, women's subordinate status has not changed throughout his-tory).

The different types and degrees of danger confronting Skokie and Minneapolis point to the negative side of the psychological politics that prevailed in Minneapolis. Although meaningful social change may result when private psychological suffering is transformed into public language, such politics can also unleash an emotionalism and intolerance which threaten the perspective and civility required by healthy public life. "A stance of rage, incorporated within a utopian political urge, may bode ill for that civility that is necessary to a dem-ocratic politics," a democratic feminist has remarked about some as-pects of radical feminism.[77]

68   A matching intransigence marked the opposition to the anti-

pornography forces. The Minnesota Civil Liberties Union divined unacceptable danger in the ordinance itself, as well as in the task force's later concessions to compromise. The MCLU would admit no line between tolerable and intolerable expression; any effort to deal with the potential harms of certain types of pornography was a threat to intellectual freedom—*reductio ad absurdum*. The MCLU was the litigant in the suit against the opaque covers law eventually upheld by the federal court and has opposed all zoning regulations proposed. When asked if zoning might be acceptable, if properly done, MCLU executive director Matthew Stark fulminated, "You can't 'properly' have people in the community tell you what's acceptable to be in their community. . . . Bookstores cannot be censored. That's all there is to it." Stark declared himself an absolutist:

> I don't want the majority of an elected body to determine
> what I can't be. That's what we come down to. It's thought
> control. We want to keep certain ideas from other people.
> It's the worst form of government oppression. [Question:
> Is hard-core pornography an idea?] I don't know what
> hard-core pornography is. I thought the MacKinnon/
> Dworkin ordinance was hard-core porno. . . . Once you
> allow a simple majority to determine what is unacceptable
> for others to read, you're developing an administrative
> process to which there is no end. And it's got to be stopped
> every time it comes up. . . . People say "it's hard-core
> porno," then all of a sudden its not the hard-core, it's the
> violence. And they just don't know what they are talking
> about.[78]

Stark's views represent in unalloyed form what has been called the "liberal approach" to sexuality and sexual depictions. The liberal approach tolerates any consensual or voluntary form of adult sexual activity as a legitimate expression of individual preference: "although some liberals may believe that some sexually-oriented materials are disgusting and offensive, the problem is seen as an issue of taste, not morality."[79] They tend to interpret pornography in relativistic, individualistic terms. Moral judgments or values are mere "metaphysics."[80] Accordingly, the modern liberal approach frowns on any restriction of sexual materials for consenting adults, including obscenity law, even though obscenity law today represents a tenuous balance between liberal and conservative values that largely favors liberalism.

Uncompromising rage is not the only problem raised by the type of psychological anti-pornography politics that prevailed at Minneapolis. According to feminist Ann Snitow, the advantages achieved by discovering and publicizing oppression can be offset by a reaction that recoils before the partial truths unveiled. "Visibility created new consciousness, but also new fear—and new forms of old sexual terrors: sexual harassment was suddenly everywhere; rape was endemic; pornography was a violent polemic against women. . . . Pornography became the symbol of female defeat. . . . Antipornography theory offers relief in the form of clear moral categories: there are victims and oppressors." Snitow fears that this posture is self-defeating because it weakens the basis for agency and change and because it ultimately exaggerates the truth: "it is hard to imagine good organizing that can emerge from this insulting presumption." [81]

Although cowed and disempowered women do tragically exist, they are likely a minority among women. To reduce the plurality of women's experience to the most extreme cases of powerlessness and silence is to deny both the complexity of social life and the full reality of women's lives.[82] Complexity and subtlety surrender to a Manichean world of irreconcilable dualism: silence/speech, power/powerlessness, men/women. As we have seen, such synecdochal reduction is central to MacKinnon and Dworkin's theory of knowledge and society.[83]

The transformation of emotion and consciousness that began in Dworkin and MacKinnon's law school classroom—"I feel so overcome that it is hard to enter into daily conversations," one student remarked—carried over into the legislative process. One journalist observed, "The Council had never held hearings like these before. With Van White and two nationally known feminists . . . presiding, the Council chambers became part tribunal, part classroom and part confessional as a succession of battered wives, girlfriends, counselors . . . rape victims, penologists, psychologists, and former prostitutes came forward. The testimony was mawkish, moving, scholarly, dull, and at times riveting. People cried and said things they had never before made public." [84] More than one witness began by stating, "I am afraid to be here and afraid not to be here." Many did not state their names. One unnamed witness divulged a litany of past abuse and trauma: "I want to tell you how pornography has affected my life, how I am fighting self-loathing, disgust and shame, how I am fighting at the beginning, and how I am fighting tearing my skin out." [85]

Of the many victims on pornography who testified, I will quote only two of the most representative statements. One witness synthesized many of the arguments that feminist theorists had been making about the links between individual and systemic harms and degradation:

70

> I have been threatened at knifepoint by a stranger in an
> attempted rape. I have been physically and verbally ha-
> rassed on the street. . . . I have experienced and continue
> to experience the humiliation, degradation, and shame
> that these acts were meant to instill in me. I believe that
> the only difference between my experiences and pornogra-
> phy was the absence or presence of a camera. This connec-
> tion became clear to me when I saw a documentary about
> pornography. . . . I realized that I was any one of the
> women in the film, at least in the eyes of those men who
> have abused me. I saw myself through the abuser's eyes
> and I felt dirty and disgusting, like a piece of meat. . . .
> The message that pornography carries is clear to me.
> There is no place in our society where it is safe to be a
> woman, not in our homes, not in the streets, not even
> within our families. Pornography promotes and creates the
> conditions that make it dangerous to be a woman.[86]

Another witness described how pornography had shattered the mutual respect and trust that once characterized her marriage, as well as
her sense of self-respect and security. Her husband began by reading
magazine stories to her about group sex, wife swapping, and bondage.
This woman's remarks typify how, in certain contexts, pornography
makes many women feel dehumanized and degraded.[87]

> I was really repulsed at the things he was reading me and I
> was really in disbelief. . . . He bought more and more
> magazines to prove to me that people weren't making it
> up, that all of these people were saying how wonderful
> these things were. . . . We would meet together as a group
> [at] pornographic adult theatres or live sex shows. Initially
> I started arguing that the women on stage looked very dev-
> astated like they were disgusted and hated it. I felt dis-
> gusted and devastated watching it. . . . About this time
> when things were getting really terrible and I was feeling
> very suicidal and very worthless as a person, at that time
> any dream that I had of a career in medicine was just to-
> tally washed away. I could not think of myself any more as
> a human being.[88]

This type of testimony brought attention to the harms caused by
pornography and to women's special sensitivities to its degrading aspects. At the same time, however, there seems to have been unleashed
a psychology of victimization that jeopardized objectivity and per-   71

spective. Councilmember Steve Cramer, the consensus-seeking politician who co-chaired the task force, believed that the process was at times more therapeutic than objective:

> To her group, [MacKinnon would] say, "This is it. We're going to get rid of pornography." And that group consisted of some troubled people, the fifty to one hundred person cadre. They came in and testified at every hearing. Some were very troubled. One of them set herself on fire here in Minneapolis. She testified at the public hearing before the council, and it was painfully obvious that she was very disturbed. . . .
>
> The process was social therapy. [They said] "if this passes, it'll excise all the demons that have plagued me all my life. This will somehow perfect society." [89]

Cramer's observations capture the all-or-nothing quality of the politics, at least at the early stages. Recall that as early as 1974, Andrea Dworkin proclaimed, "All of us who have ever tried to right a wrong recognize that truly nothing short of everything will really do." Similarly, MacKinnon had asserted, "To remake society so that women can live here requires a feminism unqualified by preexisting modifiers." [90] This type of understanding, in juxtaposition with the MCLU's own brand of absolutism, escalated the stakes for both sides.

The battle for the ordinance assumed Armageddon proportions. After the first council vote MacKinnon announced to the press, "The magnitude of what was done here today can only really be measured in hindsight. It's hard to find words to say how big it is." [91] After the affair, Theres Stanton, a prominent feminist activist and member of the Steering Committee of the Pornography Resource Center in Minneapolis, wrote a widely cited article, "Fighting for Our Existence," which described the ordinance in messianic and apocalyptic terms. Her remarks link the various themes under discussion:

> If the truth about the women who have been harmed by pornography were admitted as evidence and affirmed as actually occurring, as fact, full of precision and stubbornness, the center, volume, surface, and active, far reaching radius of the sphere of reality would be transformed. This truth, like any truth entering the world of existence, would be forced to change. . . .
>
> The male domination that has remained vague and obscure under obscenity law will no longer remain disguised as fantasy. It will be fact. [92]

If the struggle is for nothing less than "existence" and "reality," dissent and disagreement cannot be brooked. Even feminists who entertain free speech and libertarian concerns are traitors because everything is at stake:

> Opposing the ordinance in the name of feminism makes a mockery of the word itself. Women have fought long and hard, have even died, to make the word a verb, an action, and a movement in the sphere of existence. It is increasingly difficult to be a feminist in this country. It is often dangerous and terrifying. It is an act of survival.[93]

Disagreement is translated into treason and the opposition is associated with dark forces. In this vein, Andrea Dworkin publicly charged that the council had ties to the Mafia after they failed to override Fraser's second veto, although there was no evidence to substantiate the charge.[94]

Stanton's logic equates pornography with murder itself. This is an extreme version of Andrea Dworkin's rhetorical conflation of speech and action. Similarly, the head of the Pornography Resource Center told me that it was improper to accuse the ordinance of censorship because "to say that it is censorship is to say that it is censorship to prevent murder." [95] This logic is an application of Dworkin's synedochical theory of meaning, which illuminates by reducing meaning to the most extreme variable. "The eroticization of murder is the essence of pornography," Dworkin declares in *Pornography: Men Possessing Women*.[96] "In fact, it is the woman who has not been sexually abused who deviates," MacKinnon states in *Feminism Unmodified*. "And if you understand that pornography literally means what it says, you might conclude that sexuality has become the fascism of contemporary America and we are moving into the last days of Weimar." [97]

The cathartic aspect of ordinance politics spread beyond its advocates. One liberal feminist, councilmember Barbara Carlson, who eventually voted against the ordinance on liberal grounds, experienced a personal revelation at a council hearing a day before the first vote and confessed the experience to everyone present. Carlson suddenly realized that she had once been sexually abused while under the influence of alcohol. In an interview, she linked her own confession with those of others. The politics of the ordinance

> Was almost a therapeutic experience, with the intensity of the lobbying. And it's very hard to listen to painful stories about women raped, beaten, abused, mutilated. What I

73

think happened is that people often try to justify the very sad things that have happened to them and make something better. And I think these women, who were so desperate because of the terrible things that had happened to them, that they were looking for a vehicle that they could go for. That was the intensity and emotionalism of the thing.[98]

This aspect of the politics drew mixed reviews. For some, it brought an empowerment of women's voices and disclosed the truth about pornography. For others, it bred an emotionalism that was ultimately anti-political, since politics is a process of legitimate compromise, the acknowledgement of conflicting viewpoints and understandings, and an overcoming of the purely personal in favor of a communal understanding. According to Barbara Carlson, the position taken by proponents of the ordinance "was not reasonable. . . . It was 'We are going to get rid of this evil in our society.' And if you have dealt with [this], you know what the tunnel vision is. There is no compromise. . . . It was a *personal*, a *personal* issue." [99]

Thus, activists in favor of the ordinance justified their absolute and intractable stance by pointing to the serious danger posed by pornography and by asserting that intensity was necessary to overcome indifference and prejudice towards women's claims. Their critics at Minneapolis disagreed; to them, pornography did not pose a clear and present danger. As we will see in the next sections, many political and administrative leaders believed that pornography should be regulated in some form, but they found themselves stranded between the extremes represented by the ordinance activists and the MCLU.

The Council's Posture.

The preceding discussion has dealt primarily with the activists who pressured the city council. But what of the target of the pressure? The hearings and publicity had an effect, especially on certain members of the council. But only Charlee Hoyt appears to have been enthusiastic about the ordinance. Three others supported it from the start: Van White, titular head of the Operations Committee, which had jurisdiction over the issue and the hearings, although White surrendered control to Hoyt and MacKinnon; Tony Scallon, a conservative Democrat with ties to the anti-pornography neighborhood associations; and Sally Howard, a departing councilmember who felt indebted to Hoyt.[100] Despite his disapproval of Dworkin and MacKinnon's underlying theory and tactics, Scallon, who had long backed traditional regulatory efforts, supported the ordinance because he was desperate to try something new.[101] Although Van White represented a black district that distrusted the ordinance, he was swept along with the tide. He remarked, "I have had quite a few experiences in my life that I will never forget. I have been here some time on this earth. This is one of those experiences that will live with me until I shuffle off." [102]

The other three council members who voted for the ordinance took longer to reach their decisions. Democrat Walter Dziedzic, a former policeman, did not support the ordinance at first but came around after exposure to the evidence in the hearings.[103] Long-time council member Walter Rockenstein, who left office after the first vote, supported the ordinance after much thought because he thought a new approach deserved a court test. And, as we saw, council member Jackie Slater, who died shortly thereafter, voted for the measure after much equivocation and after being the target of pressure tactics.[104]

According to people who were there, First Amendment concerns received limited attention in the council. Steve Cramer remarked that while the council did address free speech implications, "those captured by the movement just dismissed that concern. Their rationale was that this was not a local governmental concern, but for the courts." The transcripts of the public hearing show no serious debate over the ordinance's implications for free speech. Charlee Hoyt maintained that First Amendment interests were considered, but she did not elaborate on the point.[105] Another observer surmised that the council majority deferred to MacKinnon's assurances that the ordinance was consistent with First Amendment precedent and principles, and that her status as a lawyer and professor reinforced the ordinance's credibility.[106]

Those who voted against the first ordinance did so for several reasons: they feared its free speech implications; they believed that the liberal doctrine of free speech is the best public philosophy for feminists and for society as a whole; they thought it futile to pursue what might prove to be an unconstitutional course. Alice Rainville, Kathy O'Brien, and Barbara Carlson opposed the ordinance from the start for these reasons.[107] O'Brien, however, might have accepted a less ideological measure that singled out violent pornography, but she was disturbed by the ordinance as it was presented:

> I voted against the ordinance not only because of civil liberties issues, but also as a feminist. That's because I believe that the position of women or anyone who has been denied access to power in a community has more opportunity for power in an open society. And I believe that in a

closed, absolutist society there is less access and power
and empowerment for women and people of color.[108]

Some prominent feminists in Minneapolis and elsewhere expressed
similar viewpoints. June Callwood, for instance, declared

Mistrust of civil liberties reveals a lack of historical perspective. The freedom enjoyed by today's feminists owes
everything to civil liberties groups who fought for the right
of marginal organizations and minorities to disagree with
the majority. . . . Feminism and civil liberties are inextricable. The goal of both is a society in which individuals are
treated justly. Civil libertarians who oppose censorship are
fighting on behalf of feminists, not against them.[109]

Councilmember Mark Kaplan opposed the ordinance after failing
in attempts to make it less vague and ambiguous and to limit its application to violent depictions.[110] Two conservatives, Dennis Schulstadt
and Patrick Daugherty, were at first sympathetic because of their dis-
like of pornography but eventually voted against the ordinance. Schulstadt was told by lawyer friends that it stood little chance in court,
and, in addition, he resented the publicity and tactics that surrounded
the issue: "It was a media event. She [Hoyt] was literally calling press
conferences to do it. . . . It [the ordinance] was being discussed on the
council floor in front of the television cameras with every one of us
posturing ourselves so we'd look good on television. But very little
work was going on in the back offices. The good work normally is
where you've got two or three members of the council, and city attorneys, and somebody from civil rights, and somebody else and you sit
down and hammer the thing out. *This* was one that was being pushed
for publicity value." [111] Schulstadt is not entirely fair—Hoyt was genuinely committed to the cause—but the issue did escalate into a true
media event.[112]

Thus a bare majority of the city council supported the ordinance in
the key first vote but most members (with the major exception of
Hoyt) were not so committed as the activists. This did not prevent the
activists from capturing the decision-making process. In allowing this
to happen, the elected lawmakers forsook their responsibility to protect constitutional interests.

Procedural Aspects: Altered Amendment Process.

Despite pleas by key administrators involved in civil liberty policy,
Charlee Hoyt and her supporters rushed the anti-pornography ordi-

nance to passage less than four weeks after Dworkin and MacKinnon presented their draft to the council. Consequently, the product that emerged was virtually identical to this draft. This rush to judgment was propelled by a sense of moral urgency and a practical desire to pass a measure before the new city council entered office. Stark of the MCLU described the two weeks leading up to Mayor Fraser's first veto as "bedlam in this city . . . at least in certain communities."[113]

According to Kathy O'Brien, a veteran Democratic councilmember and pioneer in women's rights and liberal activism in Minneapolis, the procedures surrounding passage were "extraordinary":

> *Never* in my particular experience on the council has the council voted for something so controversial in less than a four-week period, and, essentially, that's what happened. . . . The Civil Rights Commission was very concerned about the ordinance and took a position against it. They were concerned it would dilute enforcement of civil rights issues. The Library Board also took a position against it. There was very little time, though, for the Civil Rights Commission or the Library Board to be heard due to the late December timing of the hearings. They sent letters to the council, but they really did not receive an appropriate public hearing.
>
> It's *extraordinary*. Our government is very complex. Usually if another body, a Library Board or a Civil Rights Commission, sends a letter to the city council saying, "We have trouble with this. Will you postpone action on this so that we have an opportunity to appropriately participate in the discussion?" the city council will postpone it. Usually the city council will postpone if even a majority of the council is in favor of it, but even one individual council member requested more time to deliberate.
>
> This didn't happen [this time] because of the fact that five members were leaving, and that Dworkin and Mac-Kinnon were leaving, going somewhere else to teach. So that was used as an excuse for pushing it through. There was *no flexibility,* no flexibility *whatsoever.* This has not happened before in my experience. That's why I say it was extraordinary.[114]

Thus, where controversial issues and divisions among governmental offices and officials normally would have been dealt with through procedures designed to promote compromise, this did not happen when the anti-pornography ordinance was introduced. Rather, O'Brien and

77

other skeptical leaders with liberal feminist credentials found that procedures were being altered in order to disregard their views. They felt betrayed. They were not alone. Ron Edwards, the black activist who once headed the Human Relations Commission and was then president of the Minneapolis Urban League, criticized the city council and the ordinance activists for excluding input from the black community. Edwards disagreed with Hoyt and other activists who claimed that a community of interest united blacks and women on the issues of pornography, civil rights, and oppression. The activists compared pornography to racism—a claim central to modern feminism.[115] Like black leaders in Indianapolis, Edwards feared that enforcement of the ordinance would interfere with enforcement of black rights, and he complained that the black viewpoint was being ignored:

> There was so little respect for the intellect and understandings and compassion of the Black community by Dworkin and MacKinnon and others that there was never even any discussion with the Black community—not by the council, either.
> We saw this as a white folks issue at the time, and we indicated it was a watering down and dilution of the civil rights ordinance at a time when they already wanted to put a feminist in as civil rights director. . . .
> During the course of this issue as it was beginning to emerge, the discussions, the public hearings, the marches on the porn stores, etc.—at no point was the Black community felt to be important enough for dialogue.[116]

Edward's complaint illustrates the tensions that often exist among black and feminist groups over the meaning and implementation of civil liberty policy.[117] Edwards was not actively hostile to antipornography measures but feared that the ordinance would dilute enforcement of civil rights laws in blacks' behalf. Feminists like Charlee Hoyt had a point, however, in declaring that civil rights should not be for blacks only, and that women's civil rights merit attention as well.

The Minneapolis gay community joined in the hostility to the ordinance. Gay activists declared that the measure would open the door to censoring homosexual pornography. Tim Campbell, the leading gay spokesperson in Minneapolis and publisher of *GLC Voice,* the main gay newspaper, excoriated the ordinance in a fashion befitting his flamboyant style. Its definition of pornography was "blatantly sexist, un-American, fascist, antisexual, and antiheterosexual." [118] The war of words was fierce, even though it did not take place on an even battlefield.

The City Attorney's Office was also excluded from consultation, although it had played a key role in previous amendments to the city code. Assistant City Attorney David Gross, the office's leading obscenity prosecutor, criticized the speed of passage and the disregard of adverse testimony. He also underscored the conflict of interest in hiring Dworkin and MacKinnon as consultants:

> They wanted to establish the philosophy of the ordinance despite existing legal and constitutional doctrine in the state and despite the facts. It was very philosophical. And it was going to be *forced* on the people of Minneapolis despite their beliefs. . . .
>
> [Was the process biased?] Sure. They called all the witnesses they wanted at the hearings, and that was also a situation in which nobody was prepared. They talked to Al Hyatt [Gross' colleague, another assistant city attorney], but they didn't want him asking any questions—only Kitty [MacKinnon] could ask questions. And there was no cross-examination. Only anecdotal evidence was presented.
>
> It is very rare to have a public hearing in front of a whole city council. It's usually done in committees, which make their recommendations.
>
> In this case, the *consultant,* who was also the *advocate,* was paid by the council, the City of Minneapolis, to lobby the council. So you had the council lobbying itself, with scheduled hearings where all the time was taken up by the consultant advocate. I said to myself, "Well, you know what a stacked deck is. Well, that's a stacked deck!" So, factually, the council hired an advocate to consult with the City Attorney's Office. *But in actuality, we were cut off.* Comments by Al Hyatt and me [which dealt with free speech concerns and First Amendment case law] were essentially rejected out of hand. . . . And we raised the First Amendment questions very early on because they are so obvious. . . .
>
> This was an unusual process, given my experience. . . . *Since when did the advocate have such access to the council?* They were constantly lobbying—morning, noon, and night—and constantly lecturing. [119]

The *Minneapolis Star and Tribune* in March 1984 corroborates Gross's critique. The paper reported the finding of a letter that council leaders or someone close to the council had suppressed. It had been written by the city attorney to the council the previous November, warning that the ordinance could not survive a court challenge. The issue became public when someone on the council discovered the letter in March, 1984. Councilmember Carlson speculated that some members (such as Slater) would have shifted their votes had they known of the letter in December. Because the council took its legal cues from MacKinnon, suppression of the letter removed a potential source of opposition. Carlson noted, "This [letter] raises the issue in print. I had to cast a vote, and I didn't have all the information. A member of my caucus didn't share it with me. If the opponents had had this letter, we might have used it to argue against the ordinance." The newspaper account also observed "as the debate progressed in December . . . the two women [Dworkin and MacKinnon] ceased being consultants and became advocates, willing only to sell their idea to the Council as drafted and telling them that the proposal would be approved by the courts." [120]

Such tactics alienated leaders accustomed to exercising influential roles in formulating civil liberty policy and law in Minneapolis. Perhaps the most important institution so involved was the Office of Civil Rights, which would have had the major responsibility to enforce the ordinance. William Prock is associate director and head of enforcement and administration of this office; he also held a key position on the task force. Prock criticized the first stage of consideration for lacking fairness and for excluding dissent:

> [The process] was *totally outside* of the routine method for amending a civil rights ordinance. [In the past] the ordinance has been amended in two principle ways. The council would propose an amendment; it would come to the Civil Rights Department for comment, and review and drafting by the City Attorney. Or, we would generate an amendment from here, the [Civil Rights] Commission would hold hearings on it, then it would go to the City Attorney's Office for drafting, and then to the council. *This* amendment [pornography ordinance] was generated by the council, and *it bypassed this office all the way through the initial go-round.*[121]

Prock, an eight-year veteran in the department, declared that his department had always been directly involved in other civil rights amendments. In the ordinance case, however, the department did not find out about the proposal until its head read the posting for the public hearing that had already been arranged. By this time, Prock remarked, the ordinance "had a life of its own."

> It was unprecedented in terms of the process that was used—the lack of contact with the appropriate offices, mainly civil rights and thorough analysis within the city attorney's office. And in terms of an outside consultant being hired, in essence, to draft an ordinance, whereas, in fact, all other ordinances were drafted by the city attorney.[122]

These accounts indicate that activists managed to capture the council and alter normal procedures that ordinarily would facilitate the building of consensus and compromise. "If you're up against a 'true believer,' there's nothing you can do." Prock and the others were resentful because their expertise in civil liberty law was being disregarded. "I felt that our experience was being bypassed. . . . Initially, it was definitely a stacked deck."[123]

The Hearings and the Disempowerment of Dissent.

The Public Hearings on Ordinances to Add Pornography as Discrimination against Women took place on December 12 and 13, 1983. I have quoted from these hearings above. Let us now focus on their one-sidedness.

The hearings were crucial in galvanizing support for the ordinance. According to William Prock, "absent what was presented at those hearings, and the way it was subsequently summarized and interpreted, the council would not have had a basis for the ordinance. I don't think you would have found seven council members willing to vote for the ordinance absent what was presented at the hearings." A leader of the Pornography Resource Center also pointed to the importance of the hearings. "I think most of us got politicized by the hearings . . . the hearings are a fundamental thing to read."[124]

As we have seen, the hearings appear to have been structured to exclude meaningful dissent and countervailing evidence. According to two sympathetic observers, "In a quite unusual procedure, White, the committee chair, asked MacKinnon and Dworkin to conduct questioning, and intervened mainly to keep order."[125] MacKinnon introduced the proceedings by declaring, "this opportunity for our speech is precious and rare and unprecedented." She announced the two pri-

81

mary purposes of the hearings: to "provide a forum in which women could express themselves and describe the injuries inflicted by pornography"; and to give the evidence that "would 'provide a factual basis for a legally sufficient sex discrimination statute.'"[126] The evidence included both testimony linking pornography to violence and debasement and personal testimony of victims. A number of therapists and social scientists linked pornography to harmful behavior, but "only one witness expressed doubts that pornography caused violence."[127]

Like the decision-making processes of many federal commissions (including, to some extent, the 1986 Attorney General's Commission), the process at Minneapolis seemed less an open-minded, balanced inquiry than the building and buttressing of a predetermined case. As Ray C. Rist remarks, "The goal [of commissions] is less one of fact finding than of case building."[128] As we have seen, MacKinnon and Dworkin were not proponents of "objectivity," considering it a political charade that reinforced the status quo. The one-sidedness of the hearings was balanced by the one-sidedness of the entire society outside the council chambers. Because knowledge and perception are politically and socially determined, and because power is unevenly distributed in the present world, objectivity as conventionally conceived simply camouflages the inequality of the underlying order.[129]

According to Brest and Vandenberg, "The case for the ordinance was based more on the personal experiences of victims than on social science data. A recurring theme throughout the hearings was that aggressors—strangers, friends, husbands—had forced women to submit to degrading and painful scenarios taken from pornographic films and magazines. Many of the witnesses spoke not only of physical injuries, but of lasting shame and degradation. Many had never previously divulged their experiences to anyone but counselors and therapists."[130] The star witness was Linda Marciano, the "Linda Lovelace" of *Deep Throat* who later wrote a book in which she claimed that she was coerced by violence into making the movie.[131]

In truth, not all speakers at the hearings backed the ordinance. Jane Strauss, a bookstore owner, testified against it, claiming it could have widespread chilling effect on book selection. Gay activist Tim Campbell testified acerbically, as we have seen. Dick Marple, a library clerk, and Rick Osborne of the Civil Rights Commission spoke against the ordinance, although they had not been able to prepare thorough critiques.[132] But lack of notice kept other respected dissenting voices from appearing and those who did speak were drowned out by the antics of the selected audience. Brest and Vandenberg remark, "The hearings were not closed, however, and opposing voices spoke. But the audience did not want to hear. It reacted passionately against testimony that opposed *or even questioned* the proposed law. . . . The audience . . . reacted to unsympathetic testimony with booing and hissing, moaning and crying . . . the audience remained deeply engaged, emotional, and defensive. It was their moment, and no one would be permitted to diminish it." [133]

Supporters defended the emotionalism and the one-sidedness as assisting the entry of previously silenced victim's voices into the public realm. Critics derided the emotionalism and commented on the lack of sobriety and perspective. The Minneapolis reporter for the *Wall Street Journal,* a woman, charged, "Ms. MacKinnon pulled together a group of her students and paraded them as experts"; the ordinance "was born of rant and rave in place of precise thinking. Backers engaged in Mau Mau tactics instead of a properly organized campaign." [134] This is overstated—bonafide experts did speak—yet the format of the hearings apparently did disable dissent. Debate was also stigmatized by the moral imperative created by the hearings: how can moral people question the validity of the ordinance when pornography is responsible for sufferings such as these? [135] These factors compromised the hearings for Prock:

> Initially it was *definitely* a stacked deck. The public hearings were designed to do *nothing other* than provide the basis for passing the ordinance. . . . Hearings have usually been called by the appropriate council committee with appropriate public notification. . . . You don't usually walk into a hearing and find thirty to forty names all ready to testify. In this case, there were a number of people called by Dworkin and MacKinnon to testify. Oh yeah, they orchestrated the hearings. . . .
>
> I think that if the hearings had been as balanced as most hearings that I've heard, we wouldn't have seen the ordinance passed. We'd have seen the initial establishment of a task force under the guidance of the city attorney's office to research the entire concept. This is the standard process when something really controversial comes up. [136]

Other key actors concurred with Prock's observation. The views of the MCLU's Matthew Stark on this matter are corroborated by other, more disinterested participants:

> MacKinnon and Dworkin stacked the audience day after day, not to listen, but to engage in guerilla theatre. So, con-

stantly, anybody would speak, this group would get up as
though they were playing a role, and would yell and
scream and boo and hiss. It was obvious. . . . People
would have a script, and they'd get up, and they'd read the
script. They'd cry on cue before the city council.[137]

David Gross noted that the City Attorney's Office could not prepare
for the hearings because of lack of time. "Nobody was prepared" except the ordinance's supporters. "What these people were trying to do
in terms of political process was to gain political influence and then
foreclose political debate." Gross described how MacKinnon's brilliant adversarial skills enabled her to influence the testimony of some
key witnesses. One such witness was Edward Donnerstein, a psychology and communications professor at the University of Wisconsin,
Madison, and one of America's leading researchers on the attitudinal
and behavioral effects of pornography. Gross pointed out how Mac-
Kinnon guided Donnerstein's testimony and discouraged him from
qualifying his remarks:

> They [council] misinterpreted Ed's stuff. . . . I think he was
> being manipulated. He was trying to answer the questions
> that she was asking, but she wouldn't let him put in the
> limitations. . . . The questioner controls it. Put it in the
> context of her style. The answer comes out, there's an in-
> terruption in his thought, he's gathering his thoughts on
> limitations [of his point] because they would logically fol-
> low—and she *fires* the next question at him. . . . And she
> knows *exactly* what she's doing because she's not dumb.
> She's *very smart*. And she is also a very crafty trial lawyer.
> She knows all the arguments, and she was presenting her
> case in the most favorable light she could. And she's leav-
> ing it up to the other side—*which was nonexistent.* There
> was *no cross-examination, no preparation* by the other
> side, all right?—to bring out the limitations.
>
> But she was the *"consultant,"* not the *"advocate,"* and
> the question was, "What role was she playing?" So she
> used *trial advocacy* when it suited her purpose, and a *con-
> sultant's role* when it suited her purpose. And she was able
> to manipulate that situation *very, very well.* . . . But you
> had to see it in action as a dynamic process. The limita-
> tions were never made explicit or brought out.[138]

Councilmember Steve Cramer had a similar admiring impression of
MacKinnon's skills. "She responded quickly to every angle. She's got a
response, a very nimble mind. And people were predisposed to believe

what she's saying anyway. You can't really defeat her in debate. She's sort of invincible up there—a very powerful figure." [139]

These observations reveal how the council allowed the activists to supervise the process that led to the first vote. Councilmember Schulstadt, who planned to support the ordinance until the last moment although he was never a solid backer, remarked, "Charlee is the one who carried it. But 90 percent of the thought that went into it was done by the others [Dworkin and MacKinnon]. It was their idea and they just did it through Charlee." [140] Council President Rainville's comment to the press in the midst of the hearings may be indicative of the body's second class status in the affair: "The Council pays these consultants, and they give the results of the study to the media before they give them to the Council." [141]

The treatment of the Minnesota Civil Liberties Union was also representative and important, because the MCLU was the most prominent opposition outside of the governmental framework. Though Matthew Stark's absolutist liberal stance and indecorous hyperbole make his opinions suspect, others confirmed the factual basis of his observations. Stark called the politics of the ordinance "extraordinary" because "it was the most appalling set of hearings ever. . . . It was an exercise in anti-intellectualism and fascism." The MCLU did not discover what was brewing until the council had formally hired Dworkin and MacKinnon as consultants, "so from an earlier date, a whole lot had been done of which we were not aware":

> From that point until about a day before the city council voted on it, [nobody ever] gave us a copy of [the ordinance]. We asked for it, but [they] kept playing games. . . . For a period of a month or more, we didn't have anything. So we made contact with the clerk or administrative assistant of the committee that was hearing it [Operations] and were given misinformation about when the hearings were. And then when we *did* find out about when they were, we made a judgment that the hearings were conducted in a way different from the way the Minneapolis City Council normally allows hearings to be conducted. One city council member [the late Jackie Slater], who was on our side of the issue but switched at the last minute, said that the hearings were the most undemocratic thing she'd ever seen. [142]

Stark and the MCLU eventually decided to boycott the hearings. Instead, they began to directly lobby the council, the Civil Rights

Commission, the City Attorney's Office, and the mayor's office.[143] After Fraser's veto, the MCLU's intransigence did not permit them to celebrate. They felt betrayed at Fraser's taking two weeks before vetoing the ordinance in January. Fraser's procrastination allowed pro-ordinance forces to apply pressure and create "bedlam" in town; the MCLU also felt that Fraser's claim to be studying the matter bestowed an image of legitimacy upon the ordinance and other anti-porn measures. The MCLU scorned such indecision: "He should have acted immediately. He said 'I'll let you know in two weeks.' He should have announced it [the veto] *immediately*. Because during that two weeks people went hysterical. He should have announced it the afternoon the council voted on it. The second time he vetoed it *immediately*. He learned his lesson. You don't let people think you are thinking about it." [144]

Stark also noted ironically that the council had violated the city's affirmative action guidelines in hiring Dworkin and MacKinnon as consultants without open competition. This had happened only once before, and the legal counsel in question had resigned after the MCLU complained.[145]

The other major theatre of attack was the council chambers. Activists were able to bring incessant pressure on the council during the count-down to the first votes because Charlee Hoyt turned her office and facilities (including the photocopy machine) over to them. "This meant that any time any council member came into council chambers, [he or she] were being buttonholed." [146] This special access helped activists to exert the pressure on Councilmember Jackie Slater that compelled her to change her swing vote. The unremitting pressure angered Council President Rainville and exasperated Barbara Carlson,

> It was an interesting process, an *exhausting* process. We were lobbied *very hard*. Charlee allowed women to really *take over* city hall. You couldn't go to the bathroom without being lobbied. And we were hearing from people in California—movie stars, Rhoda, etc. We were *just hysterical* with this whole thing. And you can see why! I mean, my God, it was just *onslaught, onslaught, onslaught!* I mean literally, they were in everyone's office. A month and a half![147]

The activities never stopped. There were radio and television debates, vigils at Mayor Fraser's house and office, and demonstrations without end. At one debate between Dworkin and Stark later in the affair, activists applauded, booed, and cried "on cue."[148] They also held candlelight vigils in the council chambers during the first votes and then did something that Tony Scallon, an experienced councilmember, had never seen before: they "took over the council's [public voting] chambers. They walked up and sat down in the council, over the top of police officers. . . . They had to be arrested and taken out." They repeated this action during the second vote, which cost them their credibility. Scallon then authored regulations that limited outside access to this area. These regulations remain in effect.[149]

All this pressure was mounted by a relatively small group of activists revolving around Dworkin, MacKinnon, and Hoyt. No groundswell of support materialized in the city as a whole. Estimates of the number of activists ranged from fifty to two hundred, city-wide. Steve Cramer said, "The other aspect that is puzzling to me is that there were maybe fifty or one hundred visible, strong supporters for this thing. Beyond that, you didn't hear from anybody. . . . My reaction to MacKinnon and Dworkin and their cadre is that they were at once remarkably successful in helping to create this climate." The MCLU and the *Minneapolis Star and Tribune* maintained that there were only one hundred to two hundred supporters throughout the entire town.[150] Each council member I interviewed pointed to only minimal constituency pressure.

Local neighborhood groups did jump on the bandwagon, however, and the ordinance battle sparked creation of the Pornography Resource Center, which has built a fairly strong institutional base in the city and the neighborhoods. But neighborhood and more radical feminist groups constituted the major players, along with the city council, in the politics of the ordinance in Minneapolis. No other groups stepped forward. The National Organization for Women (NOW) did not venture an official position or embroil itself in the affair, although some individual chapters in its complex local network were active in support.[151] Nor did any other feminist group join the action. Even those who accepted the logic of the ordinance found the supporters' tactics disconcerting: "[The ordinance's] drafters, committed as well they might be to the cause of equality for women, have decided the political and artistic dialogue must proceed upon their terms exclusively . . . the council is, we're afraid, displaying an unfortunate lack of responsibility."[152] Finally, conservatives and church groups did not organize around the issue; individual conservatives in the city and on the council, did, however, support the ordinance.

So the public furor was largely a phenomenon engineered by Dworkin, MacKinnon, Hoyt, and their supporters. Government officials either opposed or questioned the ordinance, yet they had no opportunity to challenge the measure. Once the ordinance's magic struck, resistance found itself disempowered. William Prock called it "a steamroller effect . . . I was just amazed." [153] According to Steve Cramer:

> In my experience, I have seen—and still can't explain it—the political climate which was created around this issue. . . . It was absolutely a bulldozer effect for those people [on the council] who believed in the ordinance. They became very enamored of the approach very quickly. . . . They just decided this was something the city should try, even though there were substantial questions about its enforceability, its legal standing, and I think significant questions about the group from which this ordinance flowed. . . . But those captured by the movement just dismissed that concern. [154]

Charlee Hoyt had no doubts. She proclaimed that the key to the ordinance was "Empowerment. Giving [women] the law as an instrument to bring actions." [155]

The Form and Content of Progressive Censorship

If the process of decision-making at Minneapolis was one-sided from the start, its sponsors intended it to be so. In accord with the Marcusean theory of progressive censorship, they determined that the oppressors and defenders of the status quo would be silenced and the voices of the oppressed would speak out. Feminist philosopher Naomi Scheman acknowledged that dissent was quashed in the hearings:

> The city council hearings were in themselves very one-sided, meaning that the vast preponderance of the voices that were heard were proponents of the ordinance. The reason for that was the theory behind the ordinance—the ground on which its First Amendment acceptability would rest—is that in very direct and real ways pornography functions successfully to silence women's speech. And that if one is interested in protecting speech, one needs to do something about pornography that effectively silences speech. Its [the ordinance's] goal is not to restrict speech, but to facillitate speech. . . .
>   So, that was the theory behind the ordinance. *The process was expressing that theory* by saying what we need in this discussion is to hear precisely those voices that the

phenomenon we are addressing has silenced. And that's what the hearings had to do.[156]

Catharine MacKinnon offered a further explanation. Responding to Councilmember O'Brien's criticism of the lack of balance, she declared that the status of the research no longer justified doubt about pornography's pernicious effects:

> Saying a body of research is open to interpretation to which it is not open is not professional. It is not objective. It is incompetent. Andrea Dworkin and I did not waste the city council's resources with outdated and irrelevant data and investigations. *In this situation, the truth apparently is a side.*[157]

MacKinnon's contention here seems overstated. The research into the effects of violent pornography is very suggestive but there is still room for reasonable doubt even here—especially when this type of pornography is presented in an intellectual or artistic context. And there is much more room for reasonable doubt about the negative effects of other types of pornography covered by the ordinance, such as "subordinating" pornography. Most importantly, pornography, like reality itself, is complex and subject to multiple interpretations. Absolutist approaches are suspect.

With the mayor's veto and the creation of the task force to study the matter, more traditional methods of decision-making returned. The new council reconsidered the ordinance and proposed a measure more consistent with present First Amendment principles. Under the leadership of Councilmembers Tony Scallon and a reformed Charlee Hoyt, deliberations now witnessed "almost too much debate."[158] The mayor's veto seemed to have vindicated the theories of checks and balances and of democratic elitism—that political elites may have to protect civil liberties from the mass of society.[159] Mayor Fraser's action led to reconsideration and the building of consensus based on compromise, benefits not appreciated by Professor Tribe in his unfair rebuke. Activists saw the compromise forged by the council and the task force as a violation of principle. Nevertheless, the second stage returned to a more responsible approach that allowed reasonable dissenting voices to be heard. The integrity of public discourse was restored.

Conclusion

On the negative side of ordinance politics in Minneapolis, we may include the way the city council allowed itself to be captured by pro-ordinance forces and the emotional and polarizing aspect of the controversy. On the positive side, the ordinance generated discussion and reconsideration of the pornography problem across the country.

The episode suggests again that the modern doctrine of speech is more precariously situated than might have been expected: political leaders on the council, in the city, and across the country at first did not support freedom of speech or even give it adequate heed. David Bryden believes that the support received by the ordinance from the intellectual Left and certain liberals indicates that some are willing to abandon the modern doctrine when presented with a progressive enough justification. Censorship of sexual materials is no longer a dirty word for progressives.[160]

As I will maintain in Chapter 5, reconsideration of the liberal tenets of contemporary free speech law is not necessarily a bad thing, especially in the adjudication of violent sexual materials. Liberals should have no monopoly of First Amendment interpretation; and the pornography problem may reasonably occasion a rethinking of liberal precepts or obscenity doctrine. Furthermore, it is entirely reasonable to integrate feminist perspectives into First Amendment law as long as important speech values are not harmed. Feminist perspectives have broadened and enriched other areas of law and have contributed to the advance of liberty.[161] MacKinnon's formidable skills as a thinker and an actor helped change the public landscape. Like the 1970 Commission on Obscenity and Pornography, she and her allies contributed "by creating dialogue and political discussion in the public arena of this society."[162]

Unfortunately, the Minneapolis situation contained many contradictions—not least the way it furthered national debate while suppressing give and take in the city council. More substantively, as we will see in the next chapter, the federal courts struck the ordinance down primarily because it constituted "viewpoint discrimination." As Joel Grossman has pointed out, "Politicizing the definition of pornography is, however, the fatal constitutional flaw. By attributing meaning to pornography beyond its appeal to individual prurience the ordinance elevates pornography to the class of ideas which necessarily have some political and social—if not artistic or scientific—significance"[163] By, in effect, operationalizing the distinction between egalitarian and inegalitarian sexually explicit depictions, the ordinance incorporated political distinctions that struck at the heart of the modern doctrine of speech.

It is clear that the advocates intended to refashion the law governing sexually explicit materials to achieve a distinct political and theoretical purpose. In their own way, they sought to constitutionalize Marcuse's doctrine of "progressive censorship" in favor of the Left or womens' causes—an approach premised on viewpoint discrimination. This conclusion may clash with the alleged reluctance of courts to inquire into motives when they examine the constitutionality of legislative enactments pertaining to speech. But motives are often relevant to First Amendment concerns, and in fact the courts often engage in de facto consideration of purpose under the guise of questions about vagueness and overbreadth of legislation.[164] The controversy over the ordinance reveals the potential relevance of political background to First Amendment analysis.

The ordinance controversy has other important implications. As we have remarked throughout this chapter, the unseemly haste with which the Minneapolis City Council passed the controversial measure, coupled with its failure to resist the polarizing tactics of the ordinance's supporters, raises questions about the ability of democratic government to maintain constitutionalism, due process, political responsibility, and institutional integrity. In certain respects, the episode was indeed "extraordinary" as local government officials insisted; in other respects, the episode revealed something all too common in political life—the reluctance of elected officials to be found on the wrong side of an emotionally charged issue which partisans have framed as a matter of good versus evil. The vulnerability of civil discourse to capture by single-minded advocates raises disturbing questions about the possibility of maintaining respect for legal forms and the rule of law.

Certainly the quality of discourse that prevailed in Minneapolis was detrimental to democratic society and democratic feminism. As I noted in the Introduction, the modern doctrine of free speech is intended to foster public virtues, including self-restraint, reasonable tolerance, and perspective.[165] The dominant public discourse attending the anti-pornography ordinance, however, was marked by excessive zeal and incivility toward reasonable opponents. The ordinance's supporters were the major offenders in this regard, although the MCLU's intransigent, knee-jerk opposition compounded the problem. The MCLU was the most vocal opponent, constituting 99 percent of the opposition, according to Stark.[166]

In the midst of the absolutism, some anti-pornography activists have managed to keep a sense of balance. Kathleen Nichols, the fiery county supervisor of Madison, one of the first local politicians to push for gay and lesbian rights, showed how one could be a committed feminist and

91

activist without forsaking the values that bestow integrity upon public conflict. She declared that she supported the civil rights logic of the ordinance, especially its focus on violence, but disapproved of the tactics of its sponsors at Minneapolis. Her understanding of the situation recalled Weber's ethics of responsibility and ultimate ends:

> On an issue like this, there *has* to be emotion. You can't debate a subject like this without having the emotions come to the surface somewhat, because you have to demonstrate impact. If you don't demonstrate that a class of persons is being disproportionately affected by this bad material, you can't prove that it has a social, real effect.
>
> To *twist* that, till it becomes *theatre,* till it becomes a way that the political and legal process is paralyzed, *is itself* immoral because governance is, in effect, the institution of moral agreement, for the greater good.[167]

For the Minneapolis activists, equality and tolerance were to reign only within the narrow camp of the ideologically pure—what Sennett calls the "negative *gemeinschaft,*" or the exclusive community of like-minded believers who perceive disagreement as a threat and betrayal.[168] Outsiders, a designation that included many participants, were treated as obstacles to be overcome. Interestingly, the activists' lack of respect for all opposition exhibited some of the same characteristics as the pornography they attacked. This is not surprising, as the synecdochal theory of reality espoused by Dworkin and MacKinnon also forms the aesthetic structure of pornography. Ordinance politics exhibited a loss of the tension between self and other, a *depersonalization* of others, in much the same manner as certain aspects of pornography. It also represented an abandonment of the tension between competing or conflicting legitimate viewpoints (such as free speech versus equality for women). By forsaking all values except equality for women as a victimized class, the ordinance offered the paradise of an absolutist world without the tension of competing viewpoints. I will argue in the last chapter that this lack of tension between competing purposes is one of pornography's greatest lures.[169] The MCLU's position was equally absolutist: there was no tension between the benefits of free speech and the possible ill effects of pornographic material, because there were no harmful effects of pornography. Society may enjoy pornography without having to worry about the consequences.

Activists attempted to replay Minneapolis a bit later in Cambridge, Massachusetts, where Dworkin and MacKinnon joined forces with the Women's Alliance against Pornography in summer 1985 to struggle for adoption of the ordinance. This time the opposition was ready, so the debate did not proceed in a one-sided fashion. Nonetheless, the confrontation was polarizing as before, leading the Commission on the Status of Women to officially complain:

> Pornography presents issues for all of us, and we must not create monolithic campaigns which force women and men to take absolute sides. We think public education and thoughtful debate can create a basis of unity as we carefully consider whether there is a legislative option for challenging violence against women.[170]

Finally, it is, perhaps, ironic that the very people who so ably created the public arena of discourse about pornography were themselves dedicated to dominating and, in effect, ending the discourse. As we have seen, MacKinnon proclaimed that all skeptical positions were "nonobjective," "incompetent," "unprofessional," and a "waste." Although the activists' refusal to compromise enabled them to create the new public arena, this posture also led them to treat everyone outside the circle of believers with a disrespect which seemed at odds with their own goal of empowering the silenced. This treatment was justified because their opponents were seen as complicit with the forces of oppression. Because the ordinance would exorcise these forces, the ends justified the means. How can one negotiate reasonably with an established order that is essentially a reign of sexual terror? We have noted MacKinnon's declaration, "If you understand that pornography literally means what it says, you might conclude that sexuality has become the fascism of contemporary America and we are moving into the last days of Weimar."[171] From this perspective those outside the cause are not worthy of consideration. This viewpoint is questioned by many feminists. Ann Snitow, for example, asks:

> Is it in our [feminist] interests—not to mention in the interest of truth—to say that because husbands often rape wives, all marriage is rape? Or to say that women who reject this equation have been brainwashed by patriarchy? This is to deny women any agency at all in the long history of heterosexuality.[172]

If everyone is either driven or victimized by subordinating forces, there can be no democratic politics, for such politics is possible only where there is choice and rational tolerance, a sense of commonness within difference.[173]

Although significant social movements are often products of single-   93 minded commitment and intransigence, they often generate a counter-vailing absolutist opposition. That is what happened in the first stage of the ordinance controversy in Minneapolis. Such a confrontation can end only in repression or revolution, neither of which can be counte-nanced in democratic politics. Fortunately, once the issues had been defined and public attention galvanized, a more civil discourse was restored. In the second stage of the ordinance hearings in Minneapolis and in other cities around the nation where the politics of pornogra-phy have been played out, compromise and accommodation have been more evident.

FOUR

STRANGE BEDFELLOWS: THE POLITICS OF THE ORDINANCE IN INDIANAPOLIS

> The temper and integrity with which the political fight is waged is more important for the health of a society than any particular policy.
>
> Reinhold Niebuhr

In a headline story on the second version of the anti-pornography ordinance, the newspaper of a Boston gay-feminist collective compared the political climates in Indianapolis and Minneapolis:

> Observers note striking differences in social climates and organized constituencies in the first two cities to consider such legislation. Minneapolis boasts a long tradition of liberalism; well-organized and relatively influential feminist, gay and lesbian movements; and affectional preference rights protection. In contrast, Indianapolis is known for conservatism; has relatively small, low-profile feminist, gay, and lesbian communities; and lacks gay and lesbian civil rights protections. And while Moral Majoritarians remained conspicuously quiet during the Minneapolis anti-pornography proceedings, the religious right has played a major role in Indianapolis events.[1]

Despite these and other differences, the politics of the ordinance in the two cities also resembled each other in disconcerting respects. Both showed unusual haste, distracting emotion, and deliberative shortcomings.

Indianapolis is "a *very* conservative town," according to John Sample, the former executive assistant to Mayor William Hudnet.[2]

With a metropolitan population of over one million, it is the largest Republican-run city in the United States.[3] And where Minneapolis politics is marked by conflict and fragmentation, Indianapolis exhibits an unusual degree of consensus. The Republican Party has dominated since the consolidation of city and county functions in 1970 under "Unigov." Before that time, Democrats controlled local politics, but they, too, were very conservative:

> Whichever party has been in control, Indianapolis, the national home of the American Legion and founding place of the John Birch Society, traditionally has been a conservative city. When many other cities were clamoring for more federal aid, Indianapolis often chose to go ahead without outside assistance. Perhaps Paul Friggens said it best: "Indianapolis is a solid conservative community of half a million people in a historically conservative state."[4]

Unigov under Republican aegis integrated political power in the city and county and put the mayor at the center.[5] The city-county council, whose role was also enhanced by Unigov, is run by the Republican caucus, which sets the agenda and structures debate. "For most things in the city-county council, unless the issue is very parochial, generally there is an over-whelming majority," remarked Donald Miller, the majority leader; "and on this council, with a partisan makeup, sometimes the minority sticks together."[6] The city-county council follows a Nebraska style of decision-making; committees do most of the work on bills then submit a product to the full council with a recommendation to pass or not pass. Mark Dall, a former city attorney who helped defend the ordinance in court, declared, "In Marion County, we do things as a team."[7] In Indianapolis there is a great deal of interaction between the council and the mayor, the city attorney, and the prosecutor.[8] When top leadership strongly backs a measure, as it did the ordinance, consensus often ensues. Indeed, the agreement concerning the ordinance in Indianapolis was striking, especially in comparison to Minneapolis. The council supported the measure by a 24–5 vote—all twenty-three Republicans backed it and five of six Democrats voted against it. But, as we will see, the official consensus concealed actual and potential Republican dissent.

Unigov ushered in a new type of progressive Republican leadership that eschewed the doctrinaire conservatism of the past in favor of a more pragmatic pursuit of economic and cultural progress, social welfare, and civil justice. Richard Lugar, who pioneered Unigov and promised to make Indianapolis a first-class city, was the first Indianapolis mayor to use federal money for other than basic functions such as welfare. According to Sam Jones, president of the Indianapolis Urban League (a vocal opponent of the ordinance), "Lugar looked at Toronto, Dade County, Nashville, and other places where metro-government was developed. He was far-sighted. . . . So, the city started to take off and move. Change came. Money came in, and the physical side of the city took on a new shape and form. . . . Then Hudnut came in and kept it up." [9] (Lugar later went on to the U.S. Senate.)

During his term of office, 1975—1988, William Hudnut strove to make Indianapolis a national leader. He built the Hoosierdome, a large indoor football stadium, brought the NFL Colts and the 1987 Pan American Games to town, pushed economic development, presided over an ambitious new busing scheme, and backed affirmative action measures in city government despite the strong disapproval of the Reagan Justice Department.[10] Indianapolis has also achieved economic advancement. In 1982, the *Wall Street Journal* proclaimed Indianapolis the "star of the snow belt." [11]

Despite its progressive strivings, Indianapolis remains a mixture of past and present. At least three basic types of conservatives maintain an uneasy coexistence in the city: religious fundamentalists who believe in an absolutist system of right and wrong; social conservatives who espouse more secular and elite versions of traditional values; and progressive conservatives who support traditional values but are also concerned for social justice and suspicious of absolutism. Social and progressive conservatives sometimes feel uncomfortable with the fundamentalists on certain issues even if they agree with them on others. They are slightly embarrassed by the fundamentalist emphasis on religious purity and by the public perception of fundamentalism as primitive and unreasonable.[12] In his recent autobiography, for example, Hudnut, a former pastor at Indianapolis's most prestigious Presbyterian church, disavows moral and doctrinal absolutism in favor of tolerance and recognition of social complexity and pluralism, expressly disassociating his views from what he considers religious extremism.[13] All these tensions were reflected in the politics of the Indianapolis antipornography ordinance.

Ordinance politics in Indianapolis made for strange bedfellows. The leading advocate of the ordinance, and ally of radical feminist MacKinnon, was a self-proclaimed "conservative Republican" councilwoman who had chaired the successful "Stop ERA" campaign in Indiana.

Despite the differing political climates in the two cities, there were striking parallels between the events in Indianapolis and Minneapolis. In each case, the council enacted the ordinance with surprising speed and what even some council members who voted *for* passage considered a lack of adequate debate. The council in each city deliberated under emotionally charged conditions, with activist groups wielding intense pressure in an atmosphere of moral emergency. Both councils allowed Catharine MacKinnon to craft the ordinance and to assume a consultant role that led many council members to view her as a neutral expert rather than as an advocate. Although there were no charges that the politics of the ordinance deviated from traditional methods of enacting amendments to civil rights law in Indianapolis as at Minneapolis, key figures on both sides of the pornography issue—including council members and government officials—said in retrospect that the process had been too impassioned for rational discussion and reflection.

This chapter will follow a more chronological development than did the ones on Minneapolis. Most of the theoretical issues were touched on in those earlier passages. I begin by looking at the background of the pornography issue in Indianapolis, including the development of regulation and politics in the 1970s and the intensification of political activism in the 1980s. I then look at the conservative theory of sexuality and pornography, describe the politics of the ordinance, and draw some conclusions.

Earlier Pornography Politics and Law in Indianapolis

Like other cities, Indianapolis saw crime increase during the 1970s and early 80s and population move out to surrounding suburban areas.[14] As in Minneapolis, sex-oriented establishments such as bookstores, theatres, massage parlors, go-go bars, and the like became a problem for the first time in the mid-1970s, dramatizing the deterioration of neighborhoods and contributing to perceptions that the quality of life was degenerating. By 1983, one city-sponsored research report located sixty-eight "adult entertainment establishments" in the city.[15]

The first reactions came with the formation of neighborhood groups, especially on the northeast and south sides, where most of the sex establishments were located. The major groups were the Near East Side Community Organization (NESCO); the Thirty-eighth and Shadeland Neighborhood Improvement Association; the Citizens for a Clean Community, led by Reverend Greg Dixon, fundamentalist minister of the Baptist Temple on the south side and a co-founder of the national Moral Majority; and the Indianapolis branch of Citizens for Decency through Law (CDL), which was organized in 1984 just before the anti-pornography ordinance issue erupted. Most of these groups began operating in the early 1980s, although Dixon's group started in the late 1970s. The groups working separately and together have employed a number of strategies, including picketing and demonstrating around sex establishments and pressuring city officials to crack down.

Pornography became a political issue in the late 1970s, when Dixon initiated his anti-porn operations and Steven Goldsmith won the prosecutor's office after running against, among other things, pornography. Dixon campaigned for Goldsmith, partly because of Goldsmith's position on sin and sex.[16] According to Richard Kammen, the leading area attorney for pornographers and a local counsel in the ordinance court case:

> This [anti-pornography action] is something the prosecutor adopted right after he was elected. He was elected in 1979, and one of the first things he did was to raid the adult bookstores. Before this, there was no real controversy for about ten years. The first year or eighteen months a lot of the cases were lost on technicalities, bad search warrants, that sort of thing.[17]

Mayor Hudnut also pressed the pornography issue. On March 4, 1983, he ordered police to "use every available resource within the limits of the law" to shut down pornography and prostitution operations. One week later, Indianapolis vice made several arrests at adult bookstores.[18] By the late 1970s, the city was suspending licenses of sex establishments, citing illegal sexual behavior and the sale of obscenity; later the city resorted to nuisance law.[19] From 1979 to 1984, these methods managed to close six bookstores, thirty-six massage parlors (easier to close because they are, essentially, places for prostitution), and two adult theatres. But according to Sergeant Thomas Rodgers of the Indianapolis Police Department, "The problem is that this method doesn't always work effectively. It doesn't close them down. The cases hang up in the appellate process for years. By the time they end, someone else is wearing the license hat."[20] In addition, the city lost some major obscenity prosecutions, which dampened its enthusiasm for going to court. From 1979 to 1985, the prosecutor brought only two obscenity cases—winning one, which was appealed—although his office made forty-five obscenity arrests. According to a member of the CDL, obscenity cases were brought only when "gross violations" were found.[21] Other methods of control adopted in the early 1980s included increasing fees for adult bookstores (passed by a 25–0 council vote); requiring that doors on peep-show booths at adult establishments extend only half-way to the floor to discourage sexual conduct inside; and prosecuting under the obscenity provisions of Indiana's 1980 Racketeering Influenced and Corrupt Organization (RICO) statute.[22] These efforts had some effect but fell far short of their objectives. Indianapolis attorney Richard Kammen explained why:

> The prosecutor has come to several realizations. First, political—these trials are very expensive because they are controversial. Secondly, if the goal is to close the adult bookstores, it's pointless because unless you have an enormous commitment and judicial resources, you simply can't generate enough cases to do it. . . . You don't own an adult bookstore unless you understand you are buying a certain amount of legal hassle. It comes with the territory; they aren't really scared of it.[23]

In 1984, the city passed a zoning ordinance following a study conducted by the Department of Metropolitan Planning which indicated that adult entertainment businesses increase crime and lower the appreciation of property values in residential neighborhoods. The city commissioned the study to provide a basis for defending a zoning measure in court; such a basis had been previously lacking.[24] According to the *Indianapolis News,* "The ordinance [had] been drafted by the city legal department after 18 months of work to come up with more specific regulations to replace existing laws that have been tied up in legal appeals for eight years."[25] Promulgators of the ordinance and the report upon which it was based presented the ordinance as a compromise between free speech and community control; they hoped that by focusing on physical, environmental effects, the ordinance would stand a better chance of surviving constitutional challenge. Nevertheless, Hudnut defended the ordinance more broadly in speaking to the press: "These adult bookstores, adult movie theatres and other types of adult entertainment, once they have a foot in the door, tend to spread like cancer, destroying everything around them." The ordinance prohibited adult entertainment businesses from locating within 500 feet of each other or 500 feet from land zoned for residences, schools, parks, or churches.[26]

Neighborhood groups attended the council hearings on the zoning ordinance and campaigned for it on local television. Nevertheless, a decade of attempts to restrict pornography and promote traditional values seemed to have produced few results. Despite their hopes for the new zoning ordinance, the anti-pornography forces longed for a new and more effective approach. Before we consider their reception of the Minneapolis ordinance, however, let us look at the attitudes toward sexuality current in conservative thought.

Conservative Theories of Sexuality and Pornography

Conservatism is a complex movement that defies easy distinctions.[27] Among the factions that comprise the Right are the New Right, traditional conservatives, neo-conservatives, and several more, all of which disagree among themselves on social matters and in their understanding of pornography. Some center their theories of pornography and sexuality on religion, believing that divine command limits sexual expression to the context of marriage and purposes of procreation. Others downplay religion and find secular reasons for advocating a normative sexuality. The common ground is agreement on the need for values and standards in society, whether religious and moral or secular and traditional. Conservatives join in lamenting what Richard John Neuhaus has called "the naked public square." This is the situation that results from putting into practice the philosophy of liberalism, with its stress on individual autonomy and state neutrality. Deemphasizing the idea of the common good leads to self-indulgent pursuit of individual fulfillment and pleasure, the promotion of material rather than spiritual values.[28] Pornography is seen as the explosive culmination of this liberal public philosophy.

One observer of the pornography debate discerns three basic issues that activists address. According to Eric Hoffman, "The first issue is the nature and meaning of sex. The second is the function of sexual imagery, and the third is the proper role of law in the regulation of sexually-oriented materials."[29]

Conservatives tend to see sex as proper only within a relationship of interpersonal commitment. For some, who advocate the authority of religion, this means within marriage. Others do not apply religious sanctions but still disapprove of recreational sex as destructive of traditional bonds and interpersonal responsibility. In a recent conservative work, for example, Roger Scruton acknowledges positive aspects of some non-marital sex but argues that sexual passion divorced from rational commitment leads to failure to achieve one's true character

101

and virtue.[30] Though Scruton utilizes non-religious modern philosophical concepts, his argument is ultimately conservative and traditionalist because it is premised on a normative notion of human nature and sexuality. Normative sexual desire involves commitment in relationships. The conservative emphasis on commitment "is part of a larger conservative emphasis on virtue, self-control, and dignity as the basic elements of a moral and social perspective."[31]

The conservative critique of obscenity and pornography follows from this starting point, charging that the "tendency of such images is to arouse a nonspecific desire for sex rather than a desire for sexual interaction with a specific person and to degrade a private activity by making it public."[32] Pornography and obscenity divorce passion from the virtues of rationality, commitment, and maturity. They coarsen people emotionally and diminish the shame that engenders self-restraint.[33] In addition to its contribution to sexual violence, pornography is psychologically regressive, in that it appeals to immature fantasies rather than to the sympathetic recognition of one's partner that marks sexual and emotional maturity. Pornography avoids the tension between self and other that lies at the heart of emotional responsibility. It undermines psychological acceptance of the reality principle, which supports civilization. Pornography seduces individuals from the tensions of adult existence and sexuality.[34]

Finally, the conservative approach endorses the use of obscenity law as a social tool to restrict pornography because it sees law as a valid and effective means of "protecting social decency and the quality of life."[35] In defending the criminalization of moral challenges to traditional order, Lord Devlin affirmed the importance of "public morality" and a "community of ideas" to society and went on to declare, "A man who concedes that morality is necessary to society must support the use of those instruments without which morality cannot be maintained. The two instruments are those of teaching, which is doctrine, and of enforcement, which is the law."[36]

Demonstrating the complexity of the terrain, however, there is a question that divides conservatives as well as feminists and unites some conservatives with liberals: how fervently should pornography be attacked? Some conservatives and some feminists see the issue as worthy of a crusade; others are reluctant to join in a holy war. The latter are willing to temper conservative with liberal values because of their respect for some of the latter, such as freedom of expression, because of their suspicion of certain forms of moralism, and because of their skepticism about claims to possess absolute truth.[37] Unlike conservatives who bemoan the decline of an absolutist value system (either religious or philosophical in origin) they see absolutist political theories as dangerously abstract and would rather rely on tradition and incremental social change.[38] Also, many conservatives stress individual responsibility, so they are suspicious of some of the new anti-pornography arguments that put blame on social influences rather than on culpable persons.

Neighborhood Groups in Indianapolis: The Conservative Critique in Action

Anti-pornography activists in Indianapolis took both religious and non-religious approaches to the issue. The views of major local activist groups exemplify the conservative approaches to sexual material. Some espoused a libertarianism that conflicted with some conservative thought.[39] The leading anti-pornography activists in Indianapolis, however, exhibited a traditional communitarian logic based on a normative, and sometimes religious, understanding of sexuality and desire. Some governmental officials hesitated to identify with this approach, favoring a logic based on the concept of harm rather than morals.

The Thirty-eighth and Shadeland Neighborhood Improvement Association began in April 1982 and grew rapidly. It was founded by June Beechler, at the time a seventy-six-year-old widow who had developed ties with city officials during her twelve-year tenure as manager of a drivers' license branch in Indianapolis. The Shadeland group inaugurated its efforts by gathering ten-thousand signatures on an anti-pornography petition that was presented to the mayor. Beechler acted to defend the values of neighborhood quality, social morality, and religion against the bookstores, massage parlors, and go-go bars (featuring nude dancing) that had sprouted in her neighborhood:

> My main concern in the neighborhood was the effect on young people. Second, we don't live in a million-dollar neighborhood here; but I've been fifty-one years in this house, and I don't want to move. Neither do I want to be around that kind of thing. . . . It depreciated the value of homes in the area the second the bookstore opened up here on Thirty-eighth Street, and it hurt business. . . . We saw a change in our neighborhood in the matter of a few years. . . . It's not community standards. These people have lived out here, many of them twenty to fifty years—and then to see a business like that move in here. . . . Some

people are afraid to stand up against these people, but on the whole, the community is behind us. . . . I don't think that as a churchgoer I have any right to sit still and not *do something* about it. I think I'll be held responsible for it if I don't do something about it. That's one thing that keeps me on my feet. I think we're going to be held responsible for what our young people will become.[40]

About the time the Shadeland group was growing, the Near East Side Community Organization (NESCO) arose under the leadership of Jack Lian, a local businessman. By the time the anti-pornography ordinance arrived in Indianapolis in 1984, NESCO had already developed a large following with ties to local government and engaged in numerous actions against sex businesses. Lian also headed CDL for Central Indiana, so I will discuss his views when I describe that group.

The other major group, Citizens for a Clean Community, was led by the pastor of the Baptist Temple, Greg Dixon. Dixon, a co-founder with Jerry Falwell of the national Moral Majority, was the first activist to make pornography a public issue in Indianapolis. A contentious and enthusiastic public speaker, Dixon combined fundamentalist religion with vigorous political action. Membership at the Baptist Temple, about 150 when he came to town in the mid-1950s, soon leapt to over 6,000, and he was far from reluctant to use his ministry for public purposes. Other conservatives in Indianapolis sometimes were allied with Dixon on social issues, but many maintained a wary distance from him and his rhetoric. His position on pornography and society echoed Anthony Comstock's apocalyptic vision:

> I do not preach a "social gospel," let me be clear. But there *is* an *application* of the Gospel. A Christian must be concerned with the dirty here and now. All the Bible makes an application. . . . The "fundamentalists" are too concerned with getting to heaven. Faith is the key. But without works, it is dead. It needs application. The moral law of God is still alive, as in the Old Testament. . . .
>
> I have watched local trials, and I have no problem with a jury saying this is wrong for our community. [Question: Would you put *any* limits on jury discretion concerning community standards?] No. Let the jury draw the line. . . . The jury should have the determination themselves. . . . Whatever a jury happened to hold, let community standards prevail. . . .
>
> I have always seen pornography as one of the blights on society. . . . The *river of smut* that is flowing down our cit-

ies is . . . one of the greatest indications of a totally decadent society. . . . It's indicative that we have lost our moral
moorings . . . hedonistic, humanistic, materialistic, nihilistic—churches, public education, society as a whole. And if
we do not come back quickly, it's probably too late forever
for America as a society. . . .

The church won't bring in the Kingdom. I believe Christ
will return and do so, and my role is to prepare people for
it. He'll clean it up when he gets here. But I believe I ought
to be in the hindering business. I believe that I am salt, and
it doesn't take much salt to season the meat. And I believe
that as a Christian I am a salt shaker and a light bearer.
And if I do that I don't have to worry about the results.[41]

In 1984, a group of leaders from the neighborhood organizations
joined forces and established an Indianapolis branch of Citizens for
Decency through Law. CDL's membership mushroomed and formed
ties with government; two council members, William Dowden and
David McGrath, sit on its executive committee. Indianapolis CDL
leaders' higher level of professional status distinguished them from the
unintellectual image projected by some anti-pornography groups.
(The organization also operates on the national and state levels.) By
the time of the ordinance, CDL had already staged several large street
protests at sex businesses. By 1985, it was the umbrella group for most
anti-pornography efforts in Indianapolis. Its actions were patterned on
the successful efforts of the Fort Wayne CDL, which served as a consultant. The Indianapolis group intended its demonstrations to serve
as evidence which could be used in court in regard to *Miller v. California's* community standards test.[42]

This approach distinguished CDL from Dixon's group; CDL leaders
were willing to use local, state, and federal statutory and constitutional law to achieve their goals. Whereas Dixon spoke in sweeping,
evangelical terms, most CDL leaders limited their critiques to material
that violated the law *of obscenity.* Yet this reticence was belied by their
intense public support of the anti-pornography ordinance, which went
well beyond the limits of existing constitutional law. Jack Lian,
founder of CDL and NESCO in Indianapolis, talked about the problem of obscenity and his reservations about mixing religion and politics:

I had drafted a group that was a coalition of citizens. And
in that group we had the Moral Majority and the extreme
religious groups—perhaps you'd call the Baptist Temple in

Indianapolis and Greg Dixon "extreme." His [Dixon's]
concern is genuine. . . . He goes right with me on this issue. There's no question about that. But he's also labeled
as being a Baptist. And if you get religious overtones to
this, then you lose a lot of people in the community because they don't have that direct affiliation with the Baptist Temple or the Moral Majority. So I try to stay away
from labels.

Lian's strong views on the harmfulness of pornography epitomize the
conservative position:

CDL wants the public to be really aware of what pornography really is. We are talking about hard-core pornography. . . . For many of us, it's the effect it has on our children and community in general. And it is a bit addictive
because the more you see it, the more you want. . . . I
think that if you are looking at, say, the group sex that is
shown, all of a sudden the values that we have established
concerning sexual relations with one person are harmed.
So that you have a more permissive society because of
what is going on. . . . I think the old values speak for
themselves. You now have the other aspect of family life,
the breakup of families. "I'm not happy with my partner,
so I'm not going to live with him anymore." [43]

Although Lian stressed the legal aspect of the battle, he did mention
that he personally considered *Playboy* to be more harmful than hard-
core material even though it is virtually beyond the reach of contemporary obscenity law: it starts the "chain of addiction" and is widely
available.[44] Still, he said, he would not campaign against it. Paradoxically, his support of the ordinance amounted to such a campaign, as
the measure probably covered *Playboy*-style portrayals of sex and
gender.

Ron Hackler, another founder of CDL and a member of its executive committee, expressed similar views. Deeply concerned about all
pornography, Hackler nevertheless limited his policy prescriptions to
what the Supreme Court has ruled is obscene:

We're a single issue group. Our initial concern is to get rid
of the *illegal* material. This is *still* our major concern. We
picket, too. We ask people in our newsletter to write drug-
stores against pornography. . . . We know though, that if
we start attacking *Playboy*, we're going to lose credibility.
It's not illegal. I guess I feel that if we just had *Playboy*, we

could deal with it [the problem] in a more rational way. Our concern is the law. The line should be obscenity law, with community standards. I try to draw the line at hard-core that shows ultimate sex acts.[45]

Another major CDL leader, Philip Nine, has a Ph.D. in engineering and is an engineer by profession; he is also a deacon in his church. Unlike Hackler and Lian, Nine stressed the religious aspects of the movement, but, like Beechler, he bridged the social and religious aspects of the issue:

There's definitely a moral problem with our society. And if Christians won't speak out in their society about what is right and what is wrong, then we're going to leave it to those people who don't have any standards. . . . Satan is still Prince of this world. Christians are in this world, but not of this world. . . . I believe a Christian has the obligation and duty to battle pornography and other sins, no matter what it is.[46]

These views reveal the mix of moral, religious, and legal motivations among the leading anti-pornography groups in Indianapolis. All these groups supported the ordinance, although some harbored reservations, particularly because of its feminist origins.

The Political Leaders

People in government displayed a mix of attitudes similar to that of activists; however, they were more circumspect. All seemed to agree on the undesirability of sex businesses. Some who supported the anti-pornography ordinance stressed its "harms" and civil rights rationales more than a traditional moral approach. As we have seen, Mayor Hudnut viewed pornography as a moral issue; he excoriated pornography as "a cancer" and had directed the police to crack down on it. According to Hudnut's executive assistant, "The mayor took a stand very early and made it very clear that he considers pornography and obscenity things we can very certainly live without. He considers it a disgrace."[47] As a "progressive" conservative, Hudnut approached the ordinance as an innovative tool for attaining civil liberty, equality, and justice for women. When I talked with him, he underscored this aspect of the ordinance rather than the moralistic, conservative aspect.[48] One close associate of the mayor, a liberal feminist lawyer, maintained that Hudnut did not really fathom the radical pedigree of the ordinance until she apprised him of it a number of weeks into the affair.[49]

Prosecutor Goldsmith's support of the ordinance was predicated—at least publicly—more on the harms argument than the old moral one: "New studies show that when a normal male is exposed to violent sexual material over a period of time, like six weeks, there is an increase in sexual violence toward women. . . . The question is one of harm," he told the press.[50] Assistant Prosecutor Debbie Daniels, who worked closely with MacKinnon and Coughenour on the ordinance, not only stressed the harms argument over the traditional moral argument but dismissed the moral approach as unworkable and unmeaningful. The two assistant city attorneys, Mark Dall and Catherine Watson, who worked on drafting the ordinance and on its legal defense, expressed considerable ambivalence about the ordinance that they had to defend but they believed in its basic harms logic.[51] These administrative participants were younger than the private activists and more open to new theoretical approaches.[52]

The view of the City-County Council on pornography was overwhelmingly conservative. William Dowden, the influential chairman of the Public Safety and Criminal Justice Committee and a member of CDL's executive committee, said of pornography: "I feel it demeans the respect that one person has for another. This is not to say that a man should not be honest and say that he enjoys the beautiful body of his wife. . . . That should be a natural occurrence. But I think that when I start dwelling upon a woman's body just for the objective beauty or lust that occurs, I think that's degrading over time." Although Dowden felt compelled to vote for the ordinance, he disagreed with its radical feminist premises: "I see pornography as a great deal more than a violation of woman's rights. Pornography, to me in my own social-moral value system, is demeaning to men and women. And I didn't want to see it categorized in such a narrow framework." [53]

Dowden's traditional conservative views represented the dominant view of the council. Pornography is bad because it demeans and depersonalizes sexual relations and because it disregards moral community in favor of individual gratification. Stephen West, a highly respected Republican member who had served on the council since 1971, when Unigov went into effect, epitomized this non-liberal, anti-permissive logic:

> It is to try to say that everything that occurs in someone's life and experience has some effect on them. Their background and education, and especially their formative years seem to have effect everywhere else. . . . What we have traditionally through the years considered the most valuable

things in civilization did not include a high degree of pornography. . . .
Apparently the liberal groups are afraid to associate
themselves with something that involves anything but permissive behavior, any restraints on such behavior. . . . Societal norms are part of our culture that we have evolved.
The norms change a little bit with time, but culture goes
on in the process. . . . It does push to an extreme. And it
seems that whatever happens, we can withstand it. That's
the theory. But we know that human beings are not that
way. They are somewhat absorbent, as if they had a po-
rous side, and we absorb a little bit of everything that goes
on around us.[54]

Even in the Baptist Temple and the CDL executive committee, individual beliefs could not always be predicted. David McGrath, who
was a member of both, and had been a supporter of most anti–sex-
business measures passed by the city told me in an interview that he
had deep reservations about the ordinance. He described himself as "a
very conservative Republican, very conservative on economic issues,
also on social issues. But I'm very aware that we at the local level also
have to answer to the state and the federal government and to the Supreme Court." Although McGrath was a prominent member of anti-
pornography groups that disdained libertarianism, he declared himself
uncomfortable with "playing God" and telling consenting adults what
they could and could not do unless a direct harm to others would result: "My whole concern is, if a female willingly exposes herself, I
don't want to see it. But I also realize that we have only one God, and
it's not me."[55] McGrath was well placed to observe anti-porn politics
in Indianapolis; in addition to his other affiliations, he was on the Administration Committee of the city-county council that had jurisdiction over the ordinance. His knowledge and frankness were immensely
helpful to my investigation.

The final council member to be mentioned here is the most important in the politics of the ordinance. Although Beulah Coughenour had
been inconspicuous in previous anti-sex business efforts, she rose to
become the Charlee Hoyt of Indianapolis. Like Hoyt in Minneapolis,
she was a Republican in her fifties who allied herself with MacKinnon
and Dworkin and made the ordinance her own special project. She and
MacKinnon formed an unusual alliance. Coughenour headed the successful fight against ERA in Indiana and she had never before taken a
pro-feminist position on any issue. She opposed abortion and led the

Indiana delegation out of the 1977 conference on women in Houston to protest what she deemed the convention's anti-family positions. Coughenour opposed laws against rape in marriage: "I am *very* protective of the family." The radical feminist origins of the ordinance bothered her. Responding to a question about the gulf separating her from radical feminism on other issues, she replied, "I'm afraid you're right. And that does give me real pause for thought because I'm a world apart. It is dangerous. It's very dangerous." [56] But, like McGrath, Coughenour could not be easily pigeonholed. Describing herself as "a conservative Christian," she nevertheless disavowed Dixon's view that (in her words), "Pornography is linked to all problems, including the family," in favor of a less doctrinaire approach that linked *some* forms of sexual material to harms against women. In politics, she dissociated her views from Dixon's, saying that an association had been alleged by her political enemies in order to discredit her. Coughenour also considered herself a self-determined woman, with a pilot's license that symbolized her ability to make it on her own. "I always felt equal to men," she proclaimed. Her anti-ERA background made feminists in Indianapolis suspicious, and many supporters of the ordinance questioned her motives. [57] But like Charlee Hoyt, Coughenour was committed to the issue and rose to the occasion by pushing the measure through a skeptical council. Her support combined feminist and conservative logic. Coughenour distinguished "violence" ("pornography") from "erotica" in describing Indianapolis's version of the ordinance, which was narrower than Minneapolis's and dealt mainly with depictions of violence and physical harm:

> *My* ordinance does not speak to erotica or nudity. I don't
> approve of all erotica, but I don't want the law to cover it
> because you really can't show social harm in the same
> way. . . . The key is violence linked to erotica that leads to
> a different behavior. . . .
> 　The bottom line is how do you balance First Amend-
> ment protection with protections for women in society
> and their civil rights, their right to go to the grocery store
> after dark without fear, and their right to expect a fair trial
> after being raped. . . . Just having the material pushed in
> front of women at work—to me, this lessens respect for
> women and it does make a difference attitudinally. [58]

Thus, leaders in the fight against pornography in Indianapolis displayed different reasons for fighting. There was a broad consensus based on the traditional conservative view, both religious and social, but many took a harms-based feminist, civil rights approach, especially the younger legal personnel downtown—and Beulah Coughenour. Strikingly, however, the radical feminist theory that linked pornography to systemic gender domination meant little to most supporters of the ordinance in government. Oblivious to the underlying rationale of the ordinance, city leaders and other activists pounced enthusiastically on its promise to eliminate pornography. Let us now turn to that story.

Early Developments in Indianapolis

Indianapolis leaders were desperate for a new weapon to use against pornography. Assistant city attorney Catherine Watson, speaking in company with fellow city attorney Mark Dall, declared, "Our view is that the ordinance is the only view that makes sense."[59] Nonetheless, many city leaders, especially on the council and in the legal department harbored reservations about the measure; even Dall and Watson expressed some doubt when pushed. But political circumstances worked to keep most reservations unspoken in public.

Mayor Hudnut had followed the ordinance issue in Minneapolis with keen interest. In February 1984, as the task force in the northern city was conducting its investigation, he and Coughenour attended the annual National League of Cities convention in Washington, D.C., where they discussed the issue with Charlee Hoyt. Hudnut pondered whether Indianapolis should pick up the fight in the wake of Fraser's veto. He remarked to Hoyt, "I don't think I would have vetoed that ordinance." Hudnut's supporters saw him as more willing to take risks than Fraser, more willing to assume a leadership role for the nation.[60]

Given the circumstances, however, Fraser's veto displayed leadership and, moreover, was a politically courageous act. In Indianapolis, challenges to pornography were popular and Hudnut, a former pastor of the city's prestigious Second Presbyterian Church, was inclined to provide moral leadership. Also, according to Coughenour, "The mayor had had a lot of pressure from different fronts, so he was looking for a solution, probably more than I was at the time."[61] Hudnut took his time but his eventual support conferred respectability upon the ordinance. "This was direct from the mayor. There was no question when this happened that this was the mayor's decision."[62]

Hudnut introduced Hoyt to Beulah Coughenour, suggesting "Why don't you do something?" Like Hoyt, Coughenour was "struck" by the ordinance and soon decided to push it back home, especially after being shocked by a packet on the harms of pornography that Hoyt sent her.[63]

Back in Indianapolis, Hudnut asked Catherine Watson of the city legal department to discuss the issue with Coughenour. They began talks that included Mark Dall of the legal department and people in the prosecutor's office, particularly Assistant Prosecutor Debbie Daniels.[64] Head Prosecutor Goldsmith came out strongly for the ordinance early on. An intensely political man, Goldsmith had initiated many previous anti-porn efforts. Many people also remarked on the strong political competition between Goldsmith and Hudnut. One inside source declared, "There's a pretty big rivalry between the mayor and the prosecutor. [It's] generally kept on pretty friendly terms, but there's a fierce rivalry and jockeying for position. . . . Goldsmith saw this as a great opportunity. It was a no-lose situation for him because he could come out and say 'I'm for this ordinance and behind it,' knowing full well that he wouldn't have to take the responsibility for it; he wouldn't have to defend it [in court]." According to another source, "The mayor said there was 'no way Steve Goldsmith is going to take the pornography issue from me.' "[65]

Coughenour's group soon established contact with Catharine MacKinnon in Minneapolis, and MacKinnon agreed to come to Indianapolis to work on the ordinance. The group started issuing press releases, turning the issue into a major media event.[66]

As progress accelerated, Hudnut took little part because he was often out of town negotiating the deal that brought the NFL Colts to town. "The mayor didn't realize how fast the train was moving—and it just went *really fast*." [67] As events quickened, the same bandwagon that swept Minneapolis rolled through Indianapolis. According to Mark Dall:

> It was to a position where so much publicity had been generated by it, and Goldsmith was *so* out in front of this thing . . . and Beulah . . . *It just took off like lightning . . .*
> And Beulah could pressure the mayor because she knew the mayor would need her vote on other big issues at the time [she headed the key Administration Committee]. So the mayor was in a position where he had to sign it. . . .
> And besides, he didn't want to come out as being pro-pornography, and that's how some people would have taken it.[68]

By April 10, 1984, both the mayor and the prosecutor had announced their support of the ordinance.[69] With the support of Beulah Coughenour and Beurt Ser Vaas, president of the city-county council, and the swell of publicity, a public consensus was forged among top level political leaders. Nonetheless, many important participants and council members were not so enthusiastic in private.

Coughenour, Daniels, Watson, Dall, and MacKinnon continued working on the ordinance in March, while spreading the word among other politicians. Coughenour said, "I sponsored the ordinance [along with Council President Beurt SerVaas] and worked hard with Debbie Daniels of the prosecutor's office. We went over and over it, along with MacKinnon. . . . We had a very intense and concentrated time. I suppose I spent hours per day from the time before it was introduced until it was proposed in April. . . . It all happened very quickly, quite soon." [70]

Sometime in March, Dall and Watson wrote a memo to Mayor Hudnut stating their conclusion that the ordinance, as it then existed in Minneapolis (the Minneapolis measure was not narrowed until May or June 1984), would not pass constitutional muster.[71] Their position represented the view of their superiors in the legal department, in particular City Attorney John Ryan, and the council's attorney, Robert Elrod.[72] Retaining the civil rights logic, Dall and Watson suggested changes that, in their estimation, would address what they considered to be pornography's most substantial harms and tailor the ordinance to the First Amendment. Their idea, recommended to them by Harvard's Laurence Tribe, was to narrow the ordinance's scope to restricting depictions of explicit violence and physical abuse. They also wanted to narrow the definition of pornography to cover only pictures, not words, and to exempt isolated passages from the law, so that the work would have to be pornographic "as a whole." [73]

The measure that emerged was a compromise that preserved the essence of the Minneapolis ordinance. MacKinnon, now working closely with Coughenour, helped forestall any substantial alterations. MacKinnon worked more behind the scenes at Indianapolis than at Minneapolis because, with the political forces already favoring the ordinance, its supporters did not want to risk alienating the council with her radical feminism. Interestingly, key council members remarked that MacKinnon came across as a conservative, and they did not know about her background or the happenings at Minneapolis.[74] But those with whom she worked knew her intentions. According to Catherine Watson:

113

We suggested even more changes that eventually didn't make it, basically because you had Mark and me on one side telling Beulah you've got to do this, and on the other side you've got Catharine MacKinnon down here saying "No, you can't cut that out of my ordinance, that's essential because of this and that reason." And Beulah was sort of in between us. We came up with some things we thought were fabulous. . . .

Our rationale here was, "We may not get *all* of it, but we'll get the worst stuff, the pictures, a strong rationale for protecting the models [involved in making pornography], etc." And MacKinnon's rationale was, "Well, that doesn't begin to scratch the surface! Why do it *at all* if you aren't going to do it completely?" She's an activist. She's a lawyer, but an activist first.[75]

Mark Dall added that Coughenour and Daniels also strove to limit the amount of compromise. "Cathy and I came up with all these great ideas, and the prosecutor's assistant [Daniels] and Beulah would consistently overrule [us]."[76]

The more radical position prevailed in the main. The version that emerged in late March from this workgroup did excise for a time some of the broader and vaguer parts of Minneapolis's definition of pornography pertaining to such things as "picturing women as whores by nature, women's body parts shown as parts, women dehumanized as sexual objects or things, or in postures of sexual submission."[77] Still the draft had subjective and ideological elements—"women are presented as sexual objects," for example. When the ordinance was introduced before the council's Administration Committee, Coughenour told the press that the legislation was "aimed at violent pornography and not at material depicting nudity or eroticism."[78] As for enforcement, the Indianapolis ordinance, like Minneapolis's, created civil actions for four acts: "trafficking in pornography," "coercion into pornographic performance," "forcing pornography on a person," and "assault or physical attack due to pornography."[79] The ordinance's definition of pornography was based on five of the nine components of the original Minneapolis version:

Pornography shall mean the sexually explicit subordination of women, graphically or in words, that includes one or more of the following:

1. Women are presented as sexual objects who enjoy pain or humiliation; or

2. Women are presented as sexual objects who experience sexual pleasure in being raped; or

3. Women are presented as sexual objects tied up or cut up or mutilated or bruised or physically hurt, or as dismembered or truncated or fragmented or severed into body parts; or

4. Women are presented being penetrated by objects or animals; or

5. Women are presented in scenarios of degradation, injury, abasement, torture, shown as filthy or inferior, bleeding, bruised, or hurt in a context that makes these conditions sexual.[80]

This version of the ordinance included "isolated passages" and "nonpictorial printed words" that Dall and Watson wanted to exempt.

Completed in late March 1984, the original Indianapolis ordinance was introduced to the city-county council on Monday, April 9, amid much fanfare. As Hudnut and Goldsmith proclaimed support, the Indiana Civil Liberties Union's executive director, Michael Gradison, "shrilly" announced ICLU's opposition.[81] The ICLU proved to be the only organized political opposition to the ordinance, although it brought in other individuals and the president of the Indianapolis Urban League. Gradison reacted vehemently to the measure: "The terms that MacKinnon put into the ordinance have no real legal meaning or significance. They are words that wholly escape any real definition. It is extremely difficult for any legal scholar to attach any meaning to words like 'subordination' or 'foisting pornography upon any unwilling individual,' etc. . . . There's nothing in this amendment that says 'obscenity,' and nothing that says 'socially redeeming value,' or 'community standards.' It's one woman has to be offended and the OEO [Office of Equal Opportunity] must investigate."[82] Mayor Hudnut later remarked that "I was rather startled by the shrill hyperbole of the opposition."[83] But unlike MCLU Director Matthew Stark in Minneapolis, Gradison conceded the validity of obscenity law and the *Ferber* case's doctrine on child pornography, as well as such regulatory measures as zoning and opaque covers. Other ICLU spokespersons—William Marsh, Sam Jones, and Sheila Kennedy, in particular—displayed a similar balance during the controversy and appeared more reasonable and measured in their opposition than either Stark or Gradison.

Now, the issue "just took off like lightning." "There was an explosion of public opinion."[84] Coughenour and Council President Beurt SerVaas scheduled a public hearing on the ordinance for Monday afternoon, April 16, at 4 o'clock, before the Administration Committee headed by Coughenour. This meeting would be important, for the council often defered to committee recommendations. The hearing was similar to the extraordinary Government Operations Committee hearing at Minneapolis in December, as witnesses denounced pornography with wrenching and impressive testimony.

The Administration Committee Hearing

The Administration Committee hearing lasted over four hours. At the end of the testimony the committee voted 4-0-2 (two abstentions) to recommend passage of the ordinance, with only minor amendments, to the full council.[85] The meeting was unusually well attended, with a crowd of nearly two hundred—mostly conservative and anti-porn activists. Unlike the Minneapolis hearings, no feminist groups came forward to denounce pornography—indeed, no feminist group appeared in any capacity at any point in the governmental process at Indianapolis.

As at Minneapolis, the major purpose of the hearing was to marshall evidence to support the ordinance, and the emotionally-charged testimony was weighted just as strongly in favor of passage as at the Minneapolis hearings. Coughenour and MacKinnon orchestrated the presentation much as Hoyt and MacKinnon had up north. They divided the testimony into two parts: witnesses called by supporters of the ordinance and "public testimony."

The sponsors called only anti-porn witnesses. MacKinnon introduced the issue, laying out the basic logic and content of the ordinance. She spoke with intensity, passion, and rhetorical skill: pornography "defines subordination as our [women's] sexuality," she declared; "Pornography makes men want the real thing." MacKinnon also held out the same stupendous promise she advanced at Minneapolis: "If it [the ordinance] works, it will make pornography no longer available."[86] As at Minneapolis, MacKinnon invoked her expertise and informed the committee, "Anyone who tells you that the ordinance is blatantly unconstitutional is giving you something more of a personal preference than any legal analysis."[87] MacKinnon's introduction was followed by dramatic testimony on victimization that riveted the audience. First, two anonymous women related how they had suffered because of pornography. The first was "Mary," whose testimony was summarized in the Administration Committee's Notes:

> [Mary] told the Committee that she was a victim of pornography and incest since she was three years old. Her fa-

ther had two suitcases filled with pornography, so much so
that he had to sit on them to close them. Her father tied
her feet and hung her upside down from a coat hook and
inserted objects into her and also had her perform oral sex
on him. By the time she was three years old she had had
everything done to her and he had gagged her to teach her
that big girls don't cry. Her father also gave her babysitter
and her boyfriend permission to use Mary in their orgies.
Mary stated that she had been victimized as an adult, but
will always suffer mentally for what was done to her as a
child.[88]

The second anonymous woman, "Judy," testified that her daughter
was "a victim of sexual assault for four and one-half years. When the
offending man was arrested in their home, the police found a considerable amount of pornographic material in the trunk of his car. As a
victim, her daughter had been removed from their home for over two
years now. They were able to bring criminal charges against the man
and he spent one year in jail." [89]

After this searing testimony, Detective Terry Hall reported that police often discovered hard-core pornography in the homes of rapists
and that sexually abusive men often used pornography to train girls in
sexual acts.[90] Then Assistant Prosecutor Debbie Daniels disputed the
conclusions of the 1970 Commission on Obscenity and Pornography,
pointing to subsequent studies that linked "sexually explicit violent
subordination of women" and greater propensities to commit violence
against women. During her testimony, Daniels dropped a bombshell.
Revealing a previously undisclosed detail about a recent sensational
murder case, she announced, "Greagree Davis, in a confession to police after the slaying this month of Debra Weaver, said he had visited
three adult bookstores on the Eastside the day of the killing. Miss
Weaver was stabbed several times and assaulted sexually." [91] The statement stunned the audience and provided ammunition that impatient
conservative activists would soon use.

"Public testimony" came next. Six speakers spoke against the ordinance, including Professor William Marsh of the ICLU and the law
school at Indiana University at Indianapolis; John Wood, former
member of the Indianapolis Equal Opportunity Advisory Board (then
called the Human Rights Commission) and now an attorney taking
part in the suit against the ordinance; and Sam Jones, president of the
Urban League in Indianapolis. Marsh stated that the measure violated
the First Amendment; Wood predicted that it would prove difficult to

implement and would overload the Advisory Board's caseload. He also said that the civil rights enforcement mechanism was potentially a violation of fairness and due process. Jones declared that enforcement would harm OEO's ability to protect blacks, and said that he and the Urban League did not consider pornography to be a civil rights issue *per se*. Sheila Kennedy—a local feminist, attorney, former city attorney, and eventually a local counsel in the suit against the ordinance— was unable to attend but sent a prepared statement that questioned the constitutionality of the measure as well as the legality of such an exercise of civil authority by a local government in Indiana.[92]

When I talked with members of this dissenting group, as well as with Administration Committee member David McGrath (who ultimately voted for the ordinance), they pointed out that proponents of the measure dominated the time and the attention of the hearing. Also, as at Minneapolis, the dramatic quality of the testimony discouraged dissent, as criticism made the questioner appear indifferent to the personal tragedies just attributed to pornography[93]

Six members of the public then spoke in favor of the ordinance. Included in this group were Ron Hackler and Jack Lian of CDL. Hackler took up Daniel's juxtaposition of pornography and murder: "In effect, what I said that night was (with a certain level of frustration, I guess) that If you guys aren't going to pass this, what are you going to do? We've been hollering about this problem and you can see what's happened. This girl's been murdered. *What are you guys going to do about this?*"[94]

As we have seen, the Administration Committee voted 4-0-2 to recommend adoption of the ordinance, with minor amendments, to the full council, but the committee was more divided than this vote suggests. David McGrath and Harold Hawkins, the abstainers, attempted more than once to block the ordinance with parliamentary procedures. After Hawkins failed by a 2-4 vote in an attempt to send the amendment to the council without recommendation, McGrath failed by a 2-3-1 vote to table the amendment. The committee then voted to send the amended proposal to the council with a "Do Pass as Amended" recommendation.[95] The process recalled the rush to passage in Minneapolis. McGrath remembered ruefully, "Unfortunately, this whole issue was railroaded through. We spent four hours on a Monday evening in the Administration Committee, and I was a black sheep. I kept asking all of the [difficult] questions. But the people behind it, they did a real sales job."[96] Despite the Administration Committee's quick action, however, the full council's position was not yet firm. At this point, "only 11 of the 29 council members reportedly support the ordinance."[97]

Other critics of the process included members of the Equal Opportunity Advisory Board, which would have to administer the ordinance. They worried that the new responsibilities would overwhelm them and prevent their carrying out their more traditional civil rights tasks. Black leaders in Indianapolis had similar fears.[98] As at Minneapolis, members complained that the board "wasn't consulted before the proposed ordinance was introduced to the council." Martha Bullock, chief officer of the EOAB, told me she was concerned about the vagueness of the Ordinance's definitions and the problem of draining EOAB resources, but "I was not involved in the preparation of this ordinance. They talked to me afterwards. When I learned of the ordinance, I raised the question [of enforcement and resources]. Beulah did meet with me. But, really, everything had already been done from the standpoint of the ordinance itself. I did not have any input into that ordinance itself. . . . There just wasn't any thought given to it. . . . And in order to get it going they set up a mechanism to do that, and forgot all about the office that they said was going to administer it."[99] On Thursday, April 19, the board held a special meeting to discuss how to deal with the issue.[100] Bullock said that Hudnut contacted her after he read about her concern and assured her that the requisite resources would be forthcoming if the ordinance were passed.

After the committee vote, Coughenour and her supporters began politicking more aggressively. "I talked individually with council members and about what I was trying to do. You need fifteen votes, and after the hearing, I came to the council meeting with fourteen votes that I knew of, and I was concerned."[101] She also met with CDL leaders, Dixon, and McGrath, and they pledged their support. CDL issued a letter to the council at this point, urging passage: "The Citizens for Decency support this amendment. We consider this a strong tool for use by the city for the elimination of pornography and other obscene materials from the city of Indianapolis and Marion County."[102] Council members began receiving letters and phone calls from supporters.[103] At the same time, however, newspaper editorials began to criticize the ordinance although the papers were conservative and against pornography. The afternoon *Indianapolis News* questioned the ordinance's expansive scope, while the morning *Star* said the council should have exercised "unhurried care" and that the ordinance "now before the City-County Council does not sound either sufficiently narrow or well enough thought out."[104]

The Administration Committee held another meeting on April 19 at which Coughenour brought city lawyers together to explain how they would defend the ordinance, if challenged. City attorneys at this meeting supported the measure and declared that they could construct viable defenses. However, several of them were ambivalent about the measure, especially Mark Dall and John Ryan, as we have seen, and the council's chief counsel, Robert Elrod.[105] The press reported that at this meeting Elrod "declined to declare the ordinance constitutional in his view, preferring to outline defenses for challenge."[106] According to McGrath, "even at this time, our own attorney still said that it was bad. But, there again, it was railroaded through." The ICLU's Gradison remarked that, "Bob Elrod called me when the thing first broke and told me, 'Mike, give me something to work with. I'm trying to stop this thing.'"[107] The draft passed to the council included a very unusual note from the city legal department acknowledging its questionable constitutionality. Rozelle Boyd, a thoughtful, deliberate Democratic council member who had questions all along about the ordinance and the process, told me

> I think it is extremely significant that in the draft of the ordinance itself the persons that had the legal minds. . . . found it necessary to pin the comment on the ordinance that it had not been tested for constitutionality, and that they were not comfortable with it. *I have not seen that on other ordinances.* As a matter of fact, constitutionality is *always a test* for creating an ordinance in the first place. . . . They [city lawyers] did not want their professional integrity impugned.[108]

But political pressures discouraged the lawyers from stating their objections more strongly. Barrages of support now emanated from the mayor's office, the prosecutor's office, leading activist groups, and key figures on the council, including the council president and the head of the Administration Committee. McGrath remembers asking some city attorneys about the constitutional basis for Mayor Fraser's veto in Minneapolis: "Ryan, Elrod, and the others could have said to me, 'Dave, it's an exercise in futility.' But they didn't. They side-stepped it by saying, 'Dave, this guy [Fraser] is a real left-wing liberal, and you can expect that kind of thing.'"[109]

This remark reveals one of the most fascinating aspects of the situation in Indianapolis. Many of the people in government there did not realize that origins of the ordinance were much more left-wing than

Mayor Fraser, nor did they grasp the background of the high-pressure campaign that had pushed the measure through the Minneapolis city council. Two influential Republican council members in Indianapolis told me that they did not know that MacKinnon was a radical feminist. To them, her ordinance was simply a new method to restrict sexual material. Three years later, Hudnut in his autobiography could describe MacKinnon as a "liberal feminist," a label that she has rejected.[110]

MacKinnon's radical feminist credentials were not publicized at Indianapolis, making it easier for the very conservative council to accept her work. According to David McGrath, "MacKinnon portrayed herself as an ultra-conservative."[111] In Indianapolis, she did not play the advocate's role: "She did eventually leave the politicking to Beulah," said Mark Dall. "She did not lobby individual members of the city-county council. She was more elevated, 'Here's what you should do,' etc., and left the behind-the-scenes work to Beulah, whereas in Minneapolis she was more in the forefront." Catherine Watson recalls, "She acted as an expert giving testimony before the council."

As a result, most council members saw the ordinance as either a conservative or a civil liberties document (a confusion that reinforced the worry of many anti-censorship feminists that the measure could play into the hands of conservative forces).[112] William Marsh remarked, "None of the people over at the City-County Building ever saw that [radical feminism] in it at all. Had Beulah understood what they were really saying, she would have turned and run so fast!"[113] One conservative supporter evidently did just that. At the Administration Committee hearing, Henry C. Karlson, a law school professor at Indiana University in Indianapolis, spoke briefly in favor of a version of the ordinance, saying that a "properly drafted" measure that differentiated between "sadistic, masochistic types of pornography" and other types could be acceptable.[114] A short time later, after hearing MacKinnon lay out her theory more fully at a law school forum, Karlson dropped his support of the ordinance.[115]

When I spoke to her nearly a year after the vote, Beulah Coughenour acknowledged the radical pedigree of the ordinance and said that her alliance with MacKinnon had been "dangerous." Nevertheless, she defended her stance: "You have to zero in. You can't do politics if everyone has to have the same beliefs about everything."[116]

Between the Thursday committee meeting and the full council hearing and vote the following Monday, organized groups stepped up their support for the ordinance. CDL, Dixon, and neighborhood associations gathered signatures on a long petition. CDL and Dixon launched plans to bus large numbers of supporters to pressure the council at the vote. However, all this activist support was exclusively conservative. No one I talked to was aware of any groundswell of public support; and no womens' group came forward. Michael Gradison pointed out that NOW in Indianapolis was undergoing conflict and change at the time of the ordinance dispute and could not organize a position. Indianapolis had no prominent radical feminist groups, and mainstream groups, such as NOW, were not very active. The only major organization that pushed feminism in Indianapolis was the ICLU.[117] As we have seen, the only organized opposition to the ordinance came from the ICLU (with help from the Urban League; the Indianapolis NAACP did not take a stand).[118] The ICLU normally enjoyed unusually good relations with city leadership, but on this issue it did not deal with any government leaders. Instead, it sent high ranking members or supporters—Marsh, Jones, and Kennedy—to testify before the Administration Committee and the council while it worked behind the scenes with other groups to develop the impending court case. Hudnut, Coughenour, and Dall complained bitterly about the ICLU's refusal to help draft a more suitable measure, seeing this uncustomary reluctance to lend a hand to those in need as a display of bad faith.[119]

A poll of council members reported in the press on Saturday showed many still undecided, despite the political pressure. The *Indianapolis News* reported "growing support" for the ordinance but not enough to make a majority of fifteen. Thirteen yes votes were more or less assured, although some of these supporters had reservations. Seven council members indicated they would vote against the ordinance. They cited three major problems: the prospect of an expensive court fight, the danger of watering down the EOAB's enforcement of more traditional forms of racial and gender discrimination, and the infringement of free speech values.[120] Activist groups grasped the uncertainty of the situation, so they fashioned plans to pressure the vote on Monday. The *Indianapolis News* on Saturday reported that Greg Dixon "plans to have 200 to 300 supporters at Monday's council meeting" to influence the vote.[121] CDL's Ron Hackler assessed the situation this way:

> The ordinance was not a foregone conclusion, though. It's
> possible that if we [the activists] hadn't been there, it
> wouldn't have been passed. There was a lot of reticence on
> the part of the council. I called one councilman, and I

imagine Mrs. Beechler called several. . . . The council member I called said the ordinance doesn't have much to stand on. What happened, I think, is that you could see the fifteen votes were going to be there, and so you jumped from fifteen to twenty-four. And there were some who first time through didn't vote.[122]

The Council Hearings and Vote: Mirrors of Minneapolis

On the ground that sufficient testimony had already been given, the Administration Committee had declared beforehand that no testimony would take place before the vote. In a surprise move, however, the committee called for testimony from Edward Donnerstein, the leading researcher on the effects of pornography who had testified at Minneapolis. When the meeting opened, Coughenour and MacKinnon brought out Donnerstein and MacKinnon spent a long time introducing the issue. As at Minneapolis, MacKinnon questioned Donnerstein, eliciting testimony on his research to support her legal points.[123] Several who supported the ordinance mentioned that Donnerstein's testimony about the effect of violent erotic material on average males influenced their vote; they had gathered that Donnerstein's views were widely accepted in the field.[124] No counter evidence was discussed, even though disputes rage in this area of research. (At Minneapolis counter arguments about scientific research were presented, if not really heeded.)

Three other witnesses spoke against the ordinance, on short notice, squeezed in at the last moment at the behest of a Democratic council member. Asked if the hearings were one-sided, William Marsh, a careful, deliberate man, replied:

> *Oh yes—absolutely!* No question about it. The clearest example is the city council meeting where they were going to allow *no* public testimony. They announced at the meeting that the public had had a chance to speak at the [Administration] Committee meeting, so there's to be no public testimony now. And then they bring in Donnerstein, who spoke for a long time. And he's obviously not neutral. He was brought in by the proponents of the legislation.
>
> I got to speak, much to the chagrin of three-quarters of the council and 90 percent of the people in the audience, just because of Rozelle Boyd. I don' know *how* he pulled it off, but he got the floor and called on me. [He asked] "Will you come forward? I want to ask you a few questions."

123

And *all of a sudden,* I'm up there and get a chance to
speak. If he hadn't done that, there would have been no
[counter] testimony.

Sheila Kennedy and Sam Jones, the other last-minute speakers, had
similar impressions of the situation.[125]

David McGrath, the reluctant supporter, agreed that the deck was
stacked. His observation about the political orchestration resembles
the remarks of many observers of the politics in Minneapolis:

> I kept time. I knew the sponsor would play a game. All the
> people before her were going to have so much time.
> MacKinnon spent fifty-four minutes. Donnerstein spent as
> many minutes. Then, when it came to the people of the le-
> gitimate bookstores, universities, etc., she was going to cut
> them off, and I was ready for it. I brought it up and ac-
> cused them. It was so orchestrated. The way it's set up, a
> committee chairperson has a lot of clout. He or she can
> dictate. Her [Coughenour's] position was key.[126]

As at Minneapolis, intense activists packed the audience. Although
the Minneapolis vote had been very close (7-6), all but one council
member there had decided ahead of time; most of the pressure had
been applied by activists in the council offices in the days leading up to
the vote. At Indianapolis, however, many (perhaps most) Republicans
had not made up their minds, and the major pressure to that point had
been exerted by higher city leadership. Now, the Baptist Temple and
CDL brought busloads of supporters to the voting session. The pastor,
Greg Dixon, was not familiar with the precise language of the ordinance when I talked with him later, but he did endorse its basic logic—
pornography's harm "far outweighs" even the "harm of segregation,"
he believed; it threatens "the whole feminist race" [sic]).[127] This pressure by activists at the time of the vote made a significant difference.
The count was 24-5 for passage. The *Indianapolis News* reported,
"The substantial margin of the final vote on the antipornography ordinance was surprising and indicated some council members had
changed their previously announced feelings on the proposal." [128] This
margin resulted despite significant concerns about the substance of the
ordinance and the process by which it was passing. David Page, a
Democrat, summed up the plaints of Democrats and many Republicans: "I can't see why we can't wait two or three weeks or a month to
tie up every loophole." [129]

124   The council vote was taken in an atmosphere of moral urgency.

When I asked David McGrath how many council members really supported the ordinance, he answered, "In my opinion—strictly my opinion—four or five." But all twenty-three Republicans and one Democrat voted for it because "this was like an imminent and present danger. We've got to resolve all the problems tonight." [130] Michael Gradison of ICLU was not a neutral observer but his views on the pressures accompanying the vote and the council's reluctance were shared by several others, including eventual supporters:

> And the city-county council, of course, *did not want to
> pass it.* If it had been a *secret meeting,* and they didn't have
> Greg Dixon and his wife *sitting in the front row* of the
> city-county council chambers, and no media were in the
> room at all—it was so crowded, very politicized—it
> wouldn't have passed. Beulah got them all there. Dixon
> and company were there. No women's groups were there.
> He rallied his congregation, that's who was there. He filled
> the chambers. They call it "rolling the buses." And they
> *booed and hissed,* and carried on whenever our propo-
> nents started testifying. . . .
>
> Dave McGrath said to me, "I can't vote against it. I
> wouldn't dare vote against it because some of the people
> out there are my constituents! You know, I wouldn't get
> out of here alive."
>
> They fast-tracked. They passed it out of committee in
> one week, and one week later rammed it through the
> council. [131]

The two city lawyers who worked on defending the ordinance concurred with this assessment. Mark Dall supported the measure, although he favored a more moderate version:

> We did have the Moral Majority which came out literally
> in throngs to support this thing. . . . It's good to have a
> good crowd, but they're not the kind of people that we or
> the authors of the ordinance wanted there. They didn't
> read the ordinance, but are automatically *always* against
> *any* of that stuff. . . .
>
> None of the city council, other than Beulah, wanted to
> touch the thing with a ten-foot pole. None of those people,
> other than Beulah and a few others knew anything about
> it. They didn't really *want* to know a thing about it. A lot
> of them privately said, "Hey, I would like to vote against
> this thing, but I can't." The Republicans voted for it be-
> cause the mayor wanted it, and in Marion County we do

things as a team. A lot of them never read it, and didn't go to any of the hearings [Dall was there to observe this]. But then they saw that room full of people—Dixon's group dominated the crowd—all the T.V. cameras, and a *big score board* [for votes]—it's all up there—and all these cameras down there. It's very hard. You just *could not* vote against it. It was impossible. They all knew the thing wasn't going to go down [constitutionally], and they all knew they didn't like Catharine MacKinnon's approach, but they had to vote for it.[132]

William Marsh's view reveals the similarity between the processes at Indianapolis and Minneapolis:

What's really interesting is what happened once it got here. The haste with which the city acted and the commitment put into the thing was just shocking to me, the lack of deliberation—I don't think anybody listened to anybody. There were no ideas exchanged. . . . People on the council thought it was a bad idea but were afraid to be labeled "for pornography." [The issue got] picked up by Dixon, who brought busloads of people to the council chamber. People on the council were not off base if they saw these people as just labeling them "for or ag'in it." One member, Councilman Holmes, said exactly that at the vote. He said "The only issue here is whether you're for pornography or against it, and I'm against it, so I'm voting for this ordinance." Everybody had closed minds. I never talked to anybody with an open mind.

The other thing that was amazing to me was how much MacKinnon was able to come in and call the shots. She came in and she had people just eating out of her hand.[133]

As Ron Hackler of CDL pointed out, the vote was not a forgone conclusion; many members abstained from voting until the majority of fifteen had been obtained in the face of audience pressure. Jack Lian elaborated:

When NESCO and CDL come in, obviously we have the numbers behind us. So yes, we became a factor, a very strong factor because we don't want pornography. This is a community standard that we are trying to establish. And the city council looked at us and said "These people don't want pornography. They do want the ordinance, so we should act on it."

I probably had some difficulties with this ordinance standing by itself. But it gave all of us something we could hook onto. . . . It was passed because we had hundreds of people show up. And it was [laughter] *political suicide* if you voted against it. . . . We on the East Side circulated a petition in support of the ordinance and showed up with several hundred signatures. . . . So now you had standing room only. There must have been a thousand people at City Hall showing support for the ordinance, very few that were opposed. So each time a point was made we had a thousand eyes or two thousand eyes that were watching what was going on. And because of that pressure from the citizens, that ordinance passed. It was passed and went *very quickly.*[134]

William Dowden, a Republican, chairman of the Public Safety and Criminal Justice Committee, and a member of the Indianapolis CDL's executive committee, is a careful, deliberate man who was undecided until late in the game. His remarks about the council's position and the pressures of the vote are important because he is a leading and representative member of the council majority and because he is active in anti-pornography politics:

I was among the group that finally voted for it on the council. But like a lot of them, I was not enthusiastic about it because it was pointed out to us [by attorneys whom Dowden refused to identify] that it had so many constitutional flaws that it would not be upheld. And it also, in my view, addressed pornography as something other than what I see it as. I see pornography as a great deal more than a violation of a woman's rights. My own social-moral value system says that pornography is demeaning to men and women. I didn't want to see it categorized in such a narrow framework.

[Who told you it was unconstitutional?] Several very involved attorneys, let's say that. They were people who shared my view on pornography and publicly ended up supporting the ordinance, but who also said it was of very doubtful constitutionality.

[So why vote for it?] The way I understood it, I realized that to be opposed to that ordinance, since it had been portrayed as anti-pornography, anybody who voted against it was going to be brushed as one who was for pornography. And once you got to that point after weeks of

debate, once it was obvious it was going to pass, it served
no useful purpose to vote against it because it was being
portrayed as anti-pornography. . . . [A negative vote]
would have been misunderstood by many people who
thought [the ordinance] was against pornography. But
there was a great deal of discomfort with it. It created a
real problem.[135]

These observations by leading participants on different sides of the
issue reveal that, like the circumstances of the vote in Minneapolis, the
process in Indianapolis represented a failure of institutional integrity
and responsibility. The city-county council surrendered to the crisis
mentality created by the activists and voted for the measure despite
serious reservations about its substance and the lack of adequate deliberation. The council allowed Coughenour and her allies to orchestrate
the hearings, delving neither into the ideological underpinnings of the
ordinance nor into its questionable political precedents in Minneapolis. Indianapolis council members appeared to have been less beguiled
than some in Minneapolis, but the body did forsake caution and deliberation for political expediency and it permitted the doubtful promise
to purge pornography in Indianapolis to stand unquestioned.

After the vote, Democrat Rozelle Boyd offered a resolution designed
to limit the costs of defending the ordinance in court to $200,000.[136]
Indianapolis normally prides itself on fiscal conservatism. Sheila Kennedy, for example, told me that when she was City Attorney, she
worked under a strict policy of keeping down appeals expenditures;
and Mayor Hudnut affirmed that government must balance progressive programs with fiscal limits, writing that "government at all levels
must learn to practice creative frugality." [137] But this time the council
defeated Boyd's resolution, 19-7. According to Boyd,

You will not find, in *any other* place in a city action, where
we have been so cavalier about spending money. And I
think that is probably the best index you can have about
what some of the real motives were there. Because we *violated completely* what has been a fairly consistent posture
we have taken about being fairly conservative about how
we spend money.[138]

Other interviewees were bemused about the eventual cost of legal
defense. Discussing the different political climate in Minneapolis, majority leader Donald Miller laughed, "And they got off real cheap!"
He also said that the failure in the courts demonstrated that the coun-

cil should have taken more time to pass a more acceptable product.[139] And David McGrath laughed, "Minneapolis turned it down twice. The joke up there was 'Let Indianapolis pay for it.' I heard this a number of times."[140]

If the politics in Indianapolis was one-sided, it did not approach the level of incivility that characterized Minneapolis. Perhaps conservative activists in Indianapolis were less alienated from the political process and culture than the radical feminists at Minneapolis.[141] But conservative activists did boo and hiss at the hearings and votes, and their absolutist approach to the issue showed intolerance. Mayor Hudnut has been known to champion Lincolnesque values in politics: Lincoln "held to strong moral values without becoming moralistic. He proceeded firmly and responsibly to execute historic tasks, but he never became overconfident or self-righteous. . . . Lincoln could make strong moral judgments, but he did so without becoming pompous or censorious."[142] Activists and many in government did not meet this standard at Indianapolis.

The level of civility was reportedly lower in some local debates and forums outside the official political process. Sheila Kennedy experienced some rough moments in debates with Andrea Dworkin and other activists (Dworkin was less involved at Indianapolis, and avoided the Council for political reasons). "I will tell you. The gals I debated, Dworkin, Dorchin Leechold [at a Library Association debate and in other forums]—if you disagree, there's none of that inherent civility that says, 'Well, look. We may disagree, but we're still nice people.' There's a lack of humor. . . . I consider myself a feminist. What has disturbed me greatly about the kind of debate that has occurred, is the assumption or suggestion that we [liberal feminists and feminists against censorship] are not good women. But there was not one local feminist who had anything to say about this ordinance."[143]

Another problematic aspect of the politics of the vote in both cities was the presentation of the ordinance as a magic wand that would make pornography disappear. Many supporters realized the ordinance was not a cure-all and saw it as one approach among others to the problem. Mayor Hudnut was attracted to the potential of the ordinance but he understood the risks involved and appreciated the need of responsible politics for compromise and perspective. "Those of us in city government sometimes deal with people who tend to think solely in terms of 'moral' issues—like substance abuse, massage parlors, adult bookstores, that sort of thing. While these activities merit attention, they do not constitute the whole story. There is more to urban America than this." [144] And council member Stephen West said, "The ordinance was not proposed to be a magical answer. It was proposed as one part of an effort to try to take a look at some of the more blatant acts, and to put it in the framework of what it does to women, to in a sense degrade them, treat them as commercial objects." [145]

But the ordinance's supporters implied excessive promises by their very fervor. As we have seen, MacKinnon spoke of ridding Indianapolis of pornography once and for all. In David McGrath's estimation, "I was very disappointed in the people behind this because they portrayed it to the community, the bottom line, that it was going to put an end to pornography, obscenity. It was almost a panacea. They sold it as a panacea, a real handle. I don't lie. . . . The mayor had the greatest intentions in the world, but he got snowballed. . . . When we've got something that's very complicated and very involved, I think we need to look at it, not railroad it through. This is what frightens me most. . . . I will never be a proponent of railroading something through." [146]

Rozelle Boyd, a thoughtful Democrat and a member of the black community, commented on the ways the process had fallen short of the standards of a tolerant, responsible society. When I asked him how he would treat an overtly anti-black hate magazine, he replied, "My *emotional* response would be that it *should go*. My *intellectual* response would be that if that goes, then where do you draw the line? That was one of the real weaknesses of the ordinance." Regarding the vote, Boyd said that simplistic absolutism had replaced objective complexity:

> It was a kind of issue you really didn't have to think about
> because if it's pornography, it must be really evil. [It was a]
> simplistic mind many people brought to it. As an object of
> public awareness, it took a life of its own. . . . I could
> never understand the mayor's position on it and council
> persons', for it seemed absolutely clear that it would not
> pass a constitutional test. It was presented very simplis-
> tically to the public. You know, if you vote for it you are
> against pornography, and if you vote against it you are for
> pornography. It's that simple, so how are *you* going *to
> vote*? It is much easier going ahead and voting one way
> rather than trying to interpret and explain to the public
> that doesn't see the niceties of what you are doing. [147]

Unfortunately, the evidence suggests that in Indianapolis emotion and political pressure carried the day. The city's rush to judgment despite the legal reservations of many leaders and the inherent complexity of the pornography issue gives cause for concern about the status of free speech and the integrity of political forms.

The Law Suit and Amendments

Stories about the vote appeared in the local and national media as supporters and opponents continued the debate.[148] Andrea Dworkin joined in at this stage; strategists had until now kept her away from the political end of things, fearing that her style would alienate the council.

On May 1, 1984, Mayor Hudnut signed the ordinance in the presence of Beulah Coughenour and the media, vowing that the city would defend the measure all the way to the Supreme Court.[149] A group led by the American Booksellers Association (of New York) and the ICLU stood ready to hold him to his promise. They filed a lawsuit seeking preliminary and permanent injunctive relief in the U.S. District Court for the Southern District of Indiana moments after the signing. This group did not include pornographers but consisted of "legitimate" booksellers who asserted that the ordinance could be applied to them. The idea was to present as favorable a set of plaintiffs as possible.[150] The plaintiffs were represented by Michael A. Bamberger of the New York firm Finley, Kumble, Wagner, Heine, Underberg, Manley and Casey and by local counsels Sheila Kennedy and Richard Kammen. The suit charged that the ordinance went "beyond the standard for obscenity established by the U.S. Supreme Court," was "unconstitutionally vague," held a person "liable without requiring that said party have any knowledge of the nature of the offending material" [scienter], violated the commerce clause of the U.S. Constitution by "restricting the availability of First Amendment protected materials," and violated the First, Fifth, and Fourteenth Amendments.[151] Meanwhile, city lawyers prepared their defenses.

American Booksellers Ass'n. v. Hudnut was the very first case for U.S. District Judge Sarah Evans Barker, who had just been appointed by President Reagan and sworn in on March 30. On May 9, Barker issued an uncontested preliminary order enjoining the enforcement of the ordinance until the court reached a decision. Other minor legal maneuvers ensued and amicus curiae briefs started coming in, including briefs by the ICLU, Linda Marciano, and Catharine MacKinnon. By now, the issue had gained national attention; it was the subject of two pieces in the *New York Times*.[152]

Although the Indianapolis version of the ordinance was already less   131 broad than the one in Minneapolis, the prospect of defending it in court caused the city to reconsider. On May 10, Coughenour and City Counsel John Ryan introduced two amendments to the ordinance intended to "allay the fears of Mr. Gradison and other critics. The amendments . . . try to clarify exactly what is covered by the law." [153] The key restrictions included first, excluding "isolated passages" from coverage, and second, disallowing liability for damages unless the purveyor knew the material violated the ordinance (purveyors could still be stopped from selling, whatever the status of their knowledge). Dall and Watson pressed for further changes, but supporters were able to draw the line at these rather modest alterations. [154]

At the same time, however, two further changes were made that, surprisingly, expanded the definition of pornography even as the measure's sponsors were trying to limit it. First, the following phrase was added to Section 161, "Findings, policies, and purposes": pornography's effects "promote rape, battery, child abuse, kidnapping, and prostitution." [155] This addition dealt with the relation between pornography and physical abuse and was consistent with the effort to focus on physical harms, although this language was an addition, not a substitution.

The second change was a different story. Coughenour decided to add a sixth component to the definition of pornography that was much more subjective and ideological than the other five. "There was a sixth point that I took out from the original, which I thought was very broad. But when I discussed it with Catharine [MacKinnon, we put it in]," Coughenour told me. [156] This addition contradicted the intent to restrict, even though it did not apply to the "trafficking" provision, the ordinance's most ambitious enforcement section (under this only the woman actually used in the material or picture could bring an action, and she could receive no damages, only removal of the material). To the definition of pornography in Section 16-3 (q), which begins "Pornography shall mean the graphic sexually explicit subordination of women, whether in pictures or in words, that also includes one or more of the following," Subsection 6 was added: "Women are presented as sexual objects for domination, conquest, violation, exploitation, possession, or use, or through postures of servility or submission or display." [157] This language covers depictions in words or pictures which, according to the perceptions of plaintiffs and the Equal Opportunity Board, portray women in non-egalitarian ways. According to city attorneys working on the ordinance's defense, the absence of this provision from the previous version of the ordinance had amounted to the "*Playboy* exception."[158] Now, *Playboy* could be the subject of actions other than trafficking (coercion, forcing, and assault) if it depicted "submissive" sex.

The city's attorneys, who pushed for the other changes, regretted the addition of Subsection 6 to the definition of pornography. In doing so, the city endorsed a more far-reaching amendment against its better judgment even while it was attempting to limit the reach of the ordinance. Catherine Watson, committed to the ordinance as a woman and feminist, worried about the change:

> Our [original] rationale was, "We may not get *all* of it, but we'll get the worst stuff—the pictures, and we've got a very strong rationale protecting the models, etc." And MacKinnon's attitude was, "Oh, that doesn't begin to scratch the surface."
>
> If you look at the original Minneapolis draft, they include things like "women portrayed as whores by nature," and things like that. Minneapolis had nine subsections to the definition of pornography. When we got the ordinance down here, I put together a draft for Beulah and Goldsmith. I had also talked to them about this, and we cut certain of those types of pornography out, as well as made some other changes. . . . But then at the last minute, on the last amendment [June 1984], Subsection 6 came back in. . . .
>
> When we were proposing certain changes, [we were trying to focus a bit more on] the direct harms. And with Beulah and the mayor, that was the original focus: "Look, these women are being harmed. There's physical violence." But that focus takes you totally out of the focus of Dworkin and MacKinnon, which is a *political* focus.[159]

Watson's point about the difference between a "harms" and a "political" focus is the crux of the matter. Dall, Watson, and other leaders in Indianapolis focused on the harms and civil rights side of the ordinance, which is more reconcilable with a liberal interpretation of the First Amendment. MacKinnon and, to a much more limited extent, Dworkin strove to push the Indianapolis version in an ideological-political direction, which challenged the anti–viewpoint-discrimination norm of the modern doctrine of speech. As non-radical lawyers, Dall and Watson were uncomfortable with this effort. The product that emerged from this struggle in the June amendments was a sort of compromise. The definition of pornography was still shorter than the   133 original Minneapolis version, and ideologically loaded Subsection 6 did not apply to trafficking (although it could be applied to assaults "due to pornography"). Coughenour commented that "Catharine [MacKinnon] was disappointed [with these moves], but I have to know what it is I'm talking about in these first five [definitions] . . . I think anyone knows if they are seeing them." [160]

Mark Dall was more uncomfortable than Watson. He could commit himself in good faith to the ordinance by focusing on its harms provisions, but he could not escape discomfort with the ideological thrust of the measure:

> We talked with Laurence Tribe and some other people . . . and came up with a narrower approach that these people seemed to think, "Hey, you've got a really good shot. . . ." But we wanted to limit the scope of the ordinance. . . .
>
> ["You sound divided," I remarked. "As though you preferred a better piece of legislation to work with."] Oh, I think so. There's no question. We came up with a draft. The ordinance was passed in April, and the law suit was filed minutes after the mayor signed it. And we began working immediately on changes. See, Cathy [Watson] and I came up with all these great ideas, and the prosecutor's representative [Debbie Daniels] and Beulah would consistently overrule us. . . . Subsection 6, the "*Playboy* exception," they wanted in there, all this language of "women portrayed as whores." But we said, "No way." So we managed to block this the first time around. But then it *resurfaced* [in the June 11 amendments]. But we at least got a compromise, that it would not apply to a trafficking complaint. . . .
>
> I would like to see parts of it upheld, especially the coercion, forcing, and physical assaults sections. I still am ambivalent on the trafficking. I've never come to full grips with that one. . . .
>
> One thing you're getting at is "Where does this all stop?" . . . Where *do* you draw the line? And I'm still working on this. I don't know what the motivations of Catharine MacKinnon are *in the long run*. I have a feeling this [the ordinance in Indianapolis] is just the first step toward going all the way with it, and that really bothers me. . . . We've legitimized their [radical feminist] philosophy in a way. And a lot of times I think that Cathy and I are just front men, so to speak. [161]

The ordinance's multiple dimensions allowed conservatives to focus on the harms aspect, linking it to more traditional regulatory measures, and to ignore or be ignorant of its other premises.[162] But those like Sheila Kennedy, Michael Gradison, and Henry Karlson who understood the ideology were disturbed by it; and the dissonance was especially severe among those like Mark Dall and Catherine Watson who had to deal with the constitutional problems inherent in the legalization of the ideology. The ambiguity was reflected in statements to the press on the types of materials the ordinance would now cover. In one post-amendment interview, Mark Dall told the *Louisville Courier-Journal*, "Our ordinance focuses on violent sexual acts," and it did not apply to nudity in magazines such as *Playboy* and *Penthouse*. But Beulah Coughenour, who also focused on violence, followed by stating, "I think those types of magazines would have to be judged on a case-by-case basis."[163]

On June 4, the Administration Committee approved the amendments 4-0 with a recommendation that the full council adopt them. A representative of the state library associations summed up the view of critics: "The ordinance remains so broad that it would ban material that is not obscene."[164] That, of course, was precisely the ordinance's intention.

On June 11, the full council adopted the amendments by a 24-3 vote and sent the changes to Mayor Hudnut for his approval, which came immediately.[165] On the next day, the district court extended its May 9 preliminary injunction to include the changes made on June 11. Locally, debate continued about the potential costs of litigation but no new cost control measures materialized. Anti-pornography activist groups in Indianapolis and nationally carried on with their usual activities, hoping for the ordinance's success but not forsaking traditional approaches. In the meantime, all eyes were on the district court.

Defeat by the Modern Doctrine of Speech

Judge Sarah Evans Barker heard oral arguments on the ordinance on July 30, 1984. On November 19, pointing to the measure's ideological and political elements, she issued a strong decision that struck down virtually all of its provisions and endorsed the modern doctrine of speech. The ordinance's defenders had maintained that the type of expression that it covered was consistent with those types previously held by the Supreme Court not to be entitled to First Amendment protection.[166] Judge Barker disagreed.

135

She dismissed the claim that "libel" or "fighting words" were analogous to "pornography" as defined by the ordinance, because those forms of expression "by their very nature carry the immediate potential for injury." [167] Barker further noted that although obscenity might not be protected, the "defendants concede that the 'pornography' they seek to control goes beyond obscenity, as defined by the Supreme Court in *Miller v. California*." Accordingly, Barker observed, "it becomes clear that what defendants actually seek by enacting this legislation is a newly-defined class of constitutionally unprotected speech, labeled 'pornography' and characterized as sexually discriminatory." [168]

The defendants pointed to three cases to support the creation of a new category of unprotected speech: *New York v. Ferber,*[169] the child pornography case; *FCC v. Pacifica Foundation,*[170] in which the Supreme Court ruled that offensive, non-obscene speech in a broadcast, a regulated context, is not protected by the First Amendment to the same extent as in a non-regulated context; and *Young v. American Mini-Theaters, Inc.,*[171] in which the Court determined that a zoning restriction that affects non-obscene pornography does not violate the First Amendment unless it is unduly restrictive.

Barker held that none of these cases (or the rationales that led to their being cited) applied to the case at hand. *Ferber* pertained to only child pornography; and children, unlike adult women, could not be presumed to voluntarily consent to being subjects in pornography. *Pacifica* dealt only with broadcasting, which is a highly regulated area that has never enjoyed as much First Amendment protection as publishing and filmmaking. And *Young* was essentially a time, place, and manner regulation, whereas the ordinance constituted outright censorship.[172]

Because the ordinance went beyond the established categories of unprotected expression, Judge Barker had to apply the strict scrutiny mandated for proposals to restrict speech within protected categories. "The court must, therefore, examine the underlying premise of the Ordinance: that the State has so compelling an interest in regulating the sort of sex discrimination imposed and perpetuated through 'pornography' that it warrants an exception to free speech." She observed that the ordinance set out not only to protect specific, identifiable victims from the direct harms of pornography but also to protect women as a class from the sociological harm of pornography. This aspect is a species of group libel, which is now constitutionally suspect. This interpretation of sexually explicit materials is "a novel theory advanced by the defendants, an issue of first impression in the courts."[173] Judge Barker refused to grant this claim and chastised the defendants for attempting to constitutionalize what she construed to be special group preferences at the expense of the public good:

> If this court were to extend to this case the rationale in *Ferber* to uphold this Amendment, it would signal so great a potential encroachment upon First Amendment freedoms that the precious liberties reposed within those guarantees would not survive. . . . To permit every interest group, especially those who claim to be victimized by unfair expression, their own legislative exceptions to the First Amendment so long as they succeed in obtaining a majority of legislative votes in their favor demonstrates the potentially predatory nature of what defendants seek through this Ordinance.[174]

Finally, Judge Barker struck down some key provisions that transgressed the boundaries of procedural restraint. Key terms in the ordinance were excessively vague—the term "pornography" itself and its various categories: "subordination," "degradation," "abasement," and "inferior." Furthermore, the ordinance's restriction of non-obscene material made it overbroad. And enforcement through the Equal Opportunity Advisory Board amounted to prior restraint and a form of administrative harassment. This was a disappointment to the city attorneys, who had tried to harmonize the administrative features of the ordinance with prevailing First Amendment doctrine; they considered their version to be an improvement on Minneapolis in this regard.[175] The administrative aspects of the ordinance were designed to expedite state intervention in response to individual complaints—a circumvention of established, more cumbersome procedures that have prevailed in obscenity law prosecutions. Accordingly, Judge Barker declared all of the ordinance's enforcement actions—trafficking, coercion, assault, and forcing—unconstitutional.[176]

She also required the city to pay the plaintiff's court costs—a result that dismayed many council members whose support of the ordinance had been ambivalent. In February 1985, plaintiff's lawyers submitted a bill of nearly $80,000.[177] This figure—which became larger after a year of appeals—was separate from expenses incurred by the city on its own behalf.

Indianapolis filed notice of its appeal on December 19, 1984, to the U.S. Court of Appeals in Chicago (Seventh Circuit). The case was argued on June 4, 1985. Some council members and other government leaders later expressed reservations about the chances for success; others expressed optimism at that time to the press.[178]

Judge Frank Easterbrook's decision for the Court of Appeals on August 27, 1985, confirmed Barker's decision in every respect and was just as forceful and critical. Because of the similarity of the two decisions, we need look only briefly at Easterbrook's reasoning.

Easterbrook was a young, recent Reagan appointee sometimes accused of being excessively right-wing because of his sponsorship of "economic" interpretations and applications of law. The substantive part of his decision began with a quote from the famous 1943 flag salute case, in which the Supreme Court articulated the principle that was to emerge as the liberal doctrine of state and content neutrality:

> "If there is any fixed star in our constitutional constellation, it is that no official, high or petty, can prescribe what shall be orthodox in politics, nationalism, religion, or other matters of opinion or force citizens to confess by word or act their faith therein." *West Virginia State Board of Education v. Barnette,* 319 U.S. 624, 642 (1943). Under the First Amendment the government must leave to the people the evaluation of ideas. Bald or subtle, an idea is as powerful as the audience allows it to be. A belief may be pernicious—the belief of Nazis led to the death of millions, those of the Klan to the repression of millions. A pernicious belief may prevail. . . . One of the things that separates our society from theirs is our absolute right to propogate opinions that the government finds wrong or even hateful.[179]

Easterbrook declared that the ordinance, especially in its more ideological definitions, cut to the heart of this doctrine by distinguishing what its authors deemed appropriate from inappropriate sexual portrayals. Nor did the ordinance conform to the strictures of obscenity law:

> Under the ordinance graphic sexually explicit speech is "pornography" or not depending on the perspective the author adopts. Speech that "subordinates" women and also, for example, presents women as enjoying pain, humiliation, or rape, or even simply presents women in "positions of servility or submission or display" is forbidden, no matter how great the literary or political value of the work taken a whole. Speech that portrays women in posi-

138

tions of equality is lawful, no matter how graphic the sexual context. This is thought control. It establishes an "approved" view of women, of how they may react to sexual encounters, of how the sexes may relate to each other. Those who espouse the approved view may use sexual images; those who do not, may not.[180]

Easterbrook's statement assumes that state neutrality concerning content is the best policy governing the regulation of speech, and that obscenity doctrine, which is concerned with sexual explicitness, is consistent with neutral principles.[181] Of course, the fact that this doctrine currently reigns in the realm of First Amendment law does not necessarily justify it. I will discuss the propriety of the modern doctrine of speech in the next chapter.

Indianapolis appealed Easterbrook's decision to the Supreme Court. Normally, when taking a case to the Supreme Court, a city hires outside counsel that specializes in the relevant area of law and in Supreme Court litigation. Indianapolis did not do so in this case; the strength of the two lower courts' rejection of the ordinance foreshadowed the outcome and made it seem prudent to hold costs down.[182] Months later, in 1986, the Supreme Court in effect affirmed the Seventh Circuit's decision by refusing to hear the case.[183] This ended the legal odyssey of the Indianapolis anti-pornography ordinance. According to William Dowden, many council members had not reckoned on the ordinance appeal going this far. Surprisingly, however, the council engaged in little discussion about the appeals process:

> There was a great deal of discomfort with it. I didn't think it was going to be pushed that far. I really didn't. [Was there discussion about how to do it?] No. There was no discussion about how far to push it. Most of us were concerned that at whichever level of the judicial system we ended, we were going to end up paying the costs of the plaintiffs. And I did not want to see us having to spend $300,000 to $500,000 paying the court costs. It's still ending up to be almost $300,000 eventually. This wasn't our own cost, as we did not hire outside counsel. Normally, when you've got a real good case, you hire outside counsel. But we used in-house attorneys to keep the cost down for ourselves. But we ended up being ordered to pay for the plaintiff's attorneys. That was what was concerning me. This is why I say I would have preferred to have dropped it after the first court case.[184]

139

Other council leaders expressed similar discomfort. David McGrath and Rozelle Boyd, as we have seen, considered expense a major issue, especially in light of the measure's evident invalidity. And when I asked Council Majority Leader Donald Miller what had been learned from the whole experience, he said there would be greater "hesitancy about making statements," that is, about taking on pathbreaking legal issues for the benefit of the rest of the country:

> I doubt that we'll spend that kind of money again. People will say, "Well, do we really want to go all the way to the Supreme Court on this one, too, and to spend all that money on making lawyers rich?" There will be a lot of those questions asked in the future that might not have been asked if we hadn't done it [the ordinance]. And maybe sometime we'll say "Yes," and sometimes "No." But I'm sure that those questions will come into people's minds, whether it's taking on the EPA or whatever. . . . There will be more weighing of the costs of making the statement in the future. I think probably the biggest impact is this. . . . At least we're a community that tried.[185]

In September 1986, the U.S. District Court issued its final decision on legal fees. Judge Sara Barker ordered (pursuant to Sections 1983 and 1988 of the U.S. Code 42) that counsel for the American Booksellers Association be awarded $87,316 and that Richard Kammen, counsel for plaintiff Video Shack, Inc., be awarded $7,862.[186] These figures did not cover the expenses of American Booksellers' local counsel Sheila Kennedy and Richard Cardwell, which had been settled before this decision.[187] Thus, Indianapolis's bill for plaintiff's expenses was over $100,000, in addition to court costs and expenses incurred by the city itself. The total expenses exceeded $200,000.[188]

In the aftermath of the ordinance struggle, Indianapolis's leaders were wary of adopting any new radical approaches to pornography. For the time, at least, enthusiasm for the politics of pornography was at a low ebb.[189]

Conclusion

Leaders in Indianapolis disagreed about the merits of the city's endeavor with the anti-pornography ordinance. Some believed that it marked the city as a national leader, some were much less enthusiastic, and others were ambivalent. Unquestionably Indianapolis's struggle with the ordinance raised the issue of pornography and its effect on women to national prominence. The experience clarified the legal status of the ordinance's approach to the protection of women and the modern doctrine of free speech. In this respect, the ordinance case was similar to the Skokie case, for it, too, generated debate about the deeper values of free speech.

There was, however, a major difference. Skokie galvanized discussion about the limits of the modern doctrine of speech, but there most critics worked largely within the framework of the modern free speech doctrine. The ordinance's ideological sponsors sought to shatter that doctrine. Sheila Kennedy, the local counsel in the *Hudnut* case and a member of the American Jewish Community's national board at the time of Skokie, understood the difference as did few others in Indianapolis:

> Skokie was an attempt, at least by the proponents I knew, to fit Skokie into the existing constitutional framework. *This* [ordinance] is an attempt to *amend* the existing constitutional framework. This particular group of feminists is quite clear in briefs, etc., that we understand that the ordinance as framed is inconsistent with existing law. But we *want* existing law changed so that this approach would be acceptable. This is not the way that the Skokie debate was framed—in the tradition of constitutional law and its evolution.[190]

The federal courts paid particular attention to the ordinance's ideological-political aspects, thereby affirming the modern doctrine of speech's antipathy to Marcusean "progressive censorship." In the area of speech pertaining to politics, the law must maintain strict neutrality, leaving judgment to the people.[191] But the courts did not eliminate the possibility that an acceptable version of the ordinance might be based on demonstrable harm, as distinct from ideology. The Seventh Circuit Court of Appeals pointed out that a neutrally drawn ordinance might conform to present First Amendment standards.[192] This approach might require the fashioning of a new category of unprotected expression, which only the Supreme Court could institute. I consider the feasibility of this approach in the next chapter.

The Indianapolis experience included problems similar to those that beset Minneapolis. The city appears to have allowed itself to be unduly swayed by the supporters of the ordinance, even though the absence of commitment to ideological feminism made some compromises pos-

141

sible. Leaders were unprepared to deal adequately with the issue, as they did not know enough about either radical feminist political philosophy or the course of events in Minneapolis.

In the Indianapolis debate, as too often happens in ideological controversies, concern for free speech values was lost to the passions of the moment. The First Amendment seems a burden to people bent on morally urgent reform.[193] Council members told me that free speech issues were not debated very fully, and no one among the majority expressed adequate concern about the free speech implications of the ordinance. According to William Dowden, the free speech issue was "heard" but "ignored."[194] Whatever the appropriateness of prevailing doctrine, I believe that free speech values should have been discussed. Free speech as a basic concept must be respected in a free society, even though disagreement about its contours, applications, and limits may persist.[195]

Finally, the hearings of the Administration Committee and the full council demonstrated again the precarious social status of free speech as a value. The Indianapolis City-County Council is respected for its handling of most complex public policy issues; I observed both the council and the committee in action on other issues and was impressed by the level of their deliberations. But on this issue, with its serious free speech implications, Indianapolis government did not appear to have lived up to its First Amendment obligations. According to the theory of democratic elitism, political leaders' stronger support for civil liberty should save the day when people at large fail to exhibit the virtues of a tolerant society. The frequent failures of both leaders and society suggest that free speech values are perhaps less well established than is desirable.[196] Of course, one defender of free speech values was vindicated in the affair as the federal courts ruled on the validity of the ordinance without regard to its popularity. But salvation by judiciary is not always the best practice for constitutional democracy.[197]

The ordinance itself did not, of course, mark the decline of civil liberty or free speech. Civil liberty is not a one-way street. The norms of restraint and *civil* liberty apply to the citizenry as well as to the government, to opponents as well as proponents of actions. I questioned the Minnesota Civil Liberty Union's understanding of free speech because it did not recognize the dangers inherent in some expression; it seemed to disregard the plurality of values that prevail in a reasonable society, pursuing instead an absolutist ideal of liberty. The Indiana Civil Liberties Union was more credible in this regard.[198] But the standards of civility and restraint make greater demands on government than on society because the state possesses great power and it is our representative.

The manner in which Indianapolis supported the ordinance is therefore troublesome. There was the rush to judgment and haste of passage, the lack of true adversarial debate despite the unusual nature of the ordinance, the pursuit of an acknowledged unconstitutional course of action with its implications for free speech, the silent ambivalence of many Republican council members, the deference to supporters of the measure and the government's lack of understanding of its ideological underpinnings, and the atmosphere of crisis that prevailed. In all of these factors, the decision-making process at Indianapolis was as disconcerting as the one at Minneapolis.

FIVE

PORNOGRAPHY AND HARM: TOWARD A NEW CLASSIFICATION OF UNPROTECTED SPEECH?

> Good and evil we know in the field of this world grow up together almost inseparably; and the knowledge of good is so involved and interwoven with the knowledge of evil, and in so many cunning resemblances hardly to be discerned, that those seeds which were imposed on Psyche as an incessant labor to cull out and sort asunder, were not more intermixed. It was from out the rind of one apple that the knowledge of good and evil, as two twins cleaving together, leaped forth into the world. And perhaps this is that doom which Adam fell into knowing good by evil.
>
> John Milton, *Areopagitica*.

> —The pure spirit is a pure lie.
> —Everything is ensnared, entangled, enamored.
> —Nietzsche, *Thus Spake Zarathustra*.

In this chapter I address the most important policy issues raised by the new politics of pornography. Is there a rationale for censorship? If so, what types of material should be suppressed? Should "pornography" join or even replace "obscenity" as an unprotected classification of speech under the First Amendment? Is there a case for making "violent pornography" a new category of unprotected speech? In considering these questions, I discuss the sweeping innovations of the feminist-oriented anti-pornography ordinances introduced in Minneapolis and Indianapolis and offer a more modest proposal for reform of present law. I endorse keeping the basic *Miller* approach to obscenity but advocate putting special emphasis on representations of sexual violence.

144

Although some recent research suggests that depictions of explicit sexual violence may be directly associated with social harms, pornography overall is a complex phenomenon that arguably has benefits as well as drawbacks. When associated with art and ideas, it has First Amendment implications. Any solution to the pornography dilemma must balance many interests—feminist, conservative, and liberal. Enforcement is liable to prove divisive in the community and also may incur substantial financial cost. It may be well to rely chiefly on alternative methods of control—zoning, nuisance law, public health law, law requiring covers for material on public display, various forms of community action. I will not address such forms of indirect regulation except to acknowledge that they are legitimate so long as they are practiced in a principled fashion and are not smokescreens for outright censorship.

Another reason for caution in addressing pornography is that the extent of the problem is not clear. The availability of sexually explicit material has grown substantially in recent decades, and there are well-publicized cases of men using pornography to manipulate others and as a model for violent practice. But as we saw in Chapter 1, depictions of violence probably make up a smaller percentage of material available now than ten years ago, and sexual images in some obscene media may be more egalitarian than before. Although the new politics of pornography points to recent research linking sexual images to sexually violent acts, the emotionalism accompanying the issue suggests that factors other than evidence are at work. Feminist June Callwood's conclusion cannot be dismissed: "There is strong reason to doubt that pornography is as prevalent and horrific as the public has been led to believe, and arguments about its power to influence have not been convincing."[1] But neither can studies be dismissed that associate certain types of pornography with negative effects on attitude, behavior, and character. If First Amendment values demand the toleration of sexually explicit materials to a significant extent, society is still entitled to protect itself from clear and specific harms.

Before turning to issues raised by the Minneapolis/Indianapolis ordinance, we first must consider the broadest question posed by the new politics of pornography: how valid is the liberal modern doctrine of free speech? If this basic doctrine is valid, then the burden of proof is on those who advocate new approaches that would undermine or alter it. If it is invalid, radical measures like the feminist anti-pornography ordinance are less suspect.

145

In Defense of the Modern Doctrine of Speech

I believe that the basic liberal approach to the First Amendment should be preserved because it is necessary to an open society, and an open society is a necessary, if not sufficient, condition for achieving social justice. To be sure, the liberal tradition does not necessarily require the content neutrality doctrine as the basis of public policy for speech or other issues.[2] Indeed, value and political neutrality may prove inadequate in the face of social inequities, and the liberal doctrine of tolerance can border on moral indifference if not tempered by more substantive non-liberal values. As I indicated in the introduction, however, liberal tradition is not confined to the particular doctrines of individualism and state neutrality toward values. The fathers of liberal thought—including Bentham, Mill, and Dewey—emphasized the roles of society and the state in promoting personal fulfillment, character, and happiness. But in the special domain of speech and freedom of thought state neutrality is advised. Even early liberals were uncomfortable about specifying the content of the happiness the state should foster and more uncomfortable about giving the state power to favor some ideas over others.[3] In addition, the development of cultural pluralism in the twentieth century has made state neutrality toward the content of speech even more desirable. Were state action to unduly favor one side over others, it would jeopardize the speech of those who are unable to command the state's approval.

Furthermore, the modern state is not neutral in important areas of public policy other than speech. Catharine MacKinnon and similar thinkers exaggerate the pervasiveness of liberal neutrality in present-day society. For example, conservative values are expressed in criminal laws that govern sexual behavior and so-called victimless crimes like drug use and gambling; tort law is governed by a non-liberal fiduciary ethic that downplays freedom of action; and the state has been non-neutrally liberal in passing and enforcing anti-discrimination and anti-sexual harassment laws in the private sphere. But the issue for our purposes is not whether value neutrality should be preserved in all areas of social policy but rather whether such a policy is valid in the special domain of speech that has ideational or political content. Human society is too complex to be explained or governed by a single political theory, but in matters of speech about public and social issues a predominantly liberal approach should prevail for reasons I will presently discuss. This is true even when the marketplace of ideas is recognized as having definite drawbacks.

146

Some critics of value neutrality point to the uneven distribution of resources, power, and prestige in society and call for public policy that would insure a hearing for viewpoints outside the economic or political mainstream. They have proposed laws limiting the expenditures of wealthy corporations in political campaigns and laws guaranteeing the right of reply to people or positions criticized in print media, just as the fairness doctrine once mandated the inclusion of representative viewpoints on issues appearing on broadcast media.[4] Obviously, dominant discourses prevail over less dominant ones and there is not perfect competition among ideas. Further, recent outcries about increasing numbers of television programs devoted to sensational topics, news programs emphasizing entertainment values over serious information, and unrelenting commercialization of news media have sparked discussions about the need for limits on the liberal doctrine of free speech.[5] But just as Winston Churchill once declared that democracy was the worst form of government except for all the others, the liberal doctrine of speech, with all its flaws, may be superior to the alternatives.

The real question is the balance of wanted and unwanted consequences. Different realms of society may need different values.[6] One may accept the liberal doctrine of the marketplace of ideas without endorsing liberal neutrality in all areas of public life. In response to social change, the system of law has moved from a mainly liberal form stressing liberty, property values, and legal neutrality ("autonomous law") toward a form based on a sense of social justice and legal and state activism ("responsive law").[7] If the First Amendment is one of the last bastions of liberal norms, this is a further reason for preserving its tenets because they stand as a check on other forces and tendencies in society.

There are, however, more concrete reasons for preserving the modern doctrine of speech and its liberal precepts. First, there is the testimony of history. Previous non-liberal doctrines of speech not based on the direct harms doctrine of *Brandenburg* simply did not protect controversial political speech in times of social tension. The old logic of *Hicklin* in obscenity law allowed a great many artistic works involving sexuality to be censored or restricted. The early version of the "clear and present danger" test regarding political speech allowed the courts to defer to governmental repression of critical comment, particularly during the First World War and the McCarthy era in the 1950s.[8] The modern doctrine may not prove protective if a future society loses control of its fears, but it did play a crucial role in supporting dissent during the civil rights movement and the Vietnam War. Protection of dissident and controversial speech is a recent occurrence and sexual works of artistic merit have enjoyed real freedom for only about two decades (see Chapter 1). The passions unleashed by the new politics of pornography demonstrate the need for law to temper censorious urges and social fears.

As many feminist critics of the anti-pornography ordinance pointed out, feminism itself owes a substantial debt to the growth of civil liberties.[9] The development of federal statutory and constitutional law supporting womens' rights historically paralleled the institutionalization of the modern liberal doctrine of speech. This parallel raises an ironic point which may not be an accident: womens' rights rose in the 1960s and 1970 not only in conjunction with the cause of civil rights but also at the same time that pornography was exploding. Indeed, this irony permeates Andrea Dworkin's revelation that pornography is an epiphany of womens' subordination to men. Her theory is that pornography reveals an underlying condition that was previously invisible. Thus, one of pornography's historical roles has been to make the subjection of women a matter of public knowledge and so to supply the data that awaited Andrea Dworkin's authoritative interpretation.

If history points to the need for a general liberal approach to free speech, so does the problem inherent in any departure from participation in the marketplace of ideas. If society were to adopt the Marcusean sort of "progressive censorship" embodied in the anti-pornography ordinance, there could be no guarantee that those who would carry it out—the administrators, prosecutors, and courts—would pursue the goals envisioned by the reformers. This is especially the case for "progressive" or radical movements, which by definition and their own reckoning are opposed to the majoritarian status quo. The politics in Indianapolis illustrates that conservative forces were eager to exploit the radical ordinance for their own purposes, which did not include its feminist sponsors' distinction between "erotica" and "pornography." Indeed, most conservative activists who endorsed the Indianapolis ordinance did not grasp its rationale—and, given their prominence and the lack of feminist activists in the city, it would have been the conservatives who would have brought suits under the trafficking and other provisions of the law.

Content neutrality guarantees that groups competing in a context of cultural pluralism all will enjoy the right to express their views and attempt to influence public and legal opinion. The liberal modern doctrine of speech is a compromise in which each group concedes the right of speech to all other groups and no single group claims power to dictate the terms of debate. This compromise is the basis of the liberal legal order; according to Roberto Unger, the establishment of this order was an accommodation to a situation where no single group could attain complete power.[10] This compromise, or concession to reality, recognizes both the rights of others in a pluralistic society and one's own obligation to forsake the goal of political domination. It also entails accepting the limits of any one point of view. Absolutist approaches, which attempt to impose one view of right and denigrate all others, have historically led to hate, repression, and violence directed at those outside the new order.

The modern doctrine of speech is designed to prevent established ideas from completely dominating discourse and opinion. The past two hundred years have been marked by a powerful struggle among competing world views and values. The modern doctrine of speech recognizes and facilitates this competition, which, as we have seen, is far from equal. Some discourses are more privileged than others, as critics of modernist liberalism are quick to point out. Noam Chomsky is perhaps correct in observing that "freedom of speech" forces ruling interests to engage in thought control in order to preserve their interests in society. If people may speak their minds, then ruling interests (largely corporate and financial in the United States) strive to use their influence on government and the major media to limit what is on citizens' minds by narrowing the range of discussion and by presenting some opinions as respectable and others as beyond the pale. Control of values and the context of discussion can serve as well or better than state control over expression.[11] Tocqueville and Lippman understood this phenomenon in their own times. However, such a pessimistic analysis only underscores the importance of maintaining an open marketplace of ideas, for restrictions could grant even greater advantages to prevailing power.

Whatever the limitations in the marketplace of ideas, there is significant difference between a dominant discourse enforced by the unparalleled power of the state and a dominant discourse that must compete with other discourses, however unequally. This is the difference between political freedom and non-freedom in a world in which absolute freedom and equality have never and probably cannot exist. Given the course of history, the freedom we have managed to attain is too valuable to risk.

One of the most unsettling aspects of the ideological forces behind the anti-pornography ordinance was their lack of perspective and

149

sense of limits. Just as, to them, all sexuality represented the dominating extreme (sexuality = sexual violence), they did not distinguish between the regime of competing unequal discourses and a regime of one unjust dominant discourse. If all liberal reality was a hell of domination, the anti-pornography ordinance was a promise of total, utopian justice. "Nothing short of everything will really do."[12]

The content neutrality doctrine provides a means for other voices to be heard, thereby offering at least a chance for non-dominant ideas and peaceful social change. The tolerance it requires is both remarkable and fragile. Bollinger is right: the liberal doctrine of speech mandates an area of "extraordinary" tolerance in which all ideas may be heard, and the right to speak is respected even if we do not respect the ideas that ensue. It is necessary to respect the rights of some Nazis and some pornographers to ensure respect for rights of other groups.[13]

This realm of speech, utilized, of course, by proponents of the ordinance, is remarkable in that it represents unusual forbearance by society and the state toward dissenting and threatening views. Society and the state are often reluctantly dragged to this forbearance by the courts, but this merely points to the exceptional status of constitutional tolerance of free speech. Liberal doctrine constrains our passions, so it naturally arouses resistance in difficult cases. This is why difficult cases are so important, for tolerance like freedom has meaning only in contexts of tension and temptation, where its exercise depends on reason and self-control.[14] This resistance is one reason why liberals often seem to overreact to threats of censorship. They know that tolerance and forbearance are liable to be withdrawn at any time and so they believe in constant vigilance against censorious impulses. Of course, this vigilance can itself become rigid and intolerant of reasonable compromise and balance. The Minneapolis Civil Liberties Union's reaction to the pornography debate is a case in point. In a related vein, as Alan Bloom, John Schaar and others have argued, tolerance loses its vitality and moral force in an environment of moral relativism or indifference, perhaps in the same manner as freedom loses its meaning in a culture without limits or standards. Any extreme, even in the pursuit of virtue, may be suspect.

The self-denial required to control the impulse to dominate or suppress other viewpoints paradoxically contributes to self knowledge and to the gift of knowledge of the other as a person. Such an understanding underlies both Meiklejohn and Bollinger's theories of free speech.[15] Comprehending another's position and opposing it rationally can lead to respect on both sides; while censorship is an exercise of power that forecloses dialogue. And civic virtue through free speech prevails in a context of tension between or among impulses, and the consequent exercise of self-control and responsibility. Tolerance also shows respect for democratic forms and acknowledges that the means is sometimes as important as the end.[16] Like tolerance, manners and social forms are valuable ways of controlling impulses in a situation of tension. Manners give form to passion as the ego gives form to the personality by putting a face on the impulses of the id. As we will see below, pornography is sometimes held to be corruptive precisely because it bypasses the inevitable and constructive tensions between persons. Without the tension between self and other, there is no basis for mature relations and understanding. Ironically, in the public forum, the desire to have one's way without opposition or accommodation is corruptive in the same way. The politics of pornography at Minneapolis and Indianapolis was ominous for what it revealed about popular support for democratic forms and the rule of law.

The very nature of any social order makes the exercise of tolerance and forbearance tenuous.[17] If feminist critics are correct that society is dominated by the forces of male reaction, they would seem ill advised to cast away a doctrine and its institutional supports that provide their radicalism with an opportunity to be heard. Would forsaking the commitment to tolerance in speech further the interests of those whom critics assert are already without power and respect? It is far more likely that what Tocqueville designated the "tyranny of the majority" (which MacKinnon and Dworkin declare is indeed real, conservative, and oppressive) would overwhelm progressive ideas were it not for the restraints provided in the liberal modern doctrine of speech.[18] Is the remote possibility of achieving an absolute ideal worth the risk of losing the present degree of freedom? Many anti-pornography feminists, including many who were otherwise critical of liberalism, opposed the anti-liberal tenets of the ordinance precisely because they did not wish to run this risk.

Accepting the desirability of liberal First Amendment precepts does not mean setting no limits on free speech: rather, state neutrality toward the ideological content of speech (anti-viewpoint-discrimination) should be the norm unless there are strong justifications for restriction in a particular case. Their feminist critics claim that liberal principles are exercises of male values, leading to abstractionism, a split between public and private reality, autonomy, and individualism.[19] This may be true but, as we have seen, state neutrality is still necessary to any workable regime of free speech. The doctrine protects feminists as they argue against other aspects of liberalism and male power, just as it does those who make other arguments. If it compels intolerant feminists legally to bear with dissenting views, it also contributes to their self-restraint and self-enlargement.

The anti-pornography ordinance, as the federal courts understood, was unconstitutional because it was intended to separate pro-female from anti-female sexual depictions. It intentionally construed the pornography issue as a matter of political speech, thereby attacking the heart of the modern doctrine of speech. If this doctrine is necessary, the theoretical core of the ordinance was invalid. But what about its other aspects? Before we look at a more modest approach, limited to restricting what I call "violent pornography," we should look more closely at the ordinance's specific provisions.

Defining Pornography: Progressive Censorship

As we have seen, the ordinance's definition of pornography was inclusive. Parts of the definition in the original Minneapolis version were more obviously ideological than others because they dealt with the broadest and least direct aspects of harm. The following parts of the definition were problematic:

> i. women are presented as dehumanized sexual objects, things or commodities; or
> ii. women are presented as sexual objects who enjoy pain or humiliation [this definition is only partially directed at physical abuse, as the provision for "humiliation" indicates];
> v. women are presented in postures of sexual submission; or sexual servility, including by inviting penetration; or
> vi. women's body parts—including but not limited to vaginas, breasts, and buttocks—are exhibited, such that women are reduced to those parts; or
> vii. women are presented as whores by nature.

These definitions are very broad and vague and deal more with suggestions of inequality and subordination than with precise depictions of violence. Had the ordinance merely attempted to limit depictions of violence, it would also have impacted on ideas to some extent, but such an attempt would have been less overtly ideological and political than the above provisions. In addition, as we will see, the evidence of harm caused by portrayals of sexually explicit violence is less speculative than evidence of harm from "degrading" and inegalitarian portrayals. Concern about depictions of sexually explicit violence may be as neutral as concerns about obscenity that do not distinguish between egalitarian and inegalitarian forms.

These parts of the ordinance's definition of pornography are constitutionally suspect on grounds of overbreadth, vagueness, and viewpoint discrimination. As Judge Easterbrook of the Seventh Circuit Court of Appeals declared, they distinguish politically correct (egalitarian) from politically incorrect (inegalitarian) sexual depictions. This represents a significantly greater degree of viewpoint discrimination ("thought control") than is found in obscenity laws, which are enforced in a manner that does not discriminate among viewpoints. Randall Tigue points out, "What makes sexually explicit material pornography under the MacKinnon/Dworkin ordinance is not its degree of sexual explicitness, not its appeal to prurient interests, not even its lack of social value. Rather, it is the content of the ideas advocated by the material." [20]

An analogous case is *Schacht v U.S.*, in which the Supreme Court declared unconstitutional a statute that authorized the wearing of a U.S. military uniform by a non-military person in a play only if the portrayal did not tend to discredit the military.[21] Blanket prohibition of wearing the uniform might be constitutional but not selective prohibition depending on the ideas conveyed in a particular context. Similarly, an obscenity law directed at, say, "prurient appeal in a subordinating context" would constitute significantly greater viewpoint discrimination than a law covering prurient appeal in all contexts. And if the state were to prohibit only those forms of obscene expression that included "women presented as whores by nature" or "women presented as dehumanized sexual objects, things, or commodities," this would amount to distinguishing between egalitarian and non-egalitarian contexts. The distinction between obscene and non-obscene is less ideological.

Obscenity law itself, of course, is far from neutral in regard to viewpoint discrimination, as it is based on a normative notion of sexuality. But the Supreme Court has sidestepped this issue, maintaining that obscenity has nothing to do with socially valuable ideas in the first place (when it does, this social value may make it non-obscene under *Miller*). As long as obscenity laws are applied in a viewpoint neutral fashion (that is, all materials that fail the *Miller* test are obscene regardless of implicit message or context), the First Amendment does not come into play. Even if obscenity doctrine is itself value-laden, however, obscenity laws would become more content discriminatory if they incorporated the egalitarian logic of the Minneapolis ordinance. Thus, the ordinance's logic of progressive censorship constituted a greater violation of the anti-viewpoint discrimination doctrine than obscenity law as such.[22]

Other provisions of the Minneapolis ordinance were based on less obviously political ideas, as they came closer to dealing with the narrower problem of violence. More precisely tailored to depictions of specific violence, these provisions might have posed less of a constitutional problem, similar to a federal law that prohibited non-soldiers from wearing military uniforms without distinguishing between acceptable and unacceptable contexts. These provisions were:

> ii. women are presented as sexual objects who experience sexual pleasure in being raped; or
> iv. women are presented as sexual objects tied up or cut up or mutilated or bruised or physically hurt; or
> viii. women are presented being penetrated by objects or animals; or
> ix. women are presented in scenarios of degradation, injury, abasement, torture, shown as filthy or inferior, bleeding, bruised, or hurt in a context that makes these conditions sexual.[23]

Some of the content of these provisions raised problems. The language, "women are presented as sexual objects" in sections (iii) and (iv), is vague and ideological, as are the terms "degradation," "filthy or inferior" in section (ix). But the other language was less vague and more neutral in its ideas and gender politics (less discriminatory in viewpoint). On the whole it was directed at violence and physical abuse in the context of sexual arousal. Such restrictions are not completely value free (no exceptions to the First Amendment *can* be totally value free), but they are as value free as the obscenity exception based on prurient interest. Recall that the Seventh Circuit decision pointed out that a more specific ordinance might have been constitutionally acceptable. In essence, it would define a new category of expression that would be unprotected by the First Amendment, one dealing with sexual violence in a more or less viewpoint-neutral fashion. Problems still remain with this narrower approach; but it is less obviously invalid than the broader definitions we have just discussed.

Before turning to consider violent pornography, we must look at other questionable aspects of the ordinance. The ordinance's definition of pornography as discrimination was problematic. It represented Andrea Dworkin's conflation of speech and action, interpreting a form of expression as an act of discrimination. Such conflation would undermine the entire edifice of modern First Amendment doctrine and revolutionize the law of equality. This issue will be addressed in the next section.

Two related problems reveal the stunning disrespect shown by the ordinance toward art and intellectual freedom and its disdain for the links between sexual portrayal and knowledge. First, it made even isolated passages grounds for action, unlike obscenity law in which a work's dominant theme, taken as a whole, must be prurient. Second, a work could be held to be pornographic regardless of redeeming social value. These provisions betrayed a disconcerting tolerance for anti-intellectualism on the Left. Indianapolis modified the first problem in its revision of the ordinance, but the second problem remained.

Enforcement Provisions of the Anti-pornography Ordinance

Two basic issues were raised by the ordinance's enforcement provisions. The first was its general civil rights approach and mechanism; the second was the specific enforcement triggers of trafficking, coercion into pornographic performance, forcing pornography on a person, and assault or physical attack owing to pornography. The civil rights approach, in general, was problematic. Many liberal observers in responsible positions involving civil liberties have pointed out that the harms attributed to pornography are different in nature from the harms of discrimination. The availability of pornography simply does not constitute an act of discrimination in the same sense as does a refusal to hire someone who is black or Asian.

In certain contexts, however, pornography may amount to discrimination. Courts have held that display of pornography in the workplace constitutes sexual harassment under Title VII of the 1964 Civil Rights Act, and a "hostile environment" of harassment is a form of sex discrimination actionable under Title VII.[24] This approach is limited to specific environments in which expression is tantamount to action as commonly understood. For example, when hostile words are directed at a specific target, courts have construed this as "fighting words," a form of action or speech that directly incites hostile reaction. In other contexts, however, hostile words are not to be equated with action or incitement.[25]

Restricting certain forms of expression in specific limited contexts is not inconsistent with traditional First Amendment doctrine; the "cap- 155 tive audience" doctrine is a case in point. But Andrea Dworkin's theory, which does not distinguish between expression and action, would leave society paralyzed by a nervousness about the consequences of expression that would surpass even the timidity of *Hicklin*. Such conflation of speech and action would make thoughts and ideas themselves as suspect as actions. This virtually totalitarian attempt at thought control was one of the ordinance's less inspiring aspects.

In addition, as many in Minneapolis and Indianapolis pointed out, enforcing the ordinance was very likely to overload the departments assigned this responsibility. The fear that such enforcement would increase alienation among those competing for civil liberties is less compelling; as we saw in Chapter 3 civil rights should not be thought of as divisible among groups and subjected to a zero-sum logic.[26]

More importantly, enforcement of measures like the antipornography ordinance by the civil rights divisions of government is untested. This threatens unanticipated harm to free speech interests. Enforcement by criminal divisions allows for a great deal of prosecutorial and police discretion in bringing cases—a discretion that can be abused, like all authority.[27] But a civil rights enforcement mechanism would be compelled to respond to all claims brought by roving citizens, thereby making it vulnerable to use as a means of harassment.

The ordinance's supporters saw it's civil rights enforcement approach as a way to avoid the problem of censorship because it involved neither criminal prosecution nor prior restraint.[28] However, this argument amounted to a return to pre-modern First Amendment doctrine; indeed, it was Blackstonian. The Supreme Court has correctly held that civil actions can be as censorial in their effects as criminal actions and that penalties or punishments after publication can inhibit expression as effectively as prior restraint.[29] Supporters of the ordinance seemed as disingenuous concerning this issue as they were in minimizing the measure's scope despite its lack of a provision protecting material of artistic value.

Furthermore, the ordinance established a procedure, requiring a hearing to be held before a hearing committee pursuant to a probable cause determination by the relevant civil rights board or commission, that probably violated the administrative restraints required by First Amendment cases such as *Freedman v. Maryland* and *Southeastern Promotions, Ltd., v. Conrad*.[30] *Freedman* established four conditions that prior restraint must meet to pass constitutional muster: (1) the relevant agency must reach a decision as quickly as possible; (2) the law must require the administrator to establish procedures for injunctive relief; (3) any restraints imposed before a final judicial determination on the merits "must be limited by law to the preservation of the status quo for the shortest possible fixed period"; and (4) judicial review must be made readily and promptly available.[31]

The ordinance fell short of these requirements in several respects. The Minneapolis version put the burden of proof on the exhibitor/distributor to show that relevant material is non-pornographic after an initial determination had found material to be pornographic, and it did not require the Civil Rights Department to assume the burden of proof in administrative hearings. Exhibitor/distributors are guilty until proven innocent. In addition, it did not provide prompt judicial review and put the burden of appeal on the defendant.[32] This shifting of the burden of proof represented a reversal of the presumption in favor of freedom of expression to a presumption in favor of equality for women as envisioned by the ordinance. While such equality is a laudable goal, there are other (I would say better) ways to achieve it than by reversing the key administrative tenets of the modern doctrine of free speech. According to Judge Barker in Indiana, administrative procedures involved in the coercion and forcing actions of the Indianapolis Ordinance violated the *Freedman* standards, whereas the trafficking and assault provisions did not:

> First, if the Board decides in favor of the complainant, it is the responsibility of the respondant, as an aggrieved party, to initiate judicial proceedings to prove that the material is protected. Second, the prior restraint, once imposed, lasts until the pendancy of judicial review by the court. Also, the Board, in its discretion, may award to the complainant an amount to compensate for any losses, or any other relief it deems necessary. This process goes far beyond the mere preservation of the status quo. Third, there are no provisions allowing for a "prompt" judicial determination of the Board's decision.[33]

Thus, these forms of action were judged to constitute invalid prior restraints. Barker concluded that the administrative procedures of the trafficking and assault sections were more in confirmity with *Freedman* but that the defects of the other actions rendered all of them invalid.[34]

Concerning the four enforcement triggers, the two most problematic measures were the trafficking and physical assault provisions. The assault provision raised the spectre of *Hicklin,* as people involved in the making and distribution of pornography could be held liable for subsequent attacks "directly caused" by pornography. This understanding of "direct cause" went against the First Amendment assumption that individuals are responsible for their own actions. Indeed, if the pornography could be blamed, then an attacker should be able to claim diminished responsibility for his actions, similar perhaps to a defense of intoxication or extreme emotional distress. It seems highly ironic that a measure intended to reduce the subjection of women should provide excuses for rapists. This approach also undermined the doctrine that speakers cannot be held responsible for the actions of their hearers; this principle risks protecting those who would incite others to unlawful actions, but it is necessary to the preservation of the modern doctrine of speech.

The assault provision was a return to the "bad tendency" logic of *Hicklin* and early free speech cases, raising serious questions of proof and delimitation.[35] As Judge Barker remarked, "the Ordinance establishes through the legislative findings that pornography *causes a tendency* to commit these various harmful acts." Material that simply depicted women in positions of "humiliation" could have been grounds for action if some vulnerable individual committed a sexual assault after viewing or reading it. As Tigue points out, "The reaction of the most degenerate reader or viewer in society could determine what the remainder of the population would be permitted to read."[36] The Supreme Court has ruled that the "average person" test of *Roth* and *Miller* does not permit a jury to include children in the community that is to determine prurient interest, as that would reduce the level of material available to that appropriate to children.[37] Many lower courts have already rejected arguments similar to those undergirding the ordinance's assault provisions because they would jeopardize the modern doctrine of speech.[38] The fiduciary ethic of tort law has yet to invade the domain of the First Amendment. Significantly, Frederick Schauer of the 1986 Attorney General's Commission on Pornography expressly rejected using "multiple" or "probabalistic" causation as a constitutional standard, on the grounds that the First Amendment must operate on a stricter notion of causation than does social science inquiry.[39]

Action for "discrimination by trafficking in pornography" was also problematic—especially in view of the very vague and broad definitions of pornography proffered by the ordinance. First, the measure defined trafficking as "discrimination," which stretched logic in contexts outside specific environments. Second, the trafficking section went beyond any notion of direct harm; it stipulated that "any woman" (or man or transsexual) had cause for action "against the subordination of women" if she (he) discovers trafficking in pornography (defined in Minneapolis as "the production, sale, exhibition, or distribution of pornography").[40] According to one supporter, "This provision is aimed at the harm to women posed by the availability of pornography in itself."[41] Congruent with the ordinance's basic logic, this understanding conflated speech and action and expressed the expanded notion of harm endorsed by the measure's advocates. But in so doing, this approach offered weapons to witch hunters as it would have allowed private citizens to bring civil actions against all purveyors of sexual materials. Shades of Anthony Comstock! Kathleen Jones has commented on the bookstore surveillance tactics of Women against Pornography in New York, actions that were duplicated by the Attorney General's Commission on Pornography during its Houston tour.[42]

> What began with the feminist call for the construction of
> aesthetic communities of diversified practices seems to
> have been reduced to the construction of a sisterhood of
> surveillance. It is no small irony that while feminist film
> critics have argued that the inspecting gaze is a peculiarly
> male way of looking, other feminists in the anti-
> pornography movement have accepted its vision in camera
> obscura.[43]

These observations point to ways in which some feminist advocates of the ordinance opened the way for political cooptation by the Right, something that has happened to feminism before.[44] Some anti-pornography feminists have practiced an ideology of surveillance, control, and confession that mirrors the moralistic control sought by some factions on the Right.

The notion of causation and harm embodied in the trafficking provision was akin to those in the assault provision and, like them, would undermine the modern doctrine of speech. Material, its makers and distributors or exhibitors, would be held responsible for actions, in a way that would reduce the responsibility of criminals who were, or claimed to be, readers of pornography. Conservatives who trumpet the importance of individual responsibility in criminal law and tort cases should be wary of this logic. Furthermore, as we have seen, the notion

159

of multiple causality underlying the logic of the trafficking provision posed the same problems for free speech as did the *Hicklin*-like logic of the assault provision.

The ordinance's move against coersion of persons to participate in the production of pornography seemed somewhat less problematic on its face. Anyone "coerced, intimidated, or fraudulently induced . . . into performing for pornography shall have a course of action." Criminal laws in most jurisdictions already prohibit intimidation, fraud, and coercion, and such laws are utterly consistent with the liberal doctrine of speech.[45] Feminist critics charge that such laws are underenforced and fail to deal with the omnipresence of coercion in sexual contexts. The civil rights approach to coercion attempted to remedy this problem by placing the power of enforcement in the hands of women themselves and by redefining the meaning of coercion. Although the ordinance's language concerning coercion seemed traditional in some respects, its extremely broad definition of pornography, its enforcement provisions, and its association in court with the *Ferber* child pornography case placed the measure in a more radical light. Once a woman had shown that she had participated in making what the ordinance defined as pornography and showed that she was coerced, the burden shifted to the pornographer to rebut the claim. According to a supporter, "Proof of coercion is rebuttable only by a showing that the woman in fact *meaningfully* consenting to the performance."[46] The Minneapolis ordinance listed thirteen defenses or claims that would *not* suffice to demonstrate consent, including: "that the person is a woman," "that the person has attained the age of majority," "that the person actually consented to a use of the performance that is changed into pornography," "that the person showed no resistance or appeared to cooperate actively in the photographic sessions or in the sexual events that produced the pornography," "that the person signed a contract, or made statements affirming a willingness to cooperate in the production of pornography."[47] These limits on defense emulated provisions of the Supreme Court's child pornography decision: MacKinnon has said, "the best authority we have for this is the *Ferber* case."[48] This association suggests that the coercion provision virtually defined away consent as a defense.

The language of the ordinance was not explicit about this, however. The introduction of the defenses said, "Proof of one or more of the following facts or conditions shall not, without more, negate a finding of coercion."[49] This language allowed other evidence to be introduced that might show noncoercion; nevertheless, given the burden of proof and the broader presumptions established by the ordinance, any but the most obvious and clear defenses might have been extremely difficult to entertain. The coercion provision turned the tables on the general presumption in favor of liberty and consent and established a new burden of proof. Since consent had to be "meaningful," the ordinance implicitly assumed that coercion was present.

Such an assumption seems to me too broad. I favor an approach that would enforce existing coercion laws more rigorously, change the law to recognize the potential for coersion in the making of pornography (perhaps similar to the understanding of the potential of harassment in the workplace), and reform court procedures to give more credence to women's claims, similar to changes that have been adopted in cases of rape and self-defense.[50] The criminal law could well benefit from further accommodation of feminist ideas. Alternatively, established civil and statutory law regarding sexual harassment could be applied to pornography. In 1986 the Supreme Court held that the special context of a "hostile environment" in the workplace could make sexual harassment a form of discrimination under Title VII. In this same case, the Court also ruled that "the fact that sex-related conduct was 'voluntary,' in the sense that the complainant was not forced to participate against her will, is not a defense to a sexual harassment suit brought under Title VII. The gravamen of any sexual harassment claim is that the alleged sexual advances were 'unwelcome.' "[51] In this case, however, the Court was clear about the need of sufficient evidence to prove "unwelcomeness" and recognized the conflicting interests in the case: womens' right to a harassment-free work environment versus defendants' rights to fairness. Such a balance was lacking in the ordinance's approach to coercion.

The "forcing" provision of the ordinance was the least problematic. It comported in many respects with the logic and practice of sexual harassment laws and other laws protecting unwilling viewers from exposure to unwanted expression. MacKinnon has plausibly compared this provision to safeguards against sexual harassment and "fighting words," which lie outside of First Amendment protection.[52] The Minneapolis ordinance went beyond traditional limits by penalizing the use of pornography by husbands or male lovers in the privacy of the bedroom. This reform was similar to laws against marital rape; enforcement problems have arisen with such laws but that does not discredit them. The major problem with this provision was the civil rights enforcement mechanism and the broader scope of the ordinance as a whole.

161

Most of the ordinance's provisions, including the civil rights enforcement mechanism, were inconsistent with the values of an open society. Considered as a whole—its definitions, its enforcement and administrative provisions, and its failure to take account of artistic or intellectual value—the ordinance appears to have been a frontal attack on a free intellectual environment as far as sexual issues were concerned. Its radical feminist pedigree supports this conclusion. But its provisions dealing with depictions of physical abuse were at least arguably tied to subsequent actions and attitudes and did not necessarily violate the norms of free speech. This aspect of the ordinance may point the way to a new approach to the First Amendment treatment of violent pornography. Let us now consider what such an approach might be like.

A New Unprotected Classification for Erotic Violence?

Shorn of its extreme ideological elements, a more modest version of the ordinance would focus on pornography that depicts sexually oriented violence. The evidence associating this type of material with specific harms seems more plausible than for other forms of pornography. The 1986 Attorney General's Commission described "sexually violent material" in the following manner:

> The category of material on which most of the evidence
> has focused is the category of material featuring actual or
> unmistakably simulated or unmistakably threatened vio-
> lence presented in sexually explicit fashion with a predom-
> inant focus on sexually explicit violence. Increasingly, the
> most prevalent forms of pornography, as well as an in-
> creasingly prevalent body of less sexually explicit material,
> fit this description. Some of this material involves sado-
> masochistic themes, with the standard accoutrements of
> the genre, including whips, chains, devices of torture, and
> so on. But another theme of some of this material is not
> sado-masochistic, but involves instead the recurrent theme
> of a man making some sort of sexual advance to a woman,
> being rebuffed, and then raping the woman or in some
> other way violently forcing himself on the woman. In al-
> most all of this material, whether in magazine or motion
> picture form, the woman eventually becomes aroused and
> ecstatic about the initially forced sexual activity, and usu-
> ally is portrayed as begging for more. There is also a large
> body of material, more "mainstream" in its availability,

that portrays sexual activity or sexually suggestive nudity coupled with extreme violence, such as disfigurement or murder. The so-called "slasher" films fit this description, as does some sexual material, both in films and in magazines, that is less or more sexually explicit than the prototype "slasher" films.

The commission maintained, "When clinical and experimental research has focused particularly on sexually violent material, the conclusions have been virtually unanimous" that harm is caused.[53]

Cass Sunstein, a prominent legal scholar at the University of Chicago law school, has offered an abridged definition for a new category of violent materials which he argues is consistent with neutral principles and other categories of expression not protected by the First Amendment.[54] His suggestion encapsulates the approach advocated by most moderate supporters of the logic of the ordinance, and I use it as the representative proposal for a new classification. According to Sunstein, "In short, regulable pornography must (a) be sexually explicit, (b) depict women as enjoying or deserving some form of physical abuse, and (c) have the purpose and effect of producing sexual arousal." [55]

As Sunstein affirms, this approach does not address sexually explicit material that does not sexualize violence against women. It focuses on "the principle harms caused by pornography." Sunstein believes that this definition excludes material possessing social value, thereby protecting central First Amendment concerns. The definition "excludes the vast range of materials that are not sexually explicit but that do contain implicit rape themes. The requirement of sexual explicitness is thus a means of confining the definition." [56]

Any new unprotected category must surmount two burdens of proof. First, a sufficient level of harm from the material must be demonstrated to justify restriction; the level of harm need not meet the direct harms ("clear and present danger") test if the content is not the type of expression that the First Amendment is intended to protect. The "danger test" applies only when speech covered by the First Amendment is at stake (e.g. political speech, marketplace of ideas debate, etc.). The level of harm demonstrated for non-First Amendment speech, therefore, need not be exceedingly high or direct but must still be substantial. Second, the content of the material in the new category must be congruent with other exceptions derived from the two-level

163

approach of *Chaplinsky v. New Hampshire,* which distinguishes valuable from non-valuable speech.

Sunstein points out four factors that mark speech as having low First Amendment value.

1. "The speech must be far afield from the central concern of the first amendment, which, broadly speaking, is effective popular control of public affairs."

2. "A distinction is drawn between cognitive and noncognitive aspects of speech."

3. "The purpose of the speaker is relevant: if the speaker is seeking to communicate a message, he will be treated more favorably than if he is not."

4. "The various classes of low-value speech reflect judgments that in certain areas, government is likely to be acting for constitutionally impermissable reasons or producing constitutionally troublesome harms. In the cases of commercial speech, private libel, and fighting words, for example, government regulation is particularly likely to be based on legitimate reasons. Judicial scrutiny is therefore more deferential in these areas." [57]

Using these criteria, much pornography would be entitled to constitutional protection despite evidence that certain forms are related to harm. This suggests that a new class of unprotected speech based on violence is not a good idea. This is particularly true in relation to Sunstein's second and fourth criteria, concerning the cognitive value of speech and the problem of impermissable censorial motives, respectively. Much pornography does indeed possess cognitive elements, especially as these elements are understood by the depth psychologies such as psychoanalysis. And as we have seen in previous chapters, censorship of sexual expression is indeed often laden with "constitutionally impermissable" motives. Although there are reasons to be concerned about the effects of pornography, it is too simplistic to stress these concerns without also acknowledging the more ideological motives of censorship. It is surprising that Sunstein fails to grapple with the historical reality of censorship in this area of law, as the record is well known and its implications are obvious.

Depiction of violent sexual action meets the other two criteria (Sunstein's first and third) more adequately, but problems still remain with the first criterion, which deals with the central concerns of the First Amendment. While it is true that most pornography has little to do with the process of popular government, First Amendment protection is no longer limited to political speech. Since *Miller v. California,* expression possessing social value is covered. Consequently, Sunstein's first criterion, constitutionally, is largely irrelevant. Also, as I observed in Chapter 1, obscenity prosecutions historically have had political motivations. These actions bestowed a derivative political meaning upon pornography.[58] Sunstein's third criterion, concerning speakers' purposes, is most helpful because artistic content and intention are important factors in distinguishing potentially valuable and non-valuable sexual material. I believe that a defensible line separating the legally tolerated and non-tolerated can be drawn at this point.

The Evidence of Harm

In this section I discuss the academic studies concerning the harms attributable to "violent pornography." I am not an expert in this area, so I rely on recent summaries of research and some critical commentary.[59] Because I will argue against establishing a new unprotected class of "violent pornography," my analysis need not be definitive. It is enough to note that major researchers and bodies such as the 1986 Attorney General's Commission have correlated violent pornography with harm to an extent that might justify a new unprotected class of expression. This reasonable assumption provides the basis for a "strong" argument against a new class; that is, I argue that a new classification is not merited *despite* the suggestive experimental evidence of harm. I will conclude, rather, that the research and other notable analyses indicate that present obscenity law should be retained but that it should focus on violence rather than sexual explicitness. This approach synthesizes feminist and conservative concerns about maintaining norms of sexual expression; and, unlike most critics of the new anti-pornography measures, it takes account of the findings of research.[60]

If critics are too quick to dismiss evidence of harm, however, those who grasp the new evidence to support their arguments sometimes downplay two limiting factors.

First, evidence of long-term harm does not necessarily justify restriction of sexual materials, because all sorts of things—such as liquor and unemployment—are associated with harms, including aggression against women, yet they are seldom the subjects of prohibition efforts.[61] Second, even if material is associated with harm, factors such as artistic value or other functional attributes may justify toleration of the material. A work of sexual portrayal may be simultaneously good and bad like many other things in life, a consideration that is often ignored as adversaries argue past one another.

The harms attributed to pornography operate on more than one level. The first level of harm is the most direct, as women are often coerced and brutalized during the making of pornography.[62] I believe, however, that these harms are best dealt with through stronger enforcement of the criminal law of coercion, exploitation, and kidnapping. Because adult women, unlike minor children, can and legally may give consent, *Ferber's* rationale for restricting all child pornography cannot be applied to pornography made with adult women. As the courts ruled in the Indianapolis litigation, the presumption of consent and autonomy points in different directions for adult women and for children. But if a woman is able to prove coercion, fraud, or harm in the making of pornography, that should suffice to prohibit the showing or further use of that particular material. The First Amendment does not and should not protect the use of illegally produced goods. For example, the Supreme Court has ruled that advertising for jobs based on illegal gender discrimination is not protected, nor is false advertising.[63] A similar logic is at work in *Ferber,* as pornography that contains minors is in violation of the law. In this sense, *Ferber* may not constitute a new class of unprotected expression at all, but rather a further application of an existing restriction. Involving minor children in adult sexual activity is illegal in any context, not merely pornography.[64] The difference between child pornography and pornography with adult women is that adult women cannot conclusively be presumed to lack consent, so the elimination of the entire market in advance of publication is not merited. An analogous distinction is the difference between statutory and non-statutory rape: non-consent is presumed either conclusively or rebuttably in the former but not in the latter. It is at least logically consistent for some radical feminists to maintain the presumption of coercion concerning women in pornography and to see heterosexual relations as presumptively similar to rape. In both cases, however, the logic of presumptive non-consent makes adult women equivalent to minors. Thus, while harm does exist in individual cases in the very making of pornography, the nature of the harm does not justify eliminating the entire pornographic market. Harms must be addressed on a case-by-case basis. The alternative is to treat adult women like children.

Other levels of harm are less direct and are inferred from laboratory studies or psychological speculation. Among them are

1. harms to victims of sexual assault or other sex crimes that would not have occurred except for pornography. This logic is based on the logic of "multiple causation" espoused by the Attorney General's Commission;[65]

2. harms to society from the effect of pornography on attitudes about women which, in turn, generate discrimination and disrespect; and

3. harms to the moral concept and practice of sexual relationships, caused by degrading or violent obscene depictions.

The first harm is the one most likely to justify a new class of unprotected expression. The second is much less direct. But it should be acknowledged that the type of pornography under discussion, eroticized violence, certainly can depict women in dehumanized fashion and such depictions may well work against the interests of women in both the short and long term. Laboratory experiments have indicated that violent pornography does coarsen and dehumanize male attitudes toward women to a demonstrable extent.[66] But because this type of harm is so generalized, the basic liberal doctrine would suggest that censorship is too specific a remedy. Other steps may be taken to promote respect of women, efforts such as private actions against pornography, education, and "debriefing" (the use of education and other influences to counter the violent messages implicit in some popular media). I will address the third type of harm in the next section; this normative approach embraces conservative and feminist arguments to some extent.

Laboratory studies using contrived situations have suggested that significant exposure to violent pornography tends to desensitize men to sexual violence and increase their inclination to engage in aggression against women. (Aggression in these lab settings is usually measured by the willingness of the subject to administer simulated shocks to a female confederate of the researchers.) This inclination is exacerbated when tendencies toward aggression are fused with sexual arousal. Hence, pornography that depicts female arousal in reaction to rape and sexual violence appears to be the most likely to produce harmful effects. According to Donnerstein and his colleagues, "It is this unique feature of violent pornography—the presentation of the idea that women find sexual violence arousing—that plays an important role in producing violent pornography's harmful effects."[67] Exposure to such material makes men more accepting of the myth that women actually enjoy being raped even when they protest and resist, more likely to link sex with violence, and to have more violently aggressive fantasies.[68] More recent work has suggested that the violence in the depictions is the most important variable. Even minor intimations of sexuality will have effects similar to more sexually explicit depictions if violence is present. (Of course, a wide range of material fits this description, as I point out below, which raises significant First

167

Amendment problems for any effort at censorship; in such a broad context, Sunstein's and similar approaches would be too narrow to be effective.)[69]

Other recent studies suggest that sex alone has only a minimal impact on violently aggressive behavior in the laboratory. In one key study, researchers found that non-explicit depictions of sexual violence in a popular film (*The Getaway*, starring Ali McGraw and Steve McQueen) caused male viewers to be more tolerant of rape and to have negative views of women.[70] In a later study, a male or female researcher made male college students angry and then showed them one of four films: a pornography film with violent aggression, an X-rated film without violence or coercion, a film that showed violence against women but no sexual activity, or a film with neither sex nor aggression. When given an opportunity to carry out aggression against a male or female experimenter after the films, the highest levels were inflicted against the woman by those who saw the aggressive and pornographic film. The viewers of the non-sexual aggressive film were more aggressive than those who viewed the sexual but non-aggressive film. Indeed, viewers of the non-aggressive sexual film were no more aggressive against the woman than those who viewed the non-sexual and non-aggressive film.[71] These findings are important to my final conclusions, as they suggest that obscenity law is in part misguided in its exclusive focus on sex rather than violence.

The laboratory evidence is not definitive, but it is very suggestive. The duration of the negative effects, however, is not established. At this time, it is not known whether the effects of repeated exposures to violent pornography are temporary or cumulative. Nor have researchers determined the nature and extent of any possible cumulative effects. "This is one area where additional research is definitely needed. We can say with certainty [only] that there is an immediate effect, however short-lived."[72]

In addition to these laboratory studies, victim accounts and police reports of sexual crimes often link pornography to the commission of sex crimes, especially within the family. Pornography is held to incite behavior and to provide a "how-to" manual.[73] And some have found a correlation between the level of sex crimes and the availability or circulation of pornography in an area.[74]

This, then, is the testimony and the evidence that links violent pornography with harms to women. Let us now consider some of the questions that arise in regard to such a correlation. The major problems are these.

1. The evidence concerning inclinations to engage in sexual violence proves only correlation, not direct, deterministic cause. Exposure to pornography may not be the most important underlying cause of violent aggression: the vast majority of males do not become rapists after being exposed to pornography. Personal experience and previous learning may predispose a person to violence. It seems likely that other factors, such as an existing deeply rooted anger against women, are more important in causing violent aggression.[75] Pornography may only be the precipitator, if that: the choice of pornography may be the result of an existing interest rather than its cause.

2. Laboratory samples are too small to generate reliable findings. Linz, Donnerstein, and Penrod note several other problems with the special laboratory setting, as well. Subjects may not believe they are inflicting real harm. They may perceive violent aggression in the laboratory as condoned or suggested by the experimenter. Subjects are drawn from a narrow, unrepresentative segment of the population. Usually only positive results are published; negative or inconclusive results remain obscure. Finally, there is not yet an adequate operational definition of aggression as a behavioral response, nor is there an adequate definition in the relevant media of what comprises violence. Until more consistent definitions of aggression and violence are employed, the findings of researchers cannot be systematically compared; nor can general conclusions be reliably reached.[76]

3. The duration of the effects is not proved, as we have seen.[77] One study, for example, attempted to measure the relationship between long-term exposure to violent pornography and later violent aggression against women by delaying the measurement of aggression in the subjects until a week after they had viewed the violent materials. "Surprisingly, the authors found that neither subjects exposed to violent nor non-violent pornography displayed more aggression than control (no exposure) subjects."[78]

4. The laboratory setting is very artificial, with little to counteract the overpowering negative stimuli created by the experiment. Outside the lab many factors intervene and defuse the pornographic cue, as it were, weakening the effects of exposure to pornography. Extrapolation to the real world from the contrived laboratory environment is therefore problematic.

5. The violent aggression elicited in the laboratory is, in Barry Lynn's words, "only an analogy to actual aggression" because "it is allowed or encouraged by an experimenter with the guarantee that no punishment will ensue (even if the college students believed that they

169

were actually shocking their partners, itself a dubious proposition)."
There are also strong "experimenter demands" in operation: the
showing of a film depicting violence may lead subjects to assume that
the experimenter approves of, or at least permits, violence in the context of the experiment.[79]

6. For a scientific behavioral study to be really conclusive it would
have to measure effects on the same individuals over a long period of
time, probably a number of years. Such a study has not been done, and
it is unlikely that it could be accomplished.[80]

While these considerations must be acknowledged, they are not de-
terminative. If the evidence is neither certain nor definitive, it is very
suggestive as far as it goes. Unless, as in criminal law, we insist that
guilt be established beyond a reasonable doubt, we can say that significant exposure to violent pornography, particularly in the context of
arousal, is associated with negative inclinations and attitudes toward
women. If such inclinations are already present, violent pornography
may provide a model for behavior. The research, limited as it is, is too
consistent to be dismissed (unless numerous unpublished findings
show the contrary—but there is no evidence of this being the case).

Certainly the academic findings lend support to the concept of
"multiple" or "probabalistic" causality advanced by the 1986 Attorney General's Commission. This concept does not mean that pornography is one of a set of absolutely necessary conditions for sexual violence to occur or that it is one of "potentially *several* sets of conditions,
the existence of each member of any of the sets being sufficient to determine the effect."[81] Nor does multiple causality mean that a particular pornographic exposure is even likely to lead to violence. But pornography may increase the overall incidence of sexual violence in
society to some significant extent. According to Frederick Schauer, a
key member of the 1986 commission who wrote most of the *Final Report,*

> Under a probabalistic account of causation, a causal rela-
> tionship exists, for types or classes, insofar as the putative
> cause increases the incidence of the effect, and a causal re-
> lationship exists, in particular cases, insofar as the puta-
> tive cause increases the probability of the effect.[82]

In essence, there is a causal effect when a result is simply more likely
to occur if a particular factor is present. A particular cause need not
even be the major cause among the set of probabalistic causes, nor
must it lead to the effect in a significant number of cases. Lung cancer

is more likely to occur if one smokes cigarettes than if one does not, though there are many causes of lung cancer besides smoking and though many smokers do not get lung cancer. The same relation, though probably attenuated, could well be found with pornography and sexual violence.

Thus it does not appear unreasonable to accept the suggestion that violent pornography is related to sexual violence in a probabalistic or multiple causal way. There have been supporting cross-cultural and sectional studies that posit a relationship between the levels of mass pornography distribution and rape incidences. Such studies can suffer from problems of mediating cultural variables independent of pornography and the supposed correlations may prove spurious. Recent studies, however, have done a better job of controlling for other factors that may contribute to sexual violence, such as unemployment, economic inequality, hunting license purchases, television violence, sexual liberalism, and alcoholism, and have still found important correlations between pornography distribution and the frequency of rape.[83]

The problem with the probabalistic approach is that its concept of causality is very broad and less compelling than more deterministic versions of causality. Since there are likely to be many causes of sexual violence from a probabalistic perspective, pornography's role is attenuated in this framework. And cross-cultural studies are not entirely convincing; they downplay the effects of alcoholism on sexual aggression, for example, where common experience would emphasize it.[84] And it is virtually impossible for cross-cultural studies to isolate the effects of non-pornographic variables.

Schauer and others admit that demonstrating "causal" harm is not in itself sufficient to justify censorship, for the Constitution and social policy protect many rights that may lead to harms. The very possession of a right means that only a special showing of significant harm may justify restriction of the right. For example, free speech can cause definite harm, as at Skokie or in the libel of public figures, but some such harm must be tolerated to maintain First Amendment protections. Citizens' rights against unreasonable search and seizure, coerced confessions, and the like, may harm society's ability to suppress crime, but they are, nonetheless, perhaps the necessary price of constitutional liberty.[85] Given the pre-eminence of free speech in a constitutional democracy, harm resulting from multiple or probabalistic causation will seldom suffice to justify censorship. But this does not mean that there is no such thing as such harm, nor that pornography does not inflict it.

Another problem is that the discourse of harm does not encompass

171

the whole of pornography—even violent pornography. Pornography extends into the realm of artistic value, certainly in some of the films used in the experiments discussed above—*Swept Away, The Getaway,* and the like. (There are also a host of renowned films such as *Last Tango in Paris* that may be placed in this category). As a form of representation, pornography can be understood only by taking account of the interpretive, emotional, and psychological meaning of the material. Pornography's aesthetic meaning must be acknowledged.[86] As I have argued repeatedly, harms and benefits can coexist in the same material. Thus, even granting the arguments about certain types of harm would not necessarily lead to endorsing censorship, as social value might outweigh the harm. The debate must avoid the mutually exclusive extremes that too often shape perceptions in this area of law and society.

Let us now look more closely at why all but the most extreme sexual depictions should be at least legally tolerated. Law and society have wrestled with the balance between liberty and control in this area for a good reason: pornography is a complex form of representation that can include both valuable and disturbing elements that understandably evoke different responses. A monolithic policy would fail because it would not be congruent with the nature of the subject matter. The difficulty lies in drawing a line that satisfies several competing interests. Like the line that separates the sane from the insane in criminal law, the line may be redrawn as society and experience change, but the line itself should not be eliminated.

As I have mentioned, any new class of expression to be denied First Amendment protection must be consistent with other unprotected classes along the lines of *Chaplinsky*. Pornography that portrays violence while displaying no artistic pretensions does not contribute significantly to the exposition of ideas and there are reasons aside from anti-sex ideology to be concerned about the effects of such material. (Although anti-sex motives have been significant in the history of censorship and remain so, the question here is whether censorship can be justified on more general principles.) For example, the 1986 Attorney General's Commission described a sado-masochistic film involving incest that seemed to lie well outside of *Chaplinsky*'s rationale of protection. Indeed, this film (*Forgive Me—I Have Sinned*) was found obscene by a Kentucky court.[87]

There is, however, a major problem with approaches like those of Sunstein and the anti-pornography ordinance (even in Indianapolis's more modest version). They do not take adequate account of the artistic possibilities of even violent pornography—a failure of imagination also displayed by the Attorney General's Commission. The ordinance made no provision for considering artistic value; and while Sunstein exempts works with "value" from his new classification, he does not develop an analysis of the possible artistic value of some violent material. (He does, however, raise the excellent point that value and harm exist along the line of a continuum and are not matters of black and white).[88] The works of Sade, Bataille, and the author of *The Story of O* may be pathological, sexual, and violent, but they are indisputably artistic, as are movies like *Swept Away* and *Last Tango*.[89] Ernesto Sabato's classic Argentine novel *On Heroes and Tombs,* for example, deals with a multitude of important issues, including politics, philosophy, literature, religion, modernity, incest, violence, and human pathology (and some of the pathology is strangely arousing), but I can see no responsible basis for censoring it.[90] It is artful not despite its pathology but rather *because* of its treatment of pathology. As William Gass remarks in a brilliant review of this remarkable book,

> This novel not only describes, but is itself a search, a painful passage through danger and darkness, through the interior, across the spotted soul, the Africa of its author. But our problem is that *On Heroes and Tombs* is a very artful book indeed—indeed it is overly artificial and contrived, sometimes. . . .
>
> This document [the "Report on the Blind" that is the culmination of the book] . . . is a powerful, distraught, sometimes hysterical, certainly offensive, yet magnificent depiction of the realm of the unconscious; it is a descent, like Dante's, into Hell.[91]

Sabato's art is supremely modernist. It explores the existential and sexual ramifications of a world bereft of God's redemptive grace. Gass's interpretation of Sabato's masterpiece corresponds to Susan Sontag's interpretation of the modern genre of pornographic art. Sontag refers to material that is much more sexually explicit than *On Heroes and Tombs* but her conclusions are similar. She understands modernist artistic pornography as a paradoxical result of the opening of the subconscious and the destruction of social and intellectual order. While the death of God unleashes new possibilities of freedom, the path of opportunity winds along the precipice of nihilism:

> But what *Story of O* unfolds is a spiritual paradox, that of the full void and of the vacuity that is also a plenum. The

173

power of the book lies exactly in the anguish stirred up by the continuing presence of this paradox. "Pauline Reage" [the pen name of the author of *Story of O*] raises, in far more organic and sophisticated manner than Sade does, with his clumsy expositions and discourses, the question of human personality itself. . . .

Story of O, with its project for completely transcending the idea of personality, rests on the dark and complex vision of sexuality—so far removed from the hopeful view of American Freudianism and liberal culture. . . .

Bataille understood more clearly than anyone else that what pornography is really about, isn't sex, but death.[92]

Sontag's view actually dovetails with those of conservatives who maintain that modern pornographic art is nihilistic or psychologically regressive in its tendencies. George P. Elliot, for example, declares that Henry Miller's *Tropic of Cancer*—which was assiduously prosecuted in America—is "a weapon for nihilism," a "metaphysical rage." (But even he admits that the art redeems the pornographic elements of the work.)[93] Camus declared that one of the pathologies of modern life is the "metaphysical rebellion" against death and the limits of the human condition.[94] This rebellion (and the utopian and totalitarian politics that can accompany it) is futile and a retreat from responsibility.[95] Rather than justifying censorship, however, such explications should promote tolerance of works that depict this condition and hold it up for observation and understanding. If nihilistic quality were grounds for censorship, virtually all great modern works of fiction would be headed for the shredder—including, perhaps, Andrea Dworkin's works on sex and pornography.

My point is that our understanding of sex and violence in artistic contexts must not be handicapped by literal, legalistic interpretations. Any definition of pornography must expressly include a provision similar to *Miller's* condition of social value: sexually violent works that possess significant social, artistic or intellectual value would be entitled to First Amendment protection.[96]

On the other hand, attention to social value would guard against another problem that arises from Sontag's interpretation—conflating exploitation movies like *Forgive Me—I Have Sinned* and *Deep Throat* with classic novels like *Story of O*. There is a difference between these films and this novel, and the difference is the presence or absence of art. By *art* I mean a treatment of sexual reality that presents pornographic themes and scenes in an intellectual fashion which synthesizes passion and reason—a synthesis that Roger Scruton calls "desire." This synthesis places sexual art at the heart of the First Amendment.

But while this added provision would make a new unprotected category based on pornographic violence more acceptable, it also suggests that such an addition to First Amendment law might not be advisable, for two reasons.

First, if there is redeeming art, the material is presumptively worthy of protection; and second, if there is no redeeming artistic content, it is possible that the material would be found obscene under *Miller*, thereby precluding the need for a new approach. Indeed, both *Deep Throat* and *Forgive Me—I Have Sinned* have already been found obscene.[97] Nevertheless, some violent pornography may escape the strictures of obscenity law and so there may be occasion to consider treating it as a new class of unprotected expression. I will pursue this issue in the next section.

Violent Pornography as a New Unprotected Class of Speech: A Negative View

As I have indicated throughout, I do not favor making "violent pornography" a new exception to the First Amendment. I have called my argument against establishing a new class of unprotected speech "strong" because I make it despite my accepting some of the key aspects of the strongest charges against pornography. I accept these charges not simply for purpose of discussion but because they are plausible as far as they go. One charge has just been discussed: academic research has correlated violent pornography with aggressive male tendencies, desensitization to violence, and negative attitudes toward women. The 1986 Attorney General's Commission recorded a strong consensus for such a correlation among researchers in this field. The existence of this correlation is an issue independent of any social, psychological, or artist values associated with violent pornography; harms and benefits can coexist in the same material.

Second, we must consider the conservative and feminist arguments that pornography, especially when it displays no artistic or social value, models the wrong sort of sexual behavior and attitude. This point seems to me to be on the mark to a significant extent. Steven Marcus, in *The Other Victorians*, distinguishes pure pornography from art; many feminists make a distinction between pornography and erotica. Such analyses make psychological and normative sense, as long as we are careful not to fall into the trap of idealizing the sexual encounter.[98] The reason is that sexuality requires a context of social

175

order and mutual respect in order to be human. But human beings are also animals, so animality must constitute a part of sexuality. A balance between animality and human mutuality are necessary to an adequate understanding of human sexuality [99]

Some liberal critics rightly observe that these distinctions are not easy to draw in practice or application. Morse Peckham, for example, maintains that Steven Marcus is incorrect in finding lack of artistic content and form in *My Secret Life,* the nineteenth-century anonymous classic detailing autobiographical sexual exploits.[100] But when he draws parallels between this work and higher forms of Victorian literature, especially Dickens, Marcus is convincing. While Dickens engages the central social and personal dilemmas of the age, the author of *My Secret Life* retreats from these encounters to a world of sexual megalomania—a retreat that marks unartful pornography. Two points emerge from this comparison: first, even if Peckham is correct, *My Secret Life* indisputably is less artful than, say Dickens, even if it does possess some artistic qualities; second, the difference has something to do with pornography as a distinctive literary or visual form. Thus, Peckham's and Marcus's analyses are not necessarily mutually exclusive; pornography, even the hard-core variety, may possess artistic elements but the genre tends to be much less artistic than other sexual art forms. We are dealing with a continuum of meaning and effect, not polar opposites (although two extremes may be very far apart).

Marcus's psychoanalytic and literary argument is based on the concept of desublimation: he sees pure pornography, unlike art, as a regression from mature desire and sexuality. Rather than manifesting respect for the other as a person and joining desire to rational intentionality (the individuation or personalization of desire), pornography is based on denial of others as persons and denial of the limits of reality.[101] In place of the complexities and responsibilities of mature engagement, sheer pornography offers a realm of no restraints and no impediments to desire: in brief, the world of the infant. Pornography leads to an overdetermination of sex; its synecdochal structure reduces all reality to sexual appetite and the unimpeded satisfaction of the fantasizer. Depicting pornography as "pornotopia" in his famous concluding chapter, Marcus brings together some of the important conservative and feminist arguments against pornography:

> And the effort of pornography in this regard is to achieve in consciousness the condition of the unconscious mind—a condition in which all things exist in a total, simulta-

neous present. Time, then, in pornotopia is sexual time; and its real unit of measurement is an internal one. . . .

Nature, in other words, has no separate existence in pornotopia; it is not external to us, or "out there." There is no "out there" in pornography, which serves to indicate to us again in what phase of our mental existence this kind of thinking has as its origin. . . .

Inside of every pornographer there is an infant screaming for the breast from which he has been torn. Pornography represents an endless and infinitely repeated effort to recapture that breast, and the bliss it offered, as it often represents as well a revenge against the world—and the women in it—in which such cosmic injustice could occur.

Relations between human beings also take on a special appearance in pornotopia. It is in fact something of a misnomer to call these representations "relations between human beings." They are rather juxtapositions of human bodies, parts of bodies, limbs, and organs. . . .

The transactions represented in this writing are difficult to follow because so little individuation has gone into them. In a world whose organization is directed by the omnipotence of thought, no such discriminations are necessary.[102]

This Freudian perspective assumes that there is such a thing as a normative concept of sexuality—what Scruton calls "a moral philosophy of the erotic."[103] While such a theory is inescapably bound to its time and place—today's deviance can be tomorrow's accepted practice—it is a mistake to dismiss all normative approaches as misguided traditionalism. As with other normative concepts in law and social policy—insanity, mental illness, duress, consent, aspects of "specific intent," *mens rea,* and the like—the line shifts with changing social understanding but still persists. In defining ourselves as human, we necessarily posit some normative framework. Desire does not operate outside social expectations and structures. Because the standards of our own culture inevitably seem "natural" and compelling, we must always remain skeptical and reexamine our assumptions. We must not forsake the quest for standards, but we also must recognize our fallibility in determining the normative meaning of sexuality.[104]

For example, bestiality seems clearly beyond the pale of acceptable sex. Why? Not only because of the harm it might cause animals but also because of what it means for the perpetrator. Western religious tradition teaches that through the sexual act two participants become one flesh; if one is an animal, the human status of the other is compromised. This merging avoids the risk and responsibilities of an inter-human encounter; engaging with another human consciousness is inherently risky because of the possibility of rejection and judgment but it offers the possibility of a concurrent enlargement of self. This issue raises what Scruton calls the "Sartrean paradox": human sexual desire seeks to fully possess the consciousness of the other, but it cannot do so without eliminating the other as a distinct being. Complete success in possessing is had at the cost of obliterating the other.[105] Bestiality and other forms of sex with objects that cannot be "partners," a term that implies equality or reciprocity of status, are steps in this direction, as these objects of desire do not possess full, mature consciousness. They may be seen as substitutes for half-murdered human objects, as it were. Sado-masochism, which Sartre saw as inevitable in some form in human sexual relations, is another expression of this paradox. Destruction of the other is the final act of the quest for this kind of "success." *The Story of O*, for example depicts a systematic stripping away of the subjectivity of the woman, eventuating in her death in order to fulfill the will of her "masters." [106] Ironically, one loses the other in the very process of seeking total possession.

Sex with children raises similar but more complex issues. First, there is the danger of physical and psychological harm to the children. The reduction of personality on the part of the adult is somewhat different, as children are human beings and not animals or mere objects. Nevertheless, the adult is engaging in sex and merging consciousness with a being that lacks mature personality. (Again, this avoids the challenge inherent in dealing with another being of equal or greater social or mental status). The relationship is one of domination. In this latter regard, the feminist theory of pathological sex as power and domination parallels the conservative critique of depersonalization of sexuality. It is appropriate that Marcus portrays the workings of power, domination, and class in the depersonalized sexual utopia of the author of *My Secret Life*.[107] The author's gender and class allow him to treat females as powerless objects of conquest to be discarded at his discretion.

Conservatives and feminists both see the human dimension as the key to a normative concept of sexuality. The personalization of desire requires equal respect. Similarly, Marcus shows the very logic of sheer pornography to depersonalize the viewer and the objects of view. If choosing animals or children as objects of sexual desire shows immaturity, choosing pornography as an object of desire is arguably even lower, for such an object is without any consciousness whatsoever. The pornographic object requires no reaching out or enlargement of the self at all. Just as tolerance in a free society promotes enlargement of individual perspective, the tolerance or mutual respect between sexual equals promotes the enlargement of the partners.[108] This form of mutuality accords with what feminists mean by the distinction between "erotica" and "pornography" and by the "ethic of care."[109]

Pornography and obscenity may be baneful in either of two senses. First, a particular material may present a patently dehumanized model of sexuality. Second, a person may become dependent upon the material, which then serves as a substitute for relations with another person. Of course, almost any solitary activity—stamp collecting or reading detective stories—can be pursued in lieu of the risks of social life, but obscenity presents a special opportunity for substitution and immature dependency because of sexuality's power and because of the anxiety some people have about sex. Sexual practices that depend upon non-human objects for arousal (either as substitutes for human partners or as supplemental aids) take steps in this direction, as does treating women as nothing but body parts ("tits," "ass," and so forth).[110] But the law has no way of determining when the use of pornography assumes this character, unless it is willing to crash through the walls of privacy and even invade the realm of thought. Consequently, obscenity law should concern itself with only the first form of harm mentioned above.

Pornography can feed the dominating forces of one's own insecure sexual fantasies to the detriment of care and respect for other persons—a phenomenon which Freud interpreted as a form of primitive infantile sexuality. Hence, the association of pornography with masturbation: the object of desire in masturbation exists only in the will of the masturbator.[111] This is the ultimate depersonalization of desire, as the object has no independent personality whatsoever. As Scruton remarks, "Fear of the obscene is fear of the depersonalizing quality of sexual curiosity."[112] Necrophilia (sex with corpses) offers a similar advantage to the poor in spirit: "The appeal of necrophilia, like that of bestiality, lies in the freedom from the anxiety of personal knowledge."[113] Scruton's discussion of masturbation ties together all these themes:

> Masturbation exists in two forms; one in which it relieves
> a period of sexual isolation, and is guided by a fantasy of
> copulation; the other, in which masturbation replaces the
> human encounter, and perhaps makes it impossible, by re-

> inforcing the human terror, and simplifying the process, of sexual gratification. . . . In sexual fantasy, an object is represented, often by means of a picture. But the aim is to approach as nearly as possible to a substitute for the absent object: though a substitute that is free from danger.
> (Hence the necrophiliac's need for the dead body of another, the body which can no longer *discountenance* him.)
> . . . The imaginings of such a masturbator are not personal but corporeal, perhaps explicitly phallic. They exhibit the structural trait of obscenity. They exist in order to facilitate sexual gratification *without* the trouble of the human encounter, in order to turn the subject away from the pains and the rewards of interpersonal desire, towards an alternative that—while easy in itself—displays the defining feature of perversion.[114]

Scruton raises a complicating factor, however. The normative model of humanized sexuality based on equal respect is a goal or an ideal. But we cannot realize it all the time, as we cannot live always on the level of sainthood. Furthermore, animality with its diminished personalization is a part of our natures, so idealized sexual relations are not entirely human. In Nietzsche's terms, our makeup consists of both the harmonious reason of Apollo and the animality and mystery of Dionysis.[115]

While Nietzsche praised a balance of the Apollonian and Dionysian as a model of psychic health, most individuals outside Eden fall short of this ideal. Men and women are pulled in the conflicting directions of reason and irrationality, responsibility and selfishness. We define maturity as the integration of reason and desire, a unity of purpose based on inner diversity.[116] But even the most integrated individuals have moments of incompletion and inner conflict, and fall short of normative ideals that represent realistic and achievable goals.

Indeed, pornographic art is meaningful precisely because it touches this fundamental tension of the human spirit. The world of sexual relations constantly experiences the tension between objectification of others and equal respect for the partner. It would be utopian to expect human beings to completely transcend their infantile desires and animality. The project of maturation (which also is the project of civilization) is to sublimate primitive desire by means of more humane, civilized objects, but the project can never be complete.[117] This is one reason that sexual desire and arousal inescapably involve objectification as well as personalization. In Freud's understanding, fully developed sexual relations are a synthesis of mature and more primitive psychological meanings and needs, which at least partially reconciles the conflicting parts of our natures.

From this perspective, human meaning derives from the interplay of these higher and lower forces; elimination of either side of the dialectic denies the fuller dimension of human reality and represents a utopian escape from human responsibility. Anti-pornography critics often misconstrue the issue by, in effect, viewing the dialectic of our rational and animal natures as a scandal. When such critics address sexuality, they see only corruption instead of the coexistence of two potentialities: reason and passion, mind and body, can lead to either fulfillment or fragmentation.[118] Such a judgment is, ultimately, a denial of life, as astute psychologists like Nietzsche and Dostoyevsky understood. In Nietzsche's terms, such judgment is the very essence of nihilism, as it makes an affirmation of life impossible. According to this perspective, the gender separatism espoused by some radical feminists and lesbians and the sexual denial advocated by some conservatives are nihilistic because they represent a puristic recoiling from the inevitable travails of the heterosexual encounter. The absence of humor in so many of the conservative and feminist attacks on pornography is indicative of this suffocation of life, for laughter is the emotional bridge between human animality and reason. Laughter heals the pain of the cardinal split in human nature and is a sign of psychic health.[119] The absence of humor is of a piece with the failure of the Minneapolis ordinance to distinguish between artful and non-artful pornography.

But if addressing the problem of pornography demands that we recognize a healthy dialectic between equal respect and objectification, it also requires us to realize that the dialectic can go wrong. Some liberals reveal their own form of impoverished imagination by underestimating the latter possibility. All sexual phenomena can be constructive or destructive. Thus, masturbation may be part of normal sexual functioning or may weaken the ability to relate to another human being. The same can be said for other categories of sexuality. Even sadomasochism can be expressed as a game that draws on inclinations shared by many in Western culture or as abuse and denial of the humanity of others. Similarly, aggression is possibly part of the psychological structure of sexuality, but it can assume healthy or unhealthy forms. There is a difference between the normal physical and mental advances of the sexual encounter and pathological violence. Healthy people maintain a balance between integrating and disintegrating forms of sexuality; as Freud taught, psychological normality coexists

181

with degrees of abnormality.[120] Conflict between the higher and lower impulses of the self is one of the wellsprings of religion, art, and self-understanding.[121] The healthy form of the struggle leads to enlightenment; the unhealthy form leads to weakness or delusion—and the line that separates these two paths may be thin indeed.

For instance, in the domain of sexual interest in children or pedophilia, Nabokov's *Lolita* is artful and profound, but magazines depicting children in sexual relations are certainly corrupting. *Lolita* teaches something about human nature and experience and is thematically connected to larger matters of yearning, selfishness, and the ineluctable corrosions of time. The pornographic vision attempts to elude the restraints and tensions of reality—and reality's most intractable ally is time. The id—repository of the most primitive and infantile desires—does not know time, individuation, or death. Hence, the quest of Nabokov's protagonist, Humbert Humbert, is ultimately an effort to defy time and age. *Lolita* deals artfully with a form of inner fragmentation and regression that inescapably leads to Humbert's destruction. Yet the artfulness of the book avoids shrill condemnation (the praxis of some anti-pornography activists) and makes its ultimate judgment with a sense of empathy, tragedy, and humor. Lolita, after all, is alluring, and Nabokov avoids hard-core depictions that would demean Humbert's immature, obsessive love. The book's noteworthy humor pays tribute to the dialectical relation between our animality and humanity, our lower and higher selves, for laughter travels the emotional pass between the proper and the forbidden.

Lolita also reveals that the outcome of the dialectic can be a very close call, for Nabokov brings enlightenment out of forces that threaten disruption. There is no light without darkness, as Saint Augustine's teachings and personal experience reveal.[122] The difficulty lies in acknowledging the importance of the dialectic without falling prey to dissolution. In dealing with sexuality and human experience, art must avoid sliding into artless pornography and obscenity. Yet the dangers of pornographic art are worth risking because the form engages this fundamental dialectic of our natures. From this philosophical perspective, the task of censorship is to distinguish art from sheer pornography or obscenity while still accommodating the potentially productive aspects of the dark side of human nature—what Jung called "the shadow." [123]

Some conservatives recognize the dialectic that I have discussed and even build their sexual ethics upon it. But they emphasize the ideal of educating desire. Scruton's analysis of shame is one example:

Sexual shame is a special case of a more extensive phenomenon: bodily shame—the shame induced by the perception of one's body from a point of view outside it, as an
item curious in itself. . . . The child sees his body as an
"object in the eyes of the adults." . . .

We should not regret this modesty in children. On the
contrary, it is the necessary consequence of a developing
first-person perspective, and of a growing sense of responsibility towards the human world. It is the shameless child
who should awaken our distaste. If he does not feel the
tension of his embodiment it is because he lacks a crucial
mental capacity: the capacity to entertain in a single
thought the subjective and the objective view of his own
condition.[124]

From this perspective, the deeper objection to sheer pornography or
obscenity (uncoupled from the dialectical tie to art) is that it represents
a retreat from the human dilemma and the responsibility of acknowledging the tensions in our nature. Sheer pornography also reduces us
to the lower aspects of our natures by stripping away the modesty that
arises from our encounter with our animality. Far from neutralizing or
impoverishing desire, modesty enhances the allure of the sexual object.
Modesty contributes to the challenge of the sexual encounter and
heightens desire by slightly restraining it and giving it form. A measure
of restraint builds intensity, while instant gratification trivializes.
Modesty humanizes desire.

Hunting is an activity that resembles the sexual encounter in several
respects, including the pursuit of "game" by both sexes and the ambivalence of the participants toward the more visceral aspects of animal
embodiment. In an intriguing analysis, Jose Ortega y Gasset touches
on the delicate balance between primitive and civilized sensibilities in
a manner that illuminates the idea of the obscene. While the hunt is a
ritualistic reenactment of primitive man's relationship to nature, the
normal hunter is also riveted by both a sense of "orgiastic intoxication
aroused by the sight of blood" and a sense of revulsion and horror at
the killed animal's body. At this moment, the hunter experiences the
tension between primitive excitement and disgust with the obscene:

Life is the mysterious reality *par excellence,* not only in the
sense that we do not know its secret but also because life is
the only reality that has a true "inside"—an *intus* or inti-
macy. Blood, the liquid that carries and symbolizes life, is

183

meant to flow occultly, secretly, through the interior of the body. When it is spilled and the essential "within" comes outside, a reaction of disgust and terror is produced in all Nature, as if the most radical absurdity had been committed: that which is purely internal is made external.[125]

A hunter who did not feel discomfort in the face of flowing blood would not be fully human. But the hunter must resist the temptation to spare the animal, for this would not only deny the essence of the hunt but also mark a retreat from the animalistic encounter with life. Accordingly, Ortega ridicules the modern Anglo-American practices of "photographic hunting" and "mannered tenderness." The latter is "a new immorality . . . which is . . . a matter of not knowing those very conditions without which things cannot be. This is man's supreme and devastating pride, which tends not to accept limits on his desires and supposes that reality lacks any structure of its own which may be opposed to his will." And photographic hunting must be opposed because it "is not progress but rather a digression and a prudery of hideous moral style."[126] Ortega's strictures apply to many of the "progressive" critiques of sexuality and sexual art that we have discussed. These recoil from the animalistic or biological aspects of sexuality, seeking refuge in a political meaning designed to purify sexual relations in the name of equality.

For Ortega, hunting is a kind of art, for hunting, like art, is a means whereby the darker forces are put in tension with the lighter. Escape from this dialectic is tantamount to an escape from life. Sheer pornography and obscenity represent escapes to the primitive side, while sexual and other forms of prudery (analogous with photographic hunting) represent escapes via the route of moralistic utopia.

At the same time, pure pornography or obscenity amount to an attempt to escape the contours and forms of language. Language conveys the human form of desire; by putting feelings into words, we humanize and elevate our emotions at the same time that we give form to Eros (hence, barbaric individuals often lack verbal acumen, as Hannah Arendt has remarked concerning Billy Budd). By attempting to get beyond the limits of language, pure pornography attempts to escape the tensions and limits inherent in the human condition. As Steven Marcus says:

> Inexorably trapped in words, pornography, like certain kinds of contemporary literature, tries desperately to go beneath and behind language; it vainly tries to reach what

language cannot directly express but can only point toward, the primary processes of energy upon which our
whole subsequent mental life is built. This effort explains
in part why pornography is also the repository of the forbidden, tabooed words. The peculiar power of such words
has to do with their primitiveness. They have undergone
the least evolution, and retain much of their original
force.[127]

A retreat from language is a retreat from life; absolute fulfillment of
desire without the challenge and moderating influence of verbal forms
is the world of death. In psychoanalysis, desire is fulfilled only in the
paradoxical and dialectical context of periodic denial and restraint—
the interplay of the reality principle and the pleasure principle.[128] Pleasure is the obverse of burgeoning desire and the risk of nonfulfillment;
it is not the instant and guaranteed satisfaction of desire. Hence, escape to a realm of unresisted desire untainted by time and thirst is,
ironically, destructive of the very structure of desire itself. In Freud's
terms, it is an escape to the absolute pleasure principle, which is the
correlate of the death instinct.[129]

The social radical feminist view of language raises another problem.
Because the self is only a social construct, words carry only universal
categorical meanings that defy individuation, nuance, and art. Hence,
there can be no dispute over the meaning of *pornography,* and there is
no need to distinguish artful from non-artful expressions in anti-
pornography ordinances. Nor is there an occasion for humor at the
expense of sex. But this position seems extreme. Language and words
can be highly personal and non-categorical. Great poetry and art strive
to overcome (even if they cannot transcend) the sterile limits of socially
determined discourse. They contribute to the deepening of both individuality and collective existence. Limiting language—or sexuality—
to the categorical and the social stifles the dialectic between the individual and society, which is another positive tension of human existence. This is why totalitarian regimes are suspicious of art: art deals
with this dialectic. Such a limitation destroys subjectivity in the name
of restoring it, just as some critics would restrict free speech in the
name of redeeming it.[130]

Marcus's perspective meshes with Sontag's notion that there is a the-
matic relation between pornography and death, only with a more negative, uninspiring gloss. (Sontag, however, deals with pornography
that is artistic, and art is redemptive; thus, the artistic pornographic
quest of death paradoxically serves life). Peckham provides a similar

interpretation of pornography, although he holds that this meaning is a necessary and functional diversion that provides relief from the tensions of social and psychological life. Interestingly, Peckham's defense of pornography agrees with Scruton's and Marcus's criticisms—all three understand pornography as a retreat from the tensions and conflicts of mature desire. But compared to Scruton and Marcus, Peckham is more tolerant of human weakness; he does not altogether condemn the allure of the obscene. Pornography offers a release from the tensions of the human condition in a manner analogous to death. In Nietzsche's terms, pornography appeals to a decidedly weak will to power. Peckham declares, "Death is the supreme suspension of cognitive activity, the supreme elimination of feedback, the supreme destruction of all cognitive tension. What has been called the death-wish is merely a longing for such a state. . . . Man has long since mastered the functional equivalent of death in the form of religious experience, drug taking, mystic trance, sociopolitical charisma, and sexual experience." [131]

Similarly, Peckham believes that pornography depicting sadomasochism (he refers to *The Story of O*) expresses a longing to escape the tension of existence:

> Yet submission has an enormous appeal, a sweet, seductive charm, for it means to let go and to dissolve tensions. Helpless submission has the appeal of Paradise; hence the profound attraction of the crucified one to the poor in spirit. . . . Moreover, the area of sexual behavior, in its privacy, its social protection, its psychic insulation, and its discontinuity from other social relations is admirably adapted for experiencing the resolution of the conflict, in the form of either the uninhibited exercise of the will to challenge without cognitive tension, or the symmetrical exercise of the will to submit. [132]

Scruton, interestingly, also endorses a measure of sado-masochism, on the grounds that it expresses something fundamental and normal about human nature: aggression is part of sexuality, although it carries a temptation to subordination and violence. Sado-masochism has a negative form which Scruton rejects, in which the other is not acknowledged and is made into a slave or a master (as in *The Story of O*.) But, he maintains, it also has a positive form, in which "an intelligible moral relation between equals finds embodiment in a sexual act." Scruton's acceptance of a measure of sado-masochism is premised on the paradox of human nature that we have discussed: the dialectical relation of conflict and respect, of objectification and subjectivity, and the negative and positive alternatives that beckon. "In all human relations, there seems to be both an element of conflict—a desire to compel the other to give what is required—and a compulsion toward agreement, toward the mutual recognition that only what is given can be genuinely received."[133] Sado-masochism is part of this dialectic and can be normatively appropriate as long as its relation to the ideal of equal respect is maintained. In Sade, of course, the negative route is taken, although there the darkness is tempered by the redemptive quality of art, albeit of debatable quality. Interestingly, in a recent laboratory study, researchers found that women who watch R-rated "slasher" films—violent films that often involve sexual themes but are not sexually explicit—find them more enjoyable and their male companion more attractive when the men display a fearless, macho image in reaction to the violence.[134] Such results are shocking in certain respects, but they also may point to the complex makeup of sexuality in men and women.[135]

Critics and defenders of pornography sometimes actually agree that it is regressive and depersonalizing. They differ in the conclusions they draw from their understanding. Some conservatives and feminists see all pornography as marking a retreat from responsibility and the ideal of equal respect. Others see both negative and positive potential in the genre, depending on the content and its use. And theorists like Peckham argue that regression and retreat themselves serve deep psychological needs, as do other forms of symbolic activity such as religion.

Psychoanalysis provides another perspective that has multiple implications. The renunciation of infantile gratifications is inevitably painful, and the id never forgets. So one of the key functions of culture, which demands the renunciation of primitive desires, is to provide adequate civilized substitutes—that is, to provide the means for sublimation. Perhaps the recent explosion of pornography is a sign of the inadequacy of our age's substitute objects of desire, a failure of sublimation. Perhaps the spiritual vacuum left by the decline of religion and other traditional cultural forms has been filled by a quest for more primitive forms of satisfaction.[136] In this view, violent pornography may reflect a deeper social malady, and equally suspect substitute forms of expression might arise if censorship ever were to prove effective.[137] But artful pornography like *Tropic of Cancer* actually constitutes a reflection on this very dilemma of nihilism and so provides insight into our circumstances. Obviously, the waters here are deep and turbulent.

The position one takes on the pornography issue reveals how far one is willing to go in tolerating human weakness. The best position, in my estimation, is a compromise based on the paradox we have been discussing. Social policy in a liberal democracy should recognize the higher ideals of equal respect and reason but should also tolerate the human need for remissive relief and retreat. If some behavior must be restricted, thought and imagination must remain free. Animality must be acknowledged as a healthy part of our natures, although it, like our intellectual aspects, may be given constructive or destructive expression. Regarding action, there is no principled objection to laws against the most destructive forms of sexuality—necrophilia, bestiality, incest, sex with children, and the like. But pornography involves expression, not action, so a somewhat different approach is indicated. Social policy must be more tolerant in this area. (When pornography depicts actual instances of forbidden practices, such as rape or murder, those crimes are the offense and reason enough to ban the distribution of their expression.) The line drawn between acceptable and unacceptable expression must take into account artistic quality and levels of degradation. Democratic society has a right to draw the line of tolerance at the worse, most degrading depictions of sex that are unredeemed by art. These represent not the dialectic of existence but an abandonment of responsibility. But it is by now apparent that this line resembles the line already drawn by obscenity law, which is largely tolerant of sexual material up to the point I have described.

Obscenity law, however, has one gap. It leaves out an important element that feminists and academic researchers have forced us to consider: violence.[138] The evidence suggests that sexual violence is a social problem, and that certain forms of pornography are associated with violent sexual aggression in the sense of a non-deterministic "multiple" or "probabalistic" cause. In addition, violence depicted in a sexual content can be every bit as destructive as sheer obscenity. Thus, I recommend that the concept of obscenity either be broadened to include certain forms of violence or that violence be dealt with in established obscenity doctrine. Such an approach would fuse conservative, feminist, and social concerns and still provide a wide range of tolerance that would acknowledge liberal values as well. This approach could be the most effective accommodation to all interests in this inherently complex area of law and social policy. Although it could be largely symbolic, it would be a principled compromise that would acknowledge the legitimacy of competing viewpoints.

The Question of Harm and Legal Remedies

As we have seen, libertarian claims that pornography is harmless ignore significant academic research and much testimony to the contrary. These assumptions about harm, however, do not imply a need for a new unprotected class of expression under the First Amendment, even if one would be consistent with existing unprotected classifications. There are many reasons, ranging from the theoretical to the practical, to be wary of a new class of unprotected expression. On the theoretical level, the normative position represented by thinkers such as Steven Marcus actually provides a justification for pornography: when it possesses some artistic value, such material reveals something about the inner conflicts and struggles of the human being.[139] In addition, the association of some pornography with harm is not in itself a prescription for censorship. A great many activities have harmful aspects or can be pursued in harmful ways. On a more practical plane, any new unprotected class of expression that did not amount to a frontal assault on the First Amendment could hardly avoid being severely underinclusive; too much material that caused similar harm would not be covered. Let me deal with these and related objections in more detail.

A major problem with the proposed new unprotected class of expression is that restricting its coverage to sexually explicit violence would leave a large part, perhaps the majority, of violent pornography untouched. Any restriction that could be reconciled with present constitutional law would not cover the most prevalent form of violent material now available: material that depicts violence in a sexual context but is not quite sexually explicit—things like R-rated slasher films and images of violence that are omnipresent in our society. As we have noted, recent studies have suggested that violence as such is a more serious problem than sexual explicitness, although a fusion of the two is perhaps the most harmful. Donnerstein and his associates, for example, cite a recent study indicating that "for many normal individuals with already existing calloused attitudes about violence against women, just the depiction of a woman as victim of aggression *devoid of sexual content* can stimulate sexual arousal." [140] When I interviewed him, Donnerstein spoke at length about the problem of dealing with such pervasive images:

> We say that certain messages have negative attitudinal effects. The problem is that these messages are all over the

189

place, not just in pornography. For example, a recent *Time* magazine advertisement for an ABC show about a woman who fell in love with the man who raped her and killed her husband. What we're trying to say is that violent forms of pornography have that message, but, unfortunately, so does all the media. The strongest effects are from these messages or from slasher/violent R-rated films. . . . The new studies and even the old research show that there is no effect for the X-rated, per se, only with images of rape and violence, etc. Even G-rated material is this way if images of rape are shown. . . . And, in fact, new content analysis shows that X-rated material is the least violent. . . . it isn't that it is sexual . . . it is something about the violence and the combination. But you can take away the sex—a new Malamuth study shows that one third of the males get aroused just by violence. We are learning more and more. There's no question that violence is the prerequisite.[141]

A study published in 1981 by Malamuth and Check underscored both the harmful effects of violent images and their ubiquitous presence in our society. The researchers studied the effects on attitudes about sexual violence of two widely-viewed movies: *The Getaway,* starring Steve McQueen and Ali McGraw, in which a woman falls in love with the man who rapes her, thereby driving her husband to suicide, and Lina Wertmuller's *Swept Away,* in which a woman falls in love with a man who physically abuses and dominates her on an island after a shipwreck. The latter film became a *cause célèbre* for feminists although it was respectfully reviewed. According to Donnerstein, Linz, and Penrod:

> When questioned [several days later] . . . subjects reported seeing no connection between the survey and the movies they had seen earlier. The results showed that viewing the sexually aggressive films significantly increased male but not female acceptance of interpersonal violence, and tended to increase acceptance of rape myths. The important point here is that these effects happened not with X-rated materials but with images more suitable for prime time television.[142]

This finding was supported by the 1986 study of Donnerstein, Linz, and Berkowitz in which they isolated the different effects of sex and violence. As we have seen, the researchers arranged for four sets of

190

male college students to be angered by a confederate and then shown films with or without sexual violence. The students then responded differently to subsequent opportunities to express aggression against a male or female confederate of the experimenter. According to Donnerstein and company:

> The results showed that the men who viewed the aggressive pornographic film displayed the highest level of aggression against the woman, as was the case in the other studies discussed. . . . Most importantly, the aggression-only film, which was devoid of explicit sex, produced more aggression against the woman than the sexually explicit film that contained no violence or coercion. In fact, there were no differences in aggression against the female target for subjects in the sex-only film condition and the neutral film condition.[143]

These findings are consistent with earlier research.

Films stressing violence against women have also been found to desensitize men to the ethical dimensions of violence. Studies of violence on television have fairly consistently suggested that males exposed to it show subsequent desensitization and increase of aggressive tendencies (but these findings also have been criticized by responsible critics.).[144] Other studies conducted by major experimental researchers have shown desensitization, including less inclination to come to the aid of a victim in a laboratory setting.[145]

The problem of violent depictions is widespread and is far from limited to pornographic contexts. The studies conducted by Malamuth, Check, Donnerstein, Berkowitz, and Linz show that a wide variety of material may have negative effects on attitudes and inclinations; hard-core sex alone did not have as much impact as violent but artistic films such as *Swept Away*. According to Donnerstein, Linz, and Penrod, negative and aggressive attitudes "are just as likely to come about from exposure to many types of mass media—from soap operas to popular commercially released films."[146] Censorship of such material would be extremely hazardous to First Amendment interests. Some landmark films like Alfred Hitchcock's *Psycho* would fall by the wayside, as would some scenes from *Doctor Zhivago*, to name just two artistic examples from an endless list.

Relatedly, magazines like *Playboy* have been held to be more detrimental than more hard-core material because such publications foster ideologies of hedonism and manipulation. One defender of pornogra-

191

phy as an aesthetic art form agrees: "The effect of sentimentalizing materialism . . . is to transform the natural world into a pop art toy which exists for the Playboy's well-earned amusement." [147] But censoring such material would constitute a significant retreat from the restraints of *Miller;* even leaders of Citizens for Decency in Indianapolis understood the reasons to leave *Playboy* alone, and the *Final Report* of the 1986 Attorney General's Commission stressed that prosecutions of *Playboy* and related material are now rare. In this situation, a new unprotected category under the First Amendment that focused on sexually explicit violence would be largely symbolic. Is a new approach to sexual materials justified in the present risky environment if only symbolic results can be expected? [148]

Further, even if an exception to the First Amendment were stretched far enough to cover relevant material and also avoided being over-inclusive from a constitutional perspective, such a measure would simply not be effective. Enforcement would necessarily be either uneven or lax—even more than today. [149] In addition, pornographers, film makers, advertisers, and others who create sexual images would very possibly devise ways of side-stepping the law. One reason there is so much violence in depictions today is that such depictions appeal to primitive sensibilities without running afoul of obscenity law. According to Donnerstein, violent sex is a substitute for obscene sex. [150]

Another argument that should be mentioned involves the matter of harm. As we have discussed, even if violent pornography is correlated with harm, this is not in itself a reason to censor it, for many activities are so correlated. It is very likely that liquor is more strongly associated with aggression toward women than is pornography. This is reason enough to advocate and promote restraint in the use of beverage alcohol, but not to attempt to achieve prohibition. This example does not mean that censorship is always unwise or unprincipled, but the experience with the Eighteenth Amendment merits consideration when thinking about the advisability of a new classification of unprotected expression.

Further, the harms of pornography are intricately linked with individual and social benefits. Taking a new approach would mean intervening in a complex and delicate balance. The provision that any new unprotected category take account of artistic and social value would help mitigate the dangers of intervention, but the prospects of maintaining the fragile web of relationships involved seems problematic.

Finally, there are means of controlling pornography and sexual violence that may offset the need for a new constitutional approach. Anti-pornography talks and writing can affect the climate of acceptance. Protests, demonstrations, boycotts, and other private actions endorsed by the 1986 Attorney General's Commission can express and influence community standards. And what researchers call "debriefing"—efforts that include mass public information campaigns and workshops—would be of some benefit.[151] Social disapproval is normally a more effective deterrent than criminal laws, although it can cross over the line and become intolerance—a real danger, given the subtlety of issues raised in this chapter.[152] Furthermore, non-censorious regulatory measures such as zoning (especially following the 1986 *Renton* decision), nuisance laws, opaque cover laws, and special regulatory controls for new technology like telephone dial-a-porn can help limit or control the availability of pornography without attempting to eliminate it.[153] Society is not helpless in the fight against pornography, but it must recognize that it cannot eliminate all pornography for both philosophical and practical reasons.

There is one final point that militates against a new constitutional approach. Significant moral passions have been unleashed in the new politics of pornography that threaten a return to the earlier era governed by the logic of *Hicklin*. Should we seek to have courts adjudicate a wholly new, unprecedented approach in the present social and political environment?

Given the problems inherent in making violent pornography a new unprotected category under the First Amendment, should society simply tolerate all forms of sexual depiction, however degrading and violent? I do not think so. Some forms of pornography and sexual practice are indeed degrading of sensitivity and the human capacity for relationship. Because human nature is paradoxical, characterized by the pursuit of conflict (objectification of others) and agreement (respect of others in themselves), it would be irresponsible to advocate either total censorship or total tolerance. In the domain of expression, some limits are needed to acknowledge generally accepted standards of equal respect and reason. It is not irrational to be concerned about materials that seem to support or further anti-social attitudes and actions. While society must restrain the impulse to censor, it is also entitled to establish at least minimal standards of reticence and respect in the realm of expression.

The question of minimal social value is the key to an acceptable social policy. This approach brings us back to *Miller*, which is not unexplored constitutional territory but has a long history of adjudication in a progressively principled manner. It can do justice to the arguments

193

we have been considering about the utility and significance of pornography, which coexist with its harms, and about the ameliorating presence of artistic elements. Further, the *Miller* approach can be given an added gloss that addresses feminist and conservative concerns about violence. The major problem with *Miller* is that it has been couched in traditional conservative terms—"assimilationist" rather then "pluralist." [154] But as we have seen, feminist and conservative normative concepts are not necessarily mutually exclusive. It would be possible to recast *Miller* along pluralist lines to reflect feminists' understanding of equal respect in addition to its more traditional interpretations. Accepting this approach would also provide for liberal concerns to some extent: as we saw in Chapter 1, *Miller* protects the majority of sexual material, drawing a line between non-hard-core material and hardcore material unredeemed by social value. This solution acknowledges the validity of maintaining societal standards, but also recognizes the reality of legitimate competing viewpoints in a situation of cultural pluralism.

Recasting Obscenity Law: Miller with an Added Prong

Endorsing the basic *Miller* approach to the constitutional and legal treatment of sexual materials means affirming certain norms concerning sexual expressions as well as acknowledging the limits of efforts to censor in this realm of life. The acknowledgment of limits is based on normative concerns: as we have seen, much sexual material does possess appreciable social value and is entitled to protection for that reason. The sense of limits also rests on a certain pragmatic fatalism: the growth and spread of pornography have been a function of broader historical forces, including the development of new technologies and modernist forms of psychological knowledge. These factors, along with those leading to under-enforcement of present obscenity law that we discussed in Chapter 1, should contribute to a sense of modesty concerning the prospects for restricting sexual materials. From this perspective, limiting our censorship policy recommendations to the *Miller* approach is a practical compromise.

The *Miller* approach acknowledges society's interest in upholding certain values of equal respect. The *Miller* concept of obscenity as "patently offensive" hard-core depiction lacking social value provides a means of distinguishing acceptable from non-acceptable sexual depiction. To be sure, the line is not easy to draw, but if the approach is weighted on the side of free speech and is fairly well established as a

194

standard of abjudication, it offers the best available principle by which to proceed.

As we have seen, *Miller*'s logic is seen as largely conservative, embodying the more traditional understanding of normative sexuality; it also is balanced with liberal concerns. But *Miller*'s logic can also embrace the values of equal respect and personalization of desire and so meet both conservative and feminist concerns. At the same time, *Miller*'s tolerance of most forms of pornography guards against the unrealistic attempt to exclude all forms of inegalitarian and depersonalized sex. Because *Miller* is concerned with the relation of pornography to unacceptable sexual aggression and disrespect of women, its logic can be seen as reconciling feminist and conservative viewpoints in this matter as well. Nevertheless, *Miller* at present does not fully accommodate the feminist critique of violent pornography. To remedy this lack, *Miller*'s legal doctrine should be modified to cover only violent obscenity.[155]

As we have discussed, *Miller*'s test for obscenity has three major prongs: suspect material must appeal to prurient interest, give patent offense, and lack social value. Sexual depictions that portray sexual acts or genitilia in significant detail ("ultimate sex acts," "lewd exhibition") can be designated obscene.[156] And the following types of portrayals have also been found to be obscene: "photographs which focus on, exaggerate, or emphasize the genitilia or 'erogenous zones;'" "suggestive poses or lewdly intertwined bodies, even in the absence of actual sexual activity"; the "excess of detail."[157]

I recommend adding a fourth prong to the *Miller* test to deal with violent obscene depictions. This would actually narrow the test but would incorporate feminist concerns in so doing. Portrayals of murder, dismemberment, brutality, or violence in the context of obscene acts (that is, those which depict ultimate sexual acts, lewdly displayed naked bodies, or excess of sexual detail) would be subject to the designation of "violent obscenity."

This approach would differ from Sunstein's, for it would supplement and actually limit *Miller*. But it would make *Miller* more consistent with both recent research suggesting that sexually-oriented violence is more harmful than sexual depictions *per se,* and with the feminist critique that is more concerned with harm than morals. And by limiting the restriction of violent sex to obscene contexts, the relation between significant sexual arousal and violence would be under-

195

scored. Such a modification would be less risky than fashioning a new class of unprotected expression based on violent pornography as suggested by Sunstein and others, because it would not be a completely new approach but rather a further development of an established doctrine.

Miller has been adjudicated since 1973 and reflects over thirty years of Supreme Court rulings. Only hard-core materials have been the subject of convictions under *Miller*. In today's emotional climate, the standard of abjudication for sexual depictions must be responsible and settled and be able to show an established track record. A further virtue, as seen in the discussion of public opinion in chapter 1, is that there appears to be a greater social consensus for restricting violent sexual material than for other types. For this reason, prosecution of obscene violence is more likely to be effective and principled than attempts to restrict other forms of sexual materials. And the *Miller* approach appears to have provided safeguards against abuse. Where prosecutions have been reversed on appeal, the appeals courts have acted in a very principled manner.[158]

Two final points should be stressed concerning this approach. First, while most people agree that possession of artistic value should shield sexual material from prosecution, I also argue that even works that appear worthless or unimportant may actually be worthy of constitutional protection; we always should err on the side of protecting free speech. I thus agree with the recommendation of the 1986 Attorney General's commission that the printed word should be considered as completely protected by the First Amendment. Other forms of pornography, such as videos, cable television, and telephone dial-a-porn, present much larger problems than print. It is true that, because readers supply their own pictures from their imaginations, the effects of written fantasy may be more personal and powerful than those of still photographs or film.[159] Thus, the written word may actually be more harmful than pornographic pictures. But lines must be drawn somewhere, and the written word usually comes closer to art than photos or videos. Writing is inherently more abstract and symbolic: in the words of the Attorney General's Commission, "There remains a difference between reading a book and looking at pictures, even pictures printed on a page."[160]

Second, I want to make clear that my proposal for modifying *Miller* is consistent with the First Amendment and the broader purposes of the Constitution. While liberal principles are necessary to support the core areas of First Amendment protection, especially protection of speech that involves political or social issues or possesses artistic or intellectual value, a single theory cannot prevail in all domains of expression. Steven Shiffrin expresses the matter well:

> Scholar after scholar has set out to produce a different but more successful *general* theory [of speech]. All of these attempts, in my judgment, have been thwarted by the complexity of social reality. Speech interacts with the rest of our reality in too many complicated ways to allow the hope or the expectation that a single vision or a single theory could explain, or dictate helpful conclusions in, the vast terrain of speech regulation. In trying to move toward general theory, scholars have too often built abstractions without sufficient regard for the diverse contexts in which speech regulation exists.[161]

Shiffrin's position is consistent with the spheres of reality that I discussed earlier in this chapter. So while the First Amendment is—and should be—predominantly liberal, it may entertain non-liberal values in areas of expression that do not directly impinge on its political and intellectual core.

The modified, truncated liberal approach that I advocate is also consistent with the Constitution's treatment of fundamental rights. The Constitution is not premised on strict liberalism or a general right to liberty.[162] The Bill of Rights protects certain fundamental rights rather than requiring libertarianism across the board.[163] The approach of John Stuart Mill, which would limit individual liberty of association, taste, and conscience only to prevent harm to others, has proved inconsistent with the historical practice of American democracy and has found no support in American abjudication. Constitutional democracy does not disempower the branches of government from restricting liberty by law, judicial decision, and executive order. "Self government" means more than simply the libertarian right to engage in self-regarding actions.[164] Even though a predominantly liberal approach to speech is necessary to maintain an open society, the values of the open society are not exclusively libertarian. As I have argued, values of restraint based on the norms of civility and equal respect are necessary to foster a healthier society and cultural pluralism. Consequently, the restrictions inherent in the *Miller* approach are not inconsistent with a just and open society.

Conclusion

While the new politics of pornography has raised new questions about the negative effects of pornography and the modern doctrine of speech, its proponents' arguments do not justify major alterations of First Amendment principles. The measures they offer are suspect because of their unprecedented scope. The debate, although marred by lack of restraint and perspective on both sides, has at least brought a usually avoided subject to public attention and forced society to confront its attitudes toward pornography and its effects. As a result, individuals and groups have been encouraged to take action on the private level, and obscenity doctrine may be invigorated on the public level. Nevertheless, a wholly new approach to the adjudication of free speech and sexual materials—whether that of the Minneapolis/Indianapolis ordinance or the more responsible alternatives of Sunstein and others—should be greeted with great caution because of questions about its efficacy, its unpredictable consequences, and its lack of precedents. A more prudent course would be to recast the *Miller* approach, adjusting its rationale, its provisions, and its enforcement to reflect feminist values. It should focus on violent obscenity and the harm to women, while accommodating normative sexual standards.

This proposal to reform *Miller* is modest and subject to the criticism that it is largely symbolic. I have two responses. First, the obscenity exception is not simply symbolic; it is potentially enforceable, given adequate social consensus, and it does recognize the difference between constructive and destructive forms of sexual depiction. To some extent, it honors the norm of equal respect that conservatives and feminists uphold. Second, given the nature of pornography and its historical and social roles, we cannot expect to achieve definitive triumphs either in controlling sexual depictions or in distinguishing acceptable from unacceptable forms. We must err on the side of freedom without forsaking our responsibility to maintain a decent and just society. Controversy and ambiguity cannot be avoided; the struggle detailed in this book reflects the tensions in our natures and the conflict of legitimate values in society.

NOTES

Introduction

1. Minneapolis Code of Ordinances (MCO), Title 7, ch. 139.20, sec. 3, subd. (gg), (1). Specific examples and further analysis of the ordinance will be presented in Chapter 3.

2. *Miller v. California,* 413 U.S. 15 (1973), at 24. *Miller* established the present test for the determination of obscenity. See Chapter 1.

3. In this regard the ordinance reflected the feminist "ethic of care" for others and the community. See, e.g., Jean Grimshaw, *Philosophy and Feminist Thinking* (University of Minnesota Press, 1986), pp. 215–26, "On Caring." Carol Gilligan devotes a large part of her pathbreaking book on the distinctive character of women's moral thinking and the ethic of care: *In a Different Voice* (Harvard University Press, 1982), esp. chs. 3 and 6. This ethic is similar to what Jethro K. Lieberman has labeled the "fiduciary" or "environmental" ethic. This ethic, which now governs tort law to a significant extent, sees the exercise of individual liberty as fraught with risks, and favors instead restraining individual action in order to protect the community from undesired harm. See Lieberman, *The Litigious Society* (Basic Books, 1981), ch. 1.

4. *Transcript of Minneapolis Public Hearings on Ordinances to Add Pornography as Discrimination against Women,* Session 1, Monday, 12 Dec. 1983, pp. 4–6.

5. *Boston Globe,* 10 Nov. 1985, p. 33.

6. *Los Angeles Times,* 5 June 1985, sec. 2, p. 1.

7. Lynn Hanneb and Daniel Grossberg, "Porn Censors Lose in Madison: Feminists' Campaign Poses Alternatives," *Against the Current* (Center for Changes, Detroit, Michigan), Jan.-Feb. 1986, pp. 37–38; "Anti-porno law proposal readied," *Wisconsin State Journal,* 18 Oct. 1984, p. 6, sec. 1.

8. *Ms.,* April 1985, p. 47.

9. Thus the law may censor expression that meets the legal criteria for obscenity, but it cannot discriminate among viewpoints contained in (or implied by) different obscene materials; that is, "egalitarian" obscenity may not

be treated differently from "inegalitarian" obscenity. Of course, prosecutors may exercise discretion in choosing their cases and the severity of penalty when they deal with different types of obscenity. But differential enforcement cannot be written into the law, and prosecutorial discretion must not exceed reasonable limits.

10. See, e.g., David M. Rabban, "The Emergence of Modern First Amendment Doctrine," *University of Chicago Law Review* 50 (1983): 1205; Lillian BeVier, "The First Amendment and Political Speech: An Inquiry into the Substance and Limits of Principle," *Stanford Law Review* 30 (1978): 299. The proper remedy for the undesirable effects of speech—whether physical danger from action taken after the speech, harm to the reputation or status of the group spoken about, or the success of political views that most consider abhorrent—is either counter-speech or police action against those who act on the basis of speech. Legal restriction of the speech itself—unless it poses a direct and clear danger to society or is held not to meet the low threshold of intellectual value—is not allowed. Except in special limited circumstances, speech is considered distinct from action, so harms threatened by speech are dealt with differently than are harms threatened by action. Thus, it was a major victory for the tolerance of free speech when the Supreme Court began to distinguish—after a laborious struggle—the doctrine governing threatening political speech from the criminal law of attempts. See Rabban, "Modern First Amendment Doctrine," pp. 1271–73, and generally.

11. The concept of equality is relational: it is meaningful only in relation to more fundamental substantive ends or values. See, e.g., Peter Westen, "The Empty Idea of Equality," *Harvard Law Review* 95 (1982): 537; Fourteenth Amendment equal protection cases involving fundamental rights collapse into simple fundamental rights analysis because the concept of equality is without substantive content.

12. Ronald Dworkin, "Liberalism," in *Public and Private Morality,* ed. Stuart Hampshire (Cambridge University Press, 1980), p. 127. My discussion is also indebted to Robin West, "Liberalism Rediscovered: A Pragmatic Definition of the Liberal Vision," *University of Pittsburgh Law Review* 46 (1985): 673–79.

13. Dworkin, p. 127; see also West, p. 678.

14. See Catharine MacKinnon, *Feminism Unmodified: Discourses on Life and Law* (Harvard University Press, 1987), ch. 14; "Pornography, Civil Rights, and Speech," *Harvard Civil Rights-Civil Liberties Law Review* 20 (1985): 1.

15. See, e.g., Richard John Neuhaus, *The Naked Public Square: Religion and Democracy in America* (Eerdmans, 1984); Francis Canavan, *Freedom of Expression: Purpose as Limit* (Carolina Academic Press, 1984).

16. See, e.g., MacKinnon, *Feminism Unmodified,* pp. 65, 71–73, 164–70; Lorrene M. G. Clark, "Liberalism and Pornography," in *Pornography and Censorship,* ed. David Copp and Susan Wendell (Prometheus Books, 1983), pp. 45–59.

17. See, e.g., Alison Jagger, *Feminist Politics and Human Nature* (1983), esp. p. 45; Susanne Kappeler, *The Pornography of Representation* (University

of Minnesota Press, 1986); Michel Foucault, *Power/Knowledge: Selected Interviews and Other Writings, 1972–77*, ed. Colin Gordon (Pantheon, 1980).

18. Varda Burstyn, "Political Precedents and Moral Crusades: Women, Sex and the State," in *Women against Censorship*, ed. Burstyn (Douglas and McIntyre, 1985), p. 21.

19. According to Russell Hanson, periodic struggles over the meaning of democracy and the nature of power in America have been characterized by battles over the key terms to define the nature of political relationships. See Hanson, *The Democratic Imagination in America: Conversations with Our Past* (Princeton University Press, 1985).

20. Even critics of liberalism acknowledge the dangers of "post-liberal" forms of politics because of the danger that respect for individual rights that are central to liberalism will be abandoned. See Roberto Unger, *Law in Modern Society* (Free Press, 1976), ch. 3. See also Octavio Paz, *One Earth, Four or Five Worlds: Reflections on Contemporary History*, trans. Helen Lane (Harcourt, Brace, Jovanovich, 1985).

21. Anti-pornography crusades have traditionally been emotional affairs in which certain symbols are charged with energy. See Louis A. Zurcher and R. George Kirkpatrick *Citizens for Decency: Antipornography Crusades as Status Defense* (University of Texas Press, 1976). On the psychological and emotional nature of such campaigns, see Joseph Gusfield, *Symbolic Crusade: Status Politics and the American Temperance Movement* (University of Illinois Press, 1963). Note that Zurcher and Kirkpatrick display the onesidedness that I am discussing: they downplay the zeal of anti-censorship forces, which can also be unreasonable.

22. Richard Sennett, *The Fall of Public Man* (Knopf, 1974).

23. On how political elites' support for civil liberties is crucial (an aspect of the theory of democratic elitism), see, e.g., Herbert McClosky, "Consensus and Ideology in American Politics," *American Political Science Review* 58 (1964): 361; David G. Lawrence, "Procedural Norms and Tolerance: A Reassessment," *American Political Science Review* 70 (1976): 80.

24. Interviews with Matthew Stark, executive director, Minnesota Civil Liberties Union, March 1986; Michael Gradison, executive director, Indiana Civil Liberties Union, March 1985. I will discuss these post-ordinance measures in Chapter 3.

25. Free speech has normative and pragmatic or consequentialist justifications. The former pertains to the right of individuals to engage in free speech despite the empirical consequences. The latter pertains to the useful consequences or benefits presumed to flow from free speech. My argument here takes the latter approach. See Fred Berger, ed., *Freedom of Expression* (Wadsworth, 1980), intro.

26. Lee Bollinger, *The Tolerant Society: Freedom of Speech and Extremist Speech in America* (Oxford University Press, 1986). See also Alexander Meiklejohn, *Political Freedom* (Oxford University Press, 1965), and Richard Sennett, *The Uses of Disorder* (Vintage, 1970).

27. See Donald Alexander Downs, *Nazis in Skokie: Freedom, Community, and the First Amendment* (University of Notre Dame Press, 1985). For a

201

representative case, see *Vietnamese Fishermen's Association v. Knights of the Ku Klux Klan,* 543 F. Supp. 198 (S.D. Tex. 1982).

28. See Cass Sunstein, "Pornography and the First Amendment," *Duke Law Journal* (1986), p. 595.

29. See MacKinnon, *Feminism Unmodified*; Andrea Dworkin, *Pornography: Men Possessing Women* (Perigee, 1981).

30. Freud saw sexual taboos as the basis of individual psychology and of familial social order. See, e.g., *Civilization and Its Discontents* (Norton, 1961), *Totem and Taboo* (Norton, 1950).

31. See, e.g., Donald Symons, *The Evolution of Human Sexuality* (Oxford University Press, 1979); Janet Shibley Hyde, *Understanding Human Sexuality,* 3d. ed. (McGraw Hill, 1986), p. 10.

32. Lawrence Stone, "Sex in the West: The Strange History of Human Sexuality," *New Republic,* 8 July 1985, p. 36. See also pp. 25–37; and Walter Kendrick, *The Secret Museum: Pornography in Modern Culture* (Viking, 1987), pp. 33, 51.

33. See, e.g., Peter Michelson, *The Aesthetics of Pornography* (Herder and Herder, 1971). Susan Sontag, "The Pornographic Imagination," in *Perspectives on Pornography,* ed. Douglas A. Hughes (St. Martins, 1970).

34. Perhaps the most representative critique of the emotivist theory of knowledge and ethics is Alasdair MacIntyre, *After Virtue: A Study in Moral Theory* (University of Notre Dame Press, 1981).

35. On the importance of sublimation, see Freud, *Civilization and Its Discontents;* Geza Roheim, *The Origin and Function of Culture* (Nervous and Mental Disease Monographs, no. 69, 1943).

36. See *The Portable Jung,* pt. 1, ch. 6, "Aion: Phenomenology of the Self," "The Shadow," pp. 139–62.

37. The selective and irregular enforcement of certain sexual laws concerning obscenity, prostitution, varient sexual practice, etc., illustrates this ambiguity.

38. Milton, *Areopagitica,* in *The Portable Milton* (Penguin, 1976), p. 166.

39. Mary Midgley, *Beast and Man: The Roots of Human Nature* (Meridian, 1980), p. 80.

40. Weber, "Politics as a Vocation," in *Max Weber: Essays in Sociology,* ed. Girth and Mills (Oxford University Press, 1946). Weber's ethic of responsibility avoids the pitfalls of absolutism and Machiavellianism by espousing "passion and perspective," or moral commitment balanced by an objective assessment of competing values and interests in a complex world. Weber's "professional politician" possesses "the knowledge of tragedy with which all action, but especially political action, is truly interwoven." See my former teacher, William Ker Muir, *Police: Streetcorner Politicians* (University of Chicago Press, 1977), pp. 50–51.

41. According to Laurence Tribe, "the Constitution is an historically discontinuous composition; it is the product, over time, of a series of not altogether coherent compromises; it mirrors no single vision or philosophy but reflects instead a set of sometimes reinforcing and sometimes conflicting ideals and notions." *American Constitutional Law,* 2d ed. (Foundation Press, 1987),

p. 1. See also T. Alexander Aleinikoff, "Constitutional Law in the Age of Balancing," *Yale Law Journal* 96 (1987): 943.

42. *Final Report,* Attorney General's Commission on Pornography, (U.S. Department of Justice, July 1986).

Chapter One

1. The Fraser Commission in Canada was more skeptical about the harms of pornography than was the 1986 U.S. Attorney General's Commission. *Report of the Special Committee on Pornography and Prostitution,* Paul Fraser, Q. C., chairman (1985), esp. p. 99. The Williams Committee in England also came to liberal conclusions after considering the pornography issue. See A. W. B. Simpson, *Pornography and Politics: The Williams Committee in Retrospect* (Waterlow Publishers, 1983). Like the 1970 commission report in the U.S., the Williams Committee report essentially was shelved.

2. *Final Report,* Attorney General's Commission on Pornography (U.S. Department of Justice, 1986), ch. 5, esp. pp. 322–35.

3. *Final Report,* pt. 2, ch. 5.

4. *Report of the Commission on Obscenity and Pornography* (Bantam Books, 1970), pt. 2. The Williams Committee in England came to roughly similar conclusions in 1979. See Simpson, *Pornography and Politics: Report of the Home Office,* p. 6186. Most free speech theorists supported such liberalism in the 1960s and 1970s. According to Frederick Schauer, free speech theory in this period stressed "strategies for achieving maximum protection" of speech in as many areas of expression as possible. "Must Speech Be Special?" *Northwestern Law Review* 78 (1983): 1284.

5. See, e.g., Hendrick Hertzberg, "Big Boobs: Ed Meese and His Pornography Commission," *New Republic,* 14, 21 July 1986, pp. 21–24.

6. See, e.g., the approving use of the commission's conclusions by Cass Sunstein, University of Chicago Law School, in Sunstein, "Pornography and the First Amendment."

7. See, e.g., Stephen Shiffrin, "The First Amendment and Economic Regulation: Away from a General Theory of the First Amendment," *Northwestern Law Review* 78 (1983): 1212.

8. Robert Post, "Cultural Heterogeneity and the Law: Pornography, Blasphemy and the First Amendment," *California Law Review* 76 (1988), p. 125.

9. See Rogers M. Smith, *Liberalism and American Constitutional Law* (Harvard University Press, 1985), ch. 4; Post, "Cultural Heterogeneity and the Law."

10. See, e.g., *Schenck v. U.S.,* 249 U.S. 47 (1919); *Dennis v. U.S.,* 341 U.S. 494 (1951).

11. 315 U.S. 568 (1942), at 572. Of course, forms of expression tied to criminal action do not receive First Amendment protection: speech that is an integral part of solicitation, conspiracy, harassment, threat, intimidation, coercion, fraud, or misrepresentation. See Franklyn Haiman, *Speech and Law in a Free Society* (University of Chicago Press, 1981), chs. 10, 11, 13.

12. 395 U.S. 444 (1969).

13. See, e.g., *New York Times v. Sullivan,* 376 U.S. 255 (1964): libel of public officials protected unless done with malice; *Cohen v. California* 403 U.S. 15 (1971): offensive speech and fighting words given much more constitutional protection; *Memoirs v. Massachusetts,* 383 U.S. 413 (1966): new liberal test for obscenity codified.

14. See, e.g., Harry Kalven, Jr., *The Negro and the First Amendment* (University of Chicago Press, 1965).

15. See John Hart Ely, *Democracy and Distrust: A Theory of Judicial Review* (Harvard University Press, 1980), esp. ch. 5.

16. See, e.g., *New York Times v. Sullivan.* On the fiduciary ethic in contemporary tort law, see Lieberman, *The Litigious Society,* esp. ch. 1.

17. See, e.g., *Buckley v. Valeo,* 424 U.S. 1 (1976); *First National Bank of Boston v. Bellotti,* 4355 U.S. 765 (1978); *Citizens for Rent Control v. City of Berkeley,* 454 U.S. 290 (1981). One case may be construed to favor substantive equality concerns over equal liberty of expression. In *Roberts v. U.S. Jaycees,* 468 U.S. 609 (1984), the Court ruled that the Jaycees could not exclude women despite their claim that freedom of association gave them this right. The Court sidestepped the freedom of association issue by concluding that the Jaycees were not a true private association entitled to full freedom of association protections.

18. *American Booksellers Ass'n. v. Hudnut,* 598 F. Supp. 1316 (1984), aff'd 771 F. 2d 323 (7th Cir. 1985).

19. Isaiah Berlin, "Two Concepts of Liberty," in Berlin, *Four Essays on Liberty* (Oxford University Press, 1969).

20. John Stuart Mill, *On Liberty,* in *The Essential Works of John Stuart Mill* (Bantam Books, 1961); Thomas Scanlon, "A Theory of Freedom of Expression," *Philosophy and Public Affairs* 1 (1972): 204.

21. See Kenneth Karst, "Equality as a Central Principle in the First Amendment," *University of Chicago Law Review* 43 (1975): 20. Content neutrality and equality are reciprocal First Amendment values.

22. See Post, "Cultural Heterogeneity and the Law." In a recent article, Robert Cover argues that constitutional meaning is forged and elaborated by the "constant struggle" of groups to define their own meanings and constitutional principles and to "maintain the independence and authority of their *nomos.*" Cover, "Forward: Nomos and Narrative," Harvard Law Review 97 (1983): 4. But groups are not given any special First Amendment status above and beyond individuals. Similarly, the press is not given any special constitutional treatment that individuals and groups do not enjoy, although strong arguments have been made by scholars and Justice Stewart for such treatment. See, e.g., *Houchins v. KQED, Inc.,* 438 U.S. 1 (1978).

23. 458 U.S. 747 (1982). See Frederick Schauer, "Codifying the First Amendment: *New York v. Ferber,*" *Supreme Court Review* (1982), p. 285.

24. Fried, *Right and Wrong* (Harvard University Press, 1978), ch. 2. The Williams Committee in England unanimously endorsed a harms principle in its recommendations issued in 1979. See A. W. B. Simpson, *Pornography and Politics,* esp. pp. 31–33, 63–65.

25. See, e.g., Ronald Dworkin, *Taking Rights Seriously* (Harvard University Press, 1977).

26. *Beauharnais v. Illinois,* 343 U.S. 250 (1952). The federal Skokie case is *Collin v. Smith,* 447 F. Supp. 676 (N.D. Ill. 1978), aff'd 578 F. 2d 1197 (7th Cir. 1978). For another representative federal case that rejected a state restriction of expression based on group libel logic, see *Sambo's Restaurants, Inc. v. City of Ann Arbor,* 663 F. 2d 686 (6th Cir. 1981).

27. Owen Fiss, "Groups and the Equal Protection Clause," *Philosophy and Public Affairs* 5 (1976): 107. See also Van Dyke, "Justice as Fairness: For Groups?" *American Political Science Review* 69 (1976): 607 and Morton J. Horwitz, "The Jurisprudence of Brown and the Dilemmas of Liberalism," *Harvard Civil Rights–Civil Liberties Law Review* 14 (1979): 599.

28. On state neutrality toward ethnic groups as the basis of traditional liberal policy, see Nathan Glazer, *Affirmative Discrimination: Ethnic Inequality and Public Policy* (Basic Books, 1978), ch. 1. For a similar liberal theory concerning gender discrimination, see David Kirp, Mark Yudof, and Marlene Franks, *Gender Justice* (University of Chicago Press, 1986), a book that has been scathingly reviewed by some feminists.

29. See, e.g., Michael Kammen, *Spheres of Liberty: Changing Perceptions of Liberty in American Culture* (University of Wisconsin Press, 1986).

30. Mill, of course, espoused state non-interference with thought and speech in *On Liberty.* But Mill's broader social theory, which embraced utilitarianism and occasionally even conservatism, was sometimes consistent with an active state advancing substantive ends. Mill, *On Liberty,* in *The Essential Works of John Stuart Mill,* ed. Max Lerner (Bantam Books, 1961). On the inconsistency between *On Liberty* and Mill's other works of social theory, see Gertrude Himmelfarb, *On Liberty and Liberalism: The Case of John Stuart Mill* (Knopf, 1974).

31. See West, "Liberalism Rediscovered." West calls value-neutral liberalism "agnostic liberalism."

32. David Tribe, *Questions of Censorship* (George Allen & Unwin, 1973), pp. 19–20.

33. See, e.g., *Winters v. New York,* 333 U.S. 507 (1948). This case dealt with overbreadth and vagueness of a New York statute that defined depictions of violent criminal deeds as obscene.

34. Frederick Schauer, *The Law of Obscenity* (Bureau of National Affairs, 1976), p. 1.

35. Kendrick, *Secret Museum,* p. 6.

36. David Tribe, *Questions of Censorship,* pp. 19–21, 55. David Foxon, *Libertine Literature in England 1660–1745* (University Books, 1965), pp. 49–50.

37. Kendrick, *Secret Museum,* p. 33. Kendrick also holds that "our society has been unique in regarding increased license, sexual or otherwise, as a gain" (p. 51). On the role of shame in historical societies and the concomitant restriction of sex to the private realm, see Bruce Ritter, "Pornography and Privacy," in *Final Report,* Attorney General's Commission, pp. 115–34.

38. 1 *Keble* 620 (K.B.), 83 Eng. Rep. 1146 (1663). On the significance of *Sedley,* see Schauer, *Law of Obscenity,* p. 4; and the interesting account of this case and many other cases in Albert B. Gerber, *Sex, Pornography, and Justice* (Lyle Stuart, 1965).

39. Many prosecutions for obscene libel were dismissed, and successful prosecutions were politically motivated. See, e.g., *Queen v. Read,* Fortescue's Reports 93, 92 Eng. Rep. 777 (1708); *Dominus Rex. v. Curll,* 25 Str. 789, 93 Eng. Rep. 849 (1727); *The King v. John Wilkes,* 2 Wils. K.B. 151, 95 Eng. Rep. 737 (1764). See H. Montgomery Hyde, *A History of Pornography* (Dell, 1964), p. 175.

40. *Final Report,* p. 240.

41. Hyde, *History of Pornography,* pp. 176–78; Schauer, *Law of Obscenity,* p. 6.

42. Kendrick, *Secret Museum,* p. 84.

43. Peter Gay, *Education of the Senses: The Bourgeois Experience, Victoria to Freud* (Oxford University Press, 1984), p. 369.

44. L.R. 3 Q.B. (1868), at 371.

45. *Report of Commission on Obscenity,* pp. 351–52.

46. Kendrick, *Secret Museum,* p. 123.

47. Anthony Comstock, *Traps for the Young,* ed. Robert Bremner (Cambridge, Mass., 1967), p. 9. See also Kendrick, *Secret Museum,* pp. 139–40.

48. The *Lady Chatterly* case was *Commonwealth v. Delacey,* 271 Mass. 327, 171 N.E. 455 (1930). See also the portrayal of later federal actions against *Lady Chatterly* in Charles Rembar, *The End of Obscenity* (Bantam Books, 1968), pp. 111–48. The *American Tragedy* case was *Commonwealth v. Friede,* 271 Mass. 318, 171 N.E. 472 (1930). See also Tribe, *American Constitutional Law,* 1st ed., p. 658. The *Well of Loneliness* case was *People v. Friede,* 133 Misc. 611, 233 N.Y.s. 565 (Magis. Ct. 1929).

49. *U.S. v. One Book Called 'Ulysses,'* 5 F. Supp. 182 (S.D.N.Y. 1933), aff'd 72 F. 2d 705 (2d Cir. 1934). The approach in this case was suggested earlier by Judge Lerned Hand in *U.S. v. Kennerly,* 209 F. 119, 121 (S.D.N.Y. 1913).

50. See, e.g., *U.S. v. Levine,* 83 F. (2d Cir. 1936) in which a conviction for otherwise obscene material was invalidated because the *Ullysses* test was not used; *People v. Larsen,* 5 N.Y.S. 2d 55 (Ct. Spec. Sess. 1938) which held that *Life* magazine pictures of birth were not obscene; *Attorney General v. Book Named "Forever Amber,"* 323 Mass. 302, 81 N.E. 2d 663 (1948) which found *Forever Amber* not obscene even though it referred to sex acts "almost to the point of tedium." Compare: *Attorney General v. Book Named "God's Little Acre,"* 326 Mass. 282, 83 N.E. 2d 819 (1950); this found Erskine Caldwell's *God's Little Acre* obscene because of "abundance of realistic detail." On other cases, see Schauer, *Law of Obscenity,* pp. 26–27.

51. *Final Report,* p. 246.

52. In 1948, Doubleday raised a First Amendment defense in the trial of Edmund Wilson's *Memoirs of Hecate County: Doubleday & Co. v. New York,* 335 U.S. 848 (1948). The divided Court, whose decision upheld the publisher's obscenity conviction, did not address this issue.

53. *Roth v. U.S.,* 354 U.S. 476 (1957), at 484.

54. 354 U.S., at 487, 489.

55. See also *Butler v. Michigan,* 352 U.S. 380 (1957), decided earlier

that year, for a similar rejection: censorship of material across the board in order to protect children is "to burn the house to roast the pig."

56. See John E. Nowak, Ronald D. Rotunda, and J. Nelson Young, *Constitutional Law* (West Publishing, 1983), p. 1011.

57. 354 U.S., at 487. See also Harry Clor, *Obscenity and Public Morality: Censorship in a Liberal Society* (University of Chicago Press, 1969), p. 33.

58. In general, see Clor, *Obscenity and Public Morality*, pp. 35–40.

59. Kendrick, *Secret Museum*, p. 202.

60. *Smith v. California*, 361 U.S. 147 (1961), at 152–55; *Kingsley International Pictures Corp. v. Regents*, 360 U.S. 684 (1959), at 688. The film in this case was the movie version of *Lady Chatterly's Lover*.

61. 370 U.S. 478 (1962), at 482.

62. 378 U.S. 184 (1964), at 191. See also Clor, *Obscenity and Public Morality*, p. 70: the trend from *Roth* to *Jacobellis* was "libertarian one-sidedness" (p. 75).

63. 383 U.S., at 419–20, emphasis added. Justices Clark and White, in dissent, accused the Court of abandoning, in effect, *Roth*'s balancing approach. 383 U.S., at 442–45; 461.

64. Schauer, *Law of Obscenity*, p. 43.

65. Kendrick, *Secret Museum*, pp. 211–12. Two companion cases decided along with *Memoirs* seemed less liberal. In *Ginzburg v. U.S.*, 383 U.S. 463, the Court upheld a conviction for sending sexual materials through the mail, even though the material was probably not obscene in itself, because the "leer of the sensualist" had "permeated" the way the material was marketed. "Pandering" could contribute to making material obscene. 383 U.S., at 465–70. In *Mishkin v. New York*, 383 U.S. 502, the Court held that depictions of deviant sexual behavior could be prurient even though they would not be arousing to the average person in the community. Prurience is a function of the intended effect on the probable recipient. This approach is part of the "variable obscenity" doctrine—different levels for minors and pandering.

66. *Redrup v. New York*, 386 U.S. 767 (1967).

67. *Final Report*, p. 247. Schauer, *Law of Obscenity*, p. 44. See also the *Final Report*'s analysis of the pornography industry's growth after 1970, in pt. 2, ch. 4.

68. See *Final Report*, pp. 1499–1802 for numerous other examples.

69. Kendrick, *Secret Museum*, p. 212.

70. 394 U.S. 557 (1969), at 564, 568. *Stanley* is actually at least as much a "privacy" case as a free speech case. The Court (per Justice Marshall) stated that the Founding Fathers "recognized the significance of man's spiritual nature, of his feelings and his intellect" and that "our whole constitutional heritage rebels at the thought of giving government the power to control men's minds." This is strange language considering that the Court has excluded obscenity from First Amendment protection precisely because it lacks intellectual value.

71. "An Empirical Inquiry into the Effects of Miller v. California on the Control of Obscenity." New York University Obscenity Project, *New York University Law Review* 52 (1977): 843–44. The requiem was celebrated by

Engdahl, "Requiem to Roth: The Obscenity Doctrine Is Changing," *University of Michigan Law Review* 68 (1969): 185.

72. 413 U.S. 15 (1973), at 24.

73. See Schauer, *Law of Obscenity*, pp. 150–51. Not all states have abandoned *Memoirs* for *Miller*. Until very recently, California was one state (though not the only one) that maintained the old *Memoirs* approach. See *People v. Enskat*, 109 Cal. Rptr. 433, 33 Cal. 3d 900 (1973), cert. denied, 418 U.S. 937. In January 1987, however, the governor signed Senate Bill 139 which incorporated the *Miller* standards on value. See *Final Report*, p. 1290. The Wisconsin Supreme Court adopted *Miller* soon after it came down, but struck down the state obscenity law in 1980 in *State v. Princess Cinema of Milwaukee*, 96 Wis. 2d 646 (1980).

74. *Jacobellis v. Ohio*, 378 U.S. 184 (1964), at 191.

75. 413 U.S., at 25. For example, sado-masochistic materials have been added with Supreme Court approval. See *Ward v. Illinois*, 431 U.S. 767 (1977), at 773. Patent offense is a subjective standard to be applied by the jury, as is prurient interest. However, within a year the Court made these standards more matters of law (see below).

76. Schauer, *Law of Obscenity*, pp. 111–12.

77. *Final Report*, pp. 271, 1289, 1294–95. The two cases that found issues of *Penthouse* obscene (and lacking serious value) are *Penthouse International v. McAuliffe*, 610 F.2d 1353 (5th Cir. 1980) (Jan. 1978 issue), and *Penthouse International v. Webb*, 594 F. Supp. 1186 (N.D. Ga. 1984 (Sept. 1984 issue). See also *Final Report*, p. 1289. See *Final Report*, fn. 1518 (pp. 1291–93) for cases in which courts found obscenity and lack of serious value (e.g. movie *Deep Throat*, explicit intercourse, lesbian activity, etc.). See *Final Report*, fn. 1528 (p. 1295) for cases in which serious value was found. Courts have also distinguished "sham" value from "true" value: see *Final Report*, p. 1289.

78. Justice Brennan strongly dissented in *Miller*. He shed the ambiguity that had hounded him in previous obscenity cases and stressed the "severe problems arising from the lack of fair notice, from the chill on protected expression, and from the stress imposed on the state and federal judicial machinery." 413 U.S., at 93.

79. 418 U.S. 153 (1974), at 181. The Court affirmed this position in *Erznoznik v. Jacksonville*, 422 U.S. 205 (1975).

80. *Final Report*, p. 271. See also Schauer, *Law of Obscenity*, p. 115.

81. 427 U.S. 50 (1976), at 70. In 1978 the Court made an analogous decision in *FCC v. Pacifica Foundation*, 438 U.S. 726 (1978). The Court upheld the power of the FCC to regulate the use of non-obscene indecent speech on radio broadcasts.

82. *Schad v. Borough of Mount Ephraim*, 452 U.S. 61 (1981).

83. 475 U.S. 41 (1986).

84. *Renton* has encouraged judicial tolerance of zoning schemes that have more bite than previous schemes. See, e.g., *Dumas v. City of Dallas*, 648 F. Supp. 1061 (N.D. Tex. 1986), which relied heavily on *Renton* to uphold Dallas's bold new zoning measure.

85. 458 U.S. 747 (1982).

86. *Brockett v. Spokane Arcades, Inc.*, 472 U.S. 491 (1985). Another case deserves mention. In *New York v. P.J. Video, Inc.*, 475 U.S. 868 (1986), the Supreme Court reaffirmed the policy that the standard for probable cause in First Amendment cases—searches for materials claiming First Amendment status—is no different than in searches for any other allegedly illegal material: there is no special First Amendment status within the Fourth Amendment.

87. 107 S. Ct. 1918 (1987).

88. *Final Report,* p. 461. See also pt. 4, ch. 8, "Production and Distribution of Sexually Explicit Materials."

89. On decreased prosecutions, see *New York University Obscenity Project.* This study also reported overall increases in the availability of sexually explicit and obscene materials nationwide. On decreased appeals, see R. E. Riggs, "Miller v. California Revisited: An Empirical Note," *Brigham Young University Law Review* 2 (1981): 247.

90. See, e.g., Valerie P. Hans and Neil Vidmar, *Judging the Jury* (Plenum Press, 1986), pp. 120–27.

91. See *New York University Obscenity Project,* esp. conclusions on pp. 928–30; and *Final Report,* pp. 366–72.

92. Interview with David Gross, Minneapolis Assistant City Attorney, Aug. 1985; Richard Kammen, Indianapolis pornography attorney, June 1985.

93. See, e.g., Morse Peckham, *Art and Pornography* (Basic Books, 1969); Philip Rieff, *The Triumph of the Theraputic* (Harper, 1966), esp. ch. 8 on the "remissive" needs of individuals in culture.

94. Sources claim that the porn industry is at least an eight-billion dollar industry. See Galloway and Thornton, "Crackdown on Pornography—A No-Win Battle," *U.S. News and World Report,* 4 June 1984, p. 84. See also *Final Report,* pt. 2, ch. 4. The Attorney General's Commission linked the porn industry to organized crime: pt. 4, ch. 4.

95. *Report of the Commission on Obscenity,* pp. 7–8, 28, 214–18 (on the satiation effect).

96. *Report of the Commission on Obscenity,* pt. 3, ch. 1, "Traffic and Distribution of Sexually Oriented Materials in the United States." For a later overview, see Neil Malamuth, "Aggression against Women: Cultural and Individual Causes," in *Pornography and Sexual Aggression,* ed. Neil Malamuth and Edward Donnerstein (Academic Press, 1984), pp. 30–31. The works upon which the last statement is based are P. E. Dietz and B. Evans, "Pornographic Imagery and Prevalence of Paraphilia," *American Journal of Psychiatry* 139 (1982): 1493–95; and Donald Smith, "The Social Content of Pornography," *Journal of Communication* 26 (1976): 16–33.

97. See J. E. Scott and S. J. Cuvelier, "Violence in Playboy Magazine: A Longitudinal Study," Archives of Sexual Behavior (in print); and T. S. Palys, "Testing the Common Wisdom: The Social Content of Video Pornography," *Canadian Psychology* 27 (1986): 22 These studies are discussed in Daniel Linz, Steven D. Penrod, and Edward Donnerstein, "The Attorney General's Commission on Pornography: The Gaps between 'Findings' and Facts," *American Bar Foundation Research Journal* (1987), pp. 717–18.

98. Edward Donnerstein, Daniel Linz, and Steven Penrod, *The Question*   209

of Pornography: Research Findings and Policy Implications (Free Press, 1987), p. 91.

99. D. Byrne and K. Kelley, "Pornography and Sex Research," in *Pornography and Sexual Aggression,* ed. Malamuth and Donnerstein, pp. 1–2.

100. "Anti-Pornography Laws and First Amendment Values," *Harvard Law Review* 98 (1984): 478–79, esp. n. 109. See also Ann Garry, "Pornography and Respect for Women," in *Pornography and Censorship,* ed. Copp and Wendell, pp. 61–70.

101. Interviews with Edward Donnerstein, July 1985, and Daniel Linz, Sept. 1986, both in Madison, Wisconsin. This position comes close to reflecting that of the 1986 commission, except that the commission is more confident about the negative effects of degrading but non-violent materials.

102. See Barry W. Lynn, "Civil Rights Ordinances and the Attorney General's Commission: New Developments in Pornography Regulation," *Harvard Civil Rights-Civil Liberties Law Review* 21 (1986): 66–68.

103. Dan Linz interview.

104. Ed Donnerstein, perhaps the foremost researcher in the field, stressed this point again and again in my interview. See also Linz, Penrod, and Donnerstein, "The Attorney General's Commission on Pornography."

105. See Lieberman, *Litigious Society,* on environmental ethics. Pornography has been interpreted as a form of disease or moral pollution that must be purged by regulation. See Peter Gay, *Education of the Senses,* pp. 377–78.

106. Gallup Poll in *Newsweek,* 18 March 1986, p. 60. These ambiguities in public opinion are among the reasons for a lack of zeal in enforcement. See *New York University Obscenity Project,* pp. 816–17, 914.

107. *Technical Reports of the Commission on Obscenity and Pornography,* vol. 6.

108. Herbert McClosky and Alida Brill, *Dimensions of Tolerance: What Americans Believe about Civil Liberties* (Russell Sage Foundation, 1983), pp. 59–63.

109. On the "Great Awakening" theme, see James Q. Wilson, "Reagan and the Republican Revival," *Commentary,* Oct. 1980, p. 25. For a psychological interpretation, see Christopher Lasch, *Culture of Narcissism: American Society at the Breaking Point* (Norton, 1978).

110. On symbolic politics, see my colleague Murray Edelman, *The Symbolic Uses of Politics* (University of Illinois Press, 1964). On the importance of psychological boundaries to personality, see Robert Jay Lifton, *Boundaries: Psychological Man in Revolution* (Touchstone Books, 1969).

111. On Nixon and the rise of conservatism, see Kevin Phillips, *The Emerging Republican Majority* (Arlington House, 1969).

112. Zurcher and Kirkpatrick, *Citizens for Decency,* p. 115.

113. Burnham, *The Crisis in American Politics* (Oxford University Press, 1982), p. 282.

114. Kathleen Jones, "The Eye of the Beholder: Pornographic Discourse and Feminist Criticism." Paper prepared for the annual meeting, American Political Science Association, 1985, p. 13. See also Olga G. Hoyt and Edwin P. Hoyt, *Censorship in America* (Seabury Press, 1970), ch. 3; and Michel Fou-

cault's analysis of the social control of sexuality in *The History of Sexuality*, vol. 1 (Vintage, 1980).

115. See Burstyn, "Political Precedents and Moral Crusades," in *Women against Censorship*, esp. pp. 10–15.

116. Zurcher and Kirkpatrick, *Citizens for Decency*, pp. 114–15.

117. See Alan Crawford, *Thunder on the Right: the "New Right" and the Politics of Resentment* (Pantheon Books, 1980); and my colleague, Robert Booth Fowler, *A New Engagement: Evangelical Political Thought, 1966–1976* (Eerdmans, 1982), esp. ch. 10.

118. See CDL Fact Sheet; Morality in Media Pamphlet, "You Can Stop the Pornography Plague."

119. On Morality in America, see "Our West Point, Mississippi, Porno War," *Washington Post*, 14 July 1985, p. B1: On National Federation for Decency, see *NFD Journal*, April 1985. On National Consultation, see Kirk, *The Mind Polluters* (Thomas Nelson, 1985), pp. 191–93; and packet of materials, *National Consultation on Obscenity, Pornography, and Indecency*, Cincinnati, Sept. 1984.

120. Fort Wayne *CDL Fact Sheet*, 7 July 1983; Jerry R. Kirk, *Mind Polluters*, pp. 182–87; editorial, "Fort Wayne community has applied its standards," *Ft. Wayne News-Sentinel*, 21 March 1984, p. 8A; interview with Ron Hackler, CDL, Indianapolis, June 1985.

121. Kirk, *Mind Polluters*, pp. 187–91. *Final Report*, p. 365.

122. Atlanta is the most successful big city. See *Final Report*, p. 365; Kirk, *Mind Polluters*, pp. 196–97. On Phoenix, see "Outlets That Offer Explicit Sex Tapes Facing Prosecution," *New York Times*, 3 June 1985, p. 1A.

123. See *National Consultation on Obscenity, Pornography, and Indecency Report*, Cincinnati, 1984, p. 126. On the anti-pornography movement in Cincinnati, see Kirk, *Mind Polluters*, esp. ch. 11. Kirk's CCCVC (Citizens Concerned for Community Values in Cincinnati) is considered by conservative activists a model of community action.

124. Ethel Klein, *Gender Politics: From Consciousness to Mass Politics* (Harvard University Press, 1984), p. 31.

125. On the wide-ranging pluralism within the realm of feminism, see Grimshaw, *Philosophy and Feminist Thinking*. For a compilation of writings of feminists who oppose censorship for various reasons (many of whom even agree with the feminist critique of pornography reflected by the anti-pornography ordinance), see Burstyn, ed., *Women against Censorship*.

126. The types of feminism analyzed here are from Allison Jagger, "Political Philosophies of Women's Liberation," in Mary Vetterling-Braggin, Frederick A. Elliston, and Jane English, *Feminism and Philosophy* (Rowman and Littlefield, 1977), pp. 5–21. The statement comparing Leftist feminism to liberal feminism is from Kirp, et. al., *Gender Justice*, p. 47.

127. MacKinnon, *Feminism Unmodified*, p. 60.

128. Lorenne M. G. Clark, "Liberalism and Pornography," in Copp and Wendell, *Pornography and Censorship*, p. 45. See also Jo Freeman, *The Politics of Women's Liberation* (Longman, 1975).

129. June Callwood, "Feminist Debates and Civil Liberties," in *Women against Censorship*, pp. 128–29.

130. See, e.g., Lucinda Finley, "Choice and Freedom: Elusive Issues in the Search for Gender Justice," *Yale Law Journal* 96 (1987): 914. This piece is a very critical review of Kirp, et. al.'s *Gender Justice*, which endorses the liberal model of justice and feminism.

131. MacKinnon, "Pornography, Civil Rights, and Speech," *Harvard Civil Rights–Civil Liberties Law Review* 20 (1984): 4–5. Herbert Marcuse, "Repressive Tolerance," in Robert Paul Wolff, Barrington Moore, and Herbert Marcuse, *A Critique of Pure Tolerance* (Beacon Press, 1969).

132. See Kathleen B. Jones, "The Eye of the Beholder," p. 1.

133. See *University of Pittsburgh Law Review* 40 (1979): 627–50. The article that touches (however briefly) on feminist themes is Tom Gerety, "Pornography and Violence."

134. Simpson, *Pornography and Politics*, pp. 41, 67.

135. See Jo Freeman, *Politics of Womens's Liberation*, ch. 2. See also Burstyn, "Political Precedents and Moral Crusades," pp. 5–6: contemporary feminism is a "second wave" of feminism that is only twenty years old and is more radical than its first wave of the late nineteenth and early twentieth centuries.

136. See Nathan Glazer, *Affirmative Discrimination: Ethnic Inequality and Public Policy*, ch.1; and Kirp, et. al., *Gender Justice*, ch. 1.

137. Burnham, *Crisis in American Politics*, p. 297.

138. On the rift between feminists and traditional women over ERA and abortion, see Luker, *Abortion and the Politics of Motherhood* (University of California Press, 1984), ch. 6. On conflicts between feminist and Black interests in the enforcement of civil rights, see Jeremy Rabkin, "Office for Civil Rights," in *The Politics of Regulation*, ed. James Q. Wilson (Basic Books, 1980), pp. 304–53. On the travails of implementation, see my colleague Richard Champagne, "The Complex Evolution of Civil Rights Policy: 1932–1982," Ph.D. diss., Indiana University, 1986.

139. The term *rootless* is taken from my colleague, Joel B. Grossmann, in "The 'Roots' of 'Rootless Activism,'" *American Bar Foundation Research Journal* (1985), p. 147.

140. Barber, *Pornography and Society*, pp. 11, 14, 15–16. See also, for example, Hyde, *History of Pornography*. Hyde's book was once the leading work on the history of pornography. Like Barber, he depicts the politics of pornography as freedom versus reaction.

141. Barber, *Pornography and Society*, p. 14. Richard Kammen interview, June 1985.

Chapter Two

1. MacKinnon, *Sexual Harassment of Working Women* (Yale University Press, 1979). Although MacKinnon's theory of radical feminism has grown and developed over time, this work established basic premises that still animate her thought: in particular, the theory of systemic gender inequality and domination; the insufficiency of an individualistic, liberal epistemology and policy; and (perhaps paradoxically) the promise of law as a remedial tool. MacKinnon has also published a number of articles (some cited in this book)

and a recent book, *Feminism Unmodified,* consisting largely of her speeches and articles.

2. See, e.g., *Pornography; Intercourse* (Free Press, 1987).

3. Brest and Vandenberg, "Politics, Feminism, and the Constitution: The Anti-Pornography Movement in Minneapolis," *Stanford Law Review* 39 (1987): 613. My interviewees concurred to some extent on Dworkin's charm but many also found her to be intolerant and uncharitable toward dissenting positions. As we will see, she often reviled those who disagreed with her and even made what amounted to libelous statements about people in government. Brest and Vandenberg are sympathetic to the ordinance, and this sympathy may have influenced their portrayals of Dworkin and MacKinnon and their analysis of events. My portrayal, based on comments by participants, is more critical.

4. Kathleen Jones, "The Eye of the Beholder," pp. 6–7. See also Susan Brownmiller, *Against Our Will: Men, Women, and Rape* (Simon and Schuster, 1975). For a powerful Hegelian and Freudian analysis of the inevitability of male objectification of women and aggression, sexual and otherwise, see Jessica Benjamin, "Master and Slave: The Fantasy of Erotic Domination," in *The Powers of Desire,* ed. Ann Snitow (Monthly Review Press, 1983).

5. Dworkin, *Pornography,* p. 16.

6. Hoffman, "Feminism, Pornography, and the Law," p. 511, quoting a pamphlet of Women against Pornography. On the erotica/pornography distinction, see Gloria Steinem, *Outrageous Acts and Everyday Rebellions* (Holt, Rinehart, and Winston 1983), pp. 219–30.

7. Interview with Naomi Scheman, University of Minnesota Philosophy Department, Minneapolis, March 1986. On the pornographic construction of women's subjectivity, see Susanne Kappeler, *The Pornography of Representation* (University of Minnesota Press, 1986); and Kaja Silverman, "Histoire d'O: The Construction of a Female Subject," in *Pleasure and Danger: Exploring Female Sexuality* (Routledge and Kegan, 1984), pp. 320–49, on the role of pornography.

8. Morgan, "Theory and Practice: Pornography and Rape," in *Going Too Far* (Random House 1977), p. 169. "Pornography is the undiluted essence of anti-female propaganda," Susan Brownmiller asserts in her book *Against Our Will: Men, Women, and Rape,* p. 394. See also MacKinnon, *Feminism Unmodified,* ch. 2; Dworking, *Intercourse.*

9. See, e.g., MacKinnon, "Not a Moral Issue," *Yale Law and Policy Review* 2 (1984): 321; *Feminism Unmodified,* ch. 13.

10. On the male-centeredness of individualism as an ideology, see Naomi Scheman, "Individualism and the Objects of Psychology," in *Discovering Reality: Feminist Perspectives on Epistemology, Metaphysics, Methodology, and the Philosophy of Science,* ed. S. Harding and M. Hintikka (Reidel, Dordrecht, 1983); and Grimshaw, *Philosophy and Feminist Thinking,* ch. 6. On individualism and liberty as a false ideology, see MacKinnon, *Feminism Unmodified.*

11. MacKinnon, *Feminism Unmodified,* pp. 5–7. See also MacKinnon, "Feminism, Marxism, Method and the State: Toward Feminist Jurisprudence," *Signs: Journal of Women in Culture and Society* 8 (1983): 635.

12. *Feminism Unmodified,* p. 130.

13. *Feminism Unmodified,* pp. 147, 149, emphasis in original.

14. MacKinnon, Dworkin, et. al. reduce all individual meaning to the alleged broader background social meaning. The individualistic view does the opposite. Sartre confronted the dilemma of reconciling the individual and the social in *Search for a Method,* trans. H. Barnes (Vintage, 1968), which was written to account for his excessively individualistic approach in *Being and Nothingness,* trans. H. Barnes (Washington Square, 1969). The reconciliation is difficult.

15. For instances of MacKinnon's social, power-based theory of language and sexuality, see *Feminism Unmodified,* esp. ch. 3. She explains the connection between Marxism and feminism in "Feminism, Marxism, Method, and the State: An Agenda for Theory," *Signs* 7 (1982): 516–17.

16. From this perspective, heterosexual intercourse is always potentially or actually rape because of the omnipresence of male sexual threat. Thus heterosexual intercourse is presumptively rape unless the woman is the clear initiator. Robin Morgan declares that sex is rape *"when it has not been initiated by a woman, out of her own genuine affection and desire. . . .* Anything short of this is, in a radical feminist definition, rape. Because *the pressure is there* and it need not be a knifeblade against the throat." Morgan, "Theory and Practice: Pornography and Rape," in *Going Too Far,* p. 169, emphasis in original. See also Dworkin, *Intercourse; Pornography,* e.g., pp. 203–4 ("rape is absurd and incomprehensible in a male system"). On the similarities between racism and sexism and pornography, see Dworkin, *Pornography,* ch. 4; MacKinnon, *Feminism Unmodified,* pp. 66–67, 199–200; Naomi Scheman interview.

17. See Linda Lovelace and Michael McGrady, *Ordeal* (Bell Publ. Co., 1980).

18. Justice Brandeis, in *Whitney v. California,* 274 U.S. 357 (1927), at 377.

19. *Feminism Unmodified,* pp. 129–30, 140, 156. For a similar critique of the liberal theory of cause, see Morton Horwitz, "The Doctrine of Objective Causation," in *The Politics of Law,* ed. Kairys (Little, Brown, 1982).

20. See *Final Report,* pp. 309–12. Frederick Schauer, "Causation Theory and the Causes of Sexual Violence," *American Bar Foundation Research Journal* (1987), p. 737. Schauer was a significant member of the commission.

21. Dworkin, "Pornography: The New Terrorism." Speech at the University of Wisconsin, Madison, 13 Oct. 1984.

22. Dworkin, *Pornography,* pp. 200–201, citing Kate Millet, *The Prostitution Papers* (Avon, 1973), p. 95.

23. Cindy Jenefsky, "Breaking the Silence: Andrea Dworkin's Discourse on Pornography," M.A. thesis, University of Wisconsin, Madison, 1985, pp. 41, 58, emphasis in original.

24. Kenneth Burke, *A Grammar of Motives* (University of California Press, 1969), pp. 507–8.

25. Theories that male domination is biologically based create logical

problems for radical feminist theory: if gender differences are based on nature rather training or choice, of what use are political acts? The conflict between biological and political radical views is a recurring tension in feminist thought. See, e.g., Grimshaw, *Philosophy and Feminist Thinking,* ch. 4, for a critical treatment of the biological views of Mary Daly and Dworkin. For an anti-feminist critique of feminism's logically inconsistent treatment of biology and politics, see Michael Levin, *Feminism and Freedom* (Transaction Books, 1987), esp. chs. 2–4.

26. Jenefsky, "Breaking the Vessels," pp. 67–69.

27. See, e.g., Mary Daly's almost Nietzschean theory of transformation and transvaluation of values in *Gyn/Ecology: The Metaethics of Radical Feminism* (Beacon Press, 1978). Dworkin and Daly have much in common, including the desire to establish a new order based on radical feminist values. For a critique of the anti-humanist (including anti-feminist) implications of Daly's and Dworkin's theories in this regard, see Grimshaw, *Philosophy and Feminist Thinking,* ch. 5.

28. Murray Davis, *Smut: Erotic Reality/Obscene Ideology* (University of Chicago Press, 1983), p. 176. For a powerful argument that "modernism" itself has been driven by gnostic impulses (and a critique of modernism in this regard), see Eric Voegelin, *The New Science of Politics* (University of Chicago Press, 1952).

29. Dworkin, *Woman Hating* (Dutton, 1974), pp. 189–92, emphasis added.

30. Proposed Ordinance Sec. 3, to add Minneapolis City Code (MCO) Sec. 139.20 (gg). Indianapolis deleted the broader, vaguer definitions in its version of the ordinance, as we will see in Chapter 4.

31. Margaret Baldwin, "The Sexuality of Inequality: The Minneapolis Pornography Ordinance" *Law and Inequality* 2 (1984): 643.

32. The 1986 commission, for example, declared that class II ("degrading") material comprised the vast majority of material available. *Final Report,* p. 331.

33. See *Smith v. California,* 361 U.S. 147 (1959).

34. Proposed Ord. Sec. 3, to add MCO Sec. 139.40 (m). See MacKinnon, "Pornography and Speech," p. 32: "The first victims of pornography are the ones in it."

35. Baldwin, "The Sexuality of Inequality," p. 644. The ordinance states that "Any person, including transsexual, who is coerced, intimidated, or fraudulently induced (hereafter "coerced") into performing for pornography shall have a cause of action." M.C.O. Title 7, Ch. 139, Sec. 4, subd. (m).

36. Baldwin, "Sexuality of Inequality," p. 644, emphasis in original.

37. Secs. i. iii, viii, x, xi, respectively. These factors normally do provide evidence of non-coercion in traditional criminal law. The ordinance was designed to refashion the law in a feminist direction. Similar efforts, or course, have prevailed in the law of rape and self defense, often with beneficial results for the interests and perspectives of women.

38. "Pornography and Speech," p. 36, emphasis in original.

39. MCO, Title 7, Ch. 139, subd. (o). Such abuses are not common-

place, but they are not unheard of, either. Virtually every fairly large city has had a well-publicized example. See MacKinnon, "Pornography and Speech," pp. 43–50, for many examples of pornography-inspired sexual aggression.

40. See, e.g., *Olivia N. v. National Broadcasting Co.*, 126 Cal. App. 3d 488, cert. denied, 458 U.S. 1108: imitative acts following a violent sex scene in a television program are not grounds for negligence action because of the chilling effect on First Amendment values and because of inconsistency with modern free speech doctrine.

41. Randall D. B. Tigue, "Civil Rights and Censorship—Incompatible Bedfellows," *William Mitchell Law Review* 11 (1985): 104–5. Since the *Sullivan* case in 1964, the Supreme Court has insulated the First Amendment from the normal standards of tort law. The ordinance was intended to reverse this trend.

42. MCO, Title 7, Ch. 139, subd. (n).

43. See MacKinnon, "Pornography and Speech," pp. 38–43; Baldwin, "The Sexuality of Inequality," p. 638. Sexual harrassment laws against the use of pornography in the workplace are also related to this measure; courts have been willing to modify the notion of consent in the context of sexual harassment. See the discussion of this matter in Chapter 5.

44. MCO, Title 7, Ch. 139, subd. (1). Baldwin, ibid., p. 645.

45. To be sure, speech or advocacy is constitutionally restricted in certain contexts. For example, reading from pornography in the workplace could constitute sexual harassment, and job advertising that discriminates sexually is not protected by the First Amendment. But these are special contexts. Women are entitled to work free of sexual pressure and have a privacy right not to be exposed to unwanted expression in areas which they cannot leave readily. And the First Amendment has never protected false advertising, or advertising of illegal action; and it is against the law to discriminate on grounds of sex. See, e.g., Note, "Sexual Harassment Claims of Abusive Work Environment under Title VII," *Harvard Law Review* 97 (1984): 1449.

46. "Pornography and Speech," p. 59. As we have seen, the Supreme Court has not overruled *Beauharnais v. Illinois,* the group libel case. But *Beauharnais* is suspect constitutional law, in light of the modern doctrine of speech. Some advocates of sexual harassment laws endorse a group libel approach to enforcement. See Note, "Sexual Harassment Claims."

47. See Kathleen Jones's critique of the surveillance mentality of many anti-pornography feminists in "The Eye of the Beholder," p. 12.

48. MCO, Ch. 141 (1982), Sec. 141.50(a) and 141.50(d). If no probable cause is found, the complainant may appeal to a review committee, Sec. 141.50(d).

49. MCO, Ch. 141, Sec. 141.50 (h).

50. Sec. 141.50 (k) (7). For example, it may issue punitive damages of from one hundred dollars to six thousand dollars, and reasonable lawyer's fees.

51. MCO, Sec. 141.50 (l) (3).

52. Tigue, "Civil Rights and Censorship," p. 90, fn. 51.

53. See, e.g., *Freedman v. Maryland,* 380 U.S. 51 (1965), expeditious

review is required, with prompt judicial review of action provided for; Tigue, "Civil Rights and Censorship," pp. 115–17.

54. Charlee Hoyt interview.

55. Naomi Scheman interview.

56. For a more detailed analysis of the links between the ordinance and radical feminist theory, see David Bryden, "Between Two Constitutions: Feminism and Pornography," *Constitutional Commentary* 2 (1985): 147.

Chapter Three

1. Interviews with Cathy Forbes, NOW chapter leader in Minneapolis, Aug. 1985; Kathy O'Brien, Minneapolis council member Aug. 1985.

2. Interview with William Prock, Minneapolis Civil Rights Commission, April 1986.

3. Marlys McPherson, "Minneapolis: Crime in a Politically Fragmented Arena," in *Crime in City Politics,* ed. A. Heinz, H. Jacob, and R. Lineberry (Longman, 1983), p. 153.

4. McPherson, "Minneapolis," pp. 155–56.

5. *Minneapolis Tribune,* 12 Dec. 1968. McPherson, "Minneapolis," p. 158.

6. See *State of the City: A Statistical Portrait of Minneapolis* (Minneapolis City Planning Dept., 1983), pp. 3, 12–17, 143 ff.

7. McPherson, "Minneapolis," p. 174.

8. McPherson, p. 174.

9. See "IRS claims Alexander taxes near $9 million," *Minneapolis Star and Tribune,* 30 March 1985, p. 1A.

10. McPherson, "Minneapolis," p. 182. Stenvig represented the moral reaction of the middle and working classes, which Richard Nixon was attempting to integrate into a new Republican majority. See Kevin Phillips, *The Emerging Republican Majority.* On how the politics of law and order that swept the nation during and after the Nixon administration is largely symbolic, based as much on perceptions and fears as on fact, see Stuart Scheingold, *The Politics of Law and Order* (Longman, 1985).

11. The *Minneapolis Star* ran a series of front-page articles entitled "Pornography in Minnesota." The series focused on the Alexanders' power. See "Alexanders woo politicians boldly," 18 Nov. 1975; "Officials fear porn near-monopoly," 17 Nov. 1975; "Alexanders had policemen friends," 19 Nov. 1975.

12. See "Pornography arrests in city may increase after policy change," *Minneapolis Tribune,* 17 Jan. 1976.

13. See, for example, the *Minneapolis Star* series. The Alexanders' lawyer, Randall B. Tigue, refused to be interviewed. The leading porn lawyer in Indianapolis told me that the foremost weapon of pornographers is their willingness to persevere through numerous law suits, demonstrations, and other forms of legal and social harrassment. Richard Kammen interview.

14. See Lisa Duggan, "The Dangers of Coalitions," in "Is One Woman's Sexuality Another Woman's Pornography?" *Ms.,* April 1985, p. 47. I add civil libertarians to Duggan's list, although they are on the other side of the fence.

15. McPherson, "Minneapolis," p. 160.

16. Interview with Liz Anderson, Minneapolis, August 1985. See "Browsing" is the weapon women use to attack neighborhood pornography," *Minneapolis Tribune* 28 July 1979, p. 1B; "City women go 'browsing' but not for clothes," *St. Paul Dispatch,* 9 Aug. 1979, p. 1; "Porn arouses neighborhood passion," *Minneapolis Tribune,* 31 Jan. 1981, p. 2B. The recent *Renton* decision by the U.S. Supreme Court has opened the door to widespread zoning of pornographic establishments to avoid detrimental effects on neighborhood quality of life, and the Court defended this policy on the grounds that such regulatory restrictions were *not* "content based." *City of Renton v. Playtime Theatres, Inc.,* 106 S. Ct. 925 (1986).

17. Liz Anderson interview.

18. Minneapolis Code Title 7, Sec. 590.410. This type of zoning is called dispersal zoning, as it spreads sex establishments out across a city. "Concentration" zoning confines them to a specially designated area.

19. 427 U.S. 50 (1976). On how *Young* cleared the path for the first wave of pornography zoning regulations based on dispersal techniques, see "Judicial Review of Zoning." *Pepperdine Law Review* 12 (1985): 654–55. See also Jevning, "How We Got There: A Short History of Pornography Legislation in Minneapolis," Minneapolis Citizens against Pornography, Summer 1984, p. 3; this group was one of those formed as a direct result of the ordinance.

20. 531 F. Supp. 1162 (D. Minn. 1982). Many courts applied *Young* in this fashion, thereby restricting its scope. Similar *Young*-based dispersal zoning laws were struck down about the same time in Galveston, Texas, and Keego, Michigan. See *Basiardanes v. City of Galveston,* 682 F. 2d 1203 (5th Cir. 1982); *Keego Harbor Co. v. City of Keego Harbor,* 657 F. 2d 94 (6th Cir. 1981). *Renton* was meant to give *Young's* approach more potency.

21. T. McWatters III, "An Attempt to Regulate Pornography through Civil Rights Legislation: Is It Constitutional?" *Toledo Law Review* 16 (1984): 274.

22. Liz Anderson interview. Interview with Naomi Scheman, University of Minnesota, April 1986. Scheman referred to the dramatic background of the speech.

23. Liz Anderson interview.

24. "Protest equates porno, violence," *Minneapolis Star and Tribune,* 29 Aug. 1983, p. 1.

25. Comments by students and MacKinnon were in "UM class finding porn violent and disturbing," *St. Paul Sunday Pioneer Press,* 13 Nov. 1983. Comment on the law school community are from my interview with Professor David Bryden, April 1986. Bryden remarked that he had not seen such humorless "subtle censorship" before in his fifteen years at the law school, except during the conflict over the Vietnam War.

26. "Pornography class led to protest, film star visit," *Minneapolis Star and Tribune,* 10 Dec. 1983, p. 1B; the film star was Linda Marciano, once Linda Lovelace of the general-release porno film, *Deep Throat.* Marciano was a main witness on the ordinance's behalf before the council.

27. Interview with Steve Cramer, Minneapolis City Council, August 1985.

28. Interview with Charlee Hoyt, Minneapolis City Council, August 1985.

29. William Prock interview.

30. Minutes, Minneapolis Zoning and Planning Commission, Dworkin testimony, 18 Oct. 1983. See also Cindy Jenefsky, "Breaking the Silence," p. 14.

31. Minutes, Minneapolis Zoning and Planning Commission; Jenefsky, "Breaking the Silence," pp. 14–15.

32. "Pornography, Civil Rights, and Speech," pp. 11–12.

33. Charlee Hoyt interview. Brest and Vandenberg, "Anti-Pornography Movement," p. 616.

34. Liz Anderson interview, speaker's emphasis.

35. Cathy Forbes interview, speaker's emphasis.

36. Interview with Kathleen Nichols, Dane County Board of Supervisors, June 1986, speaker's emphasis.

37. Kathleen Nichols interview. See also Varda Burstyn, "Political Precedents and Moral Crusades": she finds that the first wave of feminism in the late nineteenth and early twentieth centuries was co-opted by conservative moral crusaders and fears that the same thing could happen again in the politics of pornography and the ordinance.

38. Margaret Baldwin, for example, states that "pornography is an infringement on the civil rights of women, much like, for example, segregation is an infringement on the civil rights of blacks." Baldwin, "Sexuality of Inequality," p. 630.

39. See the discussion of dissenting feminists in Brest and Vandenberg, "Anti-Pornography Movement," esp. pp. 612–13, 629–31, 637–39, 654–56.

40. Brest and Vandenberg, "Anti-Pornography Movement," p. 660. In some respects, the politics surrounding the ordinance constituted what Aristide Zolberg has respectfully called a "moment of madness"—a rare event in which social and human limitations seem temporarily suspended in an overarching social purpose that promises reconciliation of the intractable conflicts of society and human nature. See Zolberg, "Moments of Madness," *Politics and Society*, Winter 1972, pp. 183–207.

41. Ann Snitow, "Retrenchment Versus Transformation: The Politics of the Antipornography Movement," in *Women against Censorship*, ed. Burstyn, p. 113. See also Vicky Randall's portrayal of some elements of radical feminism in *Women and Politics* (St. Martin's, 1982): "the insistence that sex is the fundamental division in society to which all other differences, such as social class or race, are merely secondary. . . . From this analysis follow certain crucial implications for strategy. On one hand, since men are the enemy who will not willingly surrender their power over women, there must be no compromise with them" (p. 5). Randall does not speak of all radical feminists; this section of feminism is also complex and varied.

42. Jenefsky, "Breaking the Silence," p. 15.

43. White's support alienated many black leaders, who considered the   219

ordinance an unnecessary watering down of civil rights law and administrative machinery. Interview with Ron Edwards, president, Minneapolis Urban League, August 1985. White refused an interview.

44. *Minneapolis Star and Tribune,* 13 Dec. 1983, p. 18; *New York Times,* 18 Dec. 1983, p. 44; Jenefsky, "Breaking the Silence," p. 17.

45. Interview with Matthew Stark, executive director, Minnesota Civil Liberties Union, April 1986. See also *Minneapolis Star and Tribune,* 31 Dec. 1983, p. 1; "Last Stand at City Hall," *Twin City Reader,* 4 Jan. 1984, p. 1; and Minneapolis City Council Official Proceedings, 30 Dec. 1983, pp. 1998–99.

46. See William R. Prock, Text of Remarks Delivered to Government Operations Committee, 13 Dec. 1983. Also: Prock interview; interview with David Gross, Minneapolis Assistant City Attorney, August 1985; interview with Mayor Donald Fraser, August 1985.

47. Brest and Vandenberg, "Anti-Pornography Movement," p. 634.

48. Fraser interview; *Minneapolis Star and Tribune,* 6 Jan. 1984, p. 1A; excerpt from veto message, *Star and Tribune,* 6 Jan., p. 10A; *New York Times,* 6 Jan. 1984.

49. *Commission on Party Structure and Delegate Selection, Mandate for Reform* (Democratic National Committee, Wash., D.C., 1970). For descriptions of the commission and its work, including a portrait of Fraser, see Austin Ranney, *Curing the Mischiefs of Faction: Party Reform in America* (University of California Press, 1975); and Byron E. Schafer, *Quiet Revolution: The Struggle for the Democratic Party and the Shaping of Post-Reform Politics* (Russell Sage, 1983). Schafer's book contains extensive sections on Fraser.

50. Fraser interview; David Gross interview; Cathy O'Brien interview. The letter to the council is quoted in Bryden, "Between the Two Constitutions," p. 180. Tribe's liberal approach to obscenity law (which I drew on frequently in Chapter 1) is in *American Constitutional Law,* 1st ed., ch. 12, pp. 656–70.

51. Final Report, City of Minneapolis Task Force on Pornography. See also *Minneapolis Star and Tribune,* 2 May 1984, p. 4B, col. 5. The other council member on the task force refused to be interviewed.

52. Brest and Vandenberg, "Anti-Pornography Movement," p. 647. See also PRC brochure, "Pornography Resource Center: Organizing against Pornography," and *Minnesota Daily,* 16 Feb. 1984, p. 3. The group included neighborhood groups, Twin Cities Women for Take Back the Night, and students from Dworkin and MacKinnon's pornography class.

53. Brest and Vandenberg, "Anti-Pornography Movement," p. 647. The following analysis of the task force's procedures is taken largely from this essay, the *Final Report, City of Minneapolis Task Force on Pornography,* and interviews with William Prock, Steve Cramer, and David Gross.

54. Task Force *Final Report,* pp. 5–6.

55. Task Force *Final Report,* p. 9; Brest and Vandenberg, "Anti-Pornography Movement," p. 650.

56. Task Force *Final Report,* app. v, p. 1, and app. II, p. 2. This approach combined the civil rights enforcement procedures with the substantive limitations of *Miller,* adding a prong to deal with violent pornography; Indi-

anapolis followed a somewhat similar path. See also Brest and Vandenberg, "Anti-Pornography Movement," p. 651.

57. Cramer, Hoyt, and Dworkin, quoted in Brest and Vandenberg, "Anti-Pornography Movement," pp. 651–52. See also Steve Cramer, "Charting a middle course in the porn debate," *Minneapolis Star and Tribune*, 13 June 1984, p. 15A; Steve Cramer interview.

58. Brest and Vandenberg, "Anti-Pornography Movement," pp. 652–53.

59. William Prock interview; Brest and Vandenberg, p. 653.

60. "City Council to Vote on Anti-Porn Law July 13," Minneapolis Citizens against Pornography, Summer 1984. See also McWatters, "Attempt to Regulate Pornography," p. 282 n. 258.

61. Quoted in Brest and Vandenberg, "Anti-Pornography Movement," p. 653. On the importance of such symbols to the construction of political meaning, see my colleague, M. Crawford Young, *The Politics of Cultural Pluralism* (University of Wisconsin Press, 1976), ch. 5, "Symbols, Threats, and Identity."

62. Interview with Matthew Stark, executive director, Minnesota Civil Liberties Union, March 1986.

63. Interview with Tony Scallon, Minneapolis City Council, June 1986. *Minneapolis Star and Tribune*, 14 June 1984, p. 1A.

64. *Minneapolis Star and Tribune*, 28 July 1984, p. 1A; Fraser interview.

65. Minneapolis Resolution Stating Intent to Pass Civil Rights Porn. Ord. upon Review of Judicial Decision. 12 July 1984.

66. Minneapolis Ord. Amending Title 15, Chap. 385 of Minneap. Code of Ords. Relating to Offenses. Miscellaneous. 2 July 1984; upheld in *Upper Midwest Booksellers Assoc. v. City of Minneapolis*, 780 F. 2d 1389 (8th Cir. 1985).

67. Many of those I interviewed made this point. See also McPherson, "Minneapolis; "*Minneapolis Tribune*, 12 Dec. 1968.

68. The action of political leaders in relying on the courts to save them from constitutional irresponsibility is often criticized, yet Laurence Tribe's letter to Mayor Fraser may be construed as advocating just that: the courts, not the local executive, should decide. Tribe could not contemplate a non-judicial official authoritatively interpreting the Constitution. In a brilliant review of Tribe's recent book, *God Save This Honorable Court*, (Random House, 1985), one of my former colleagues condemns its politically and morally impoverished vision of social salvation by courts; see John H. Robinson, "Envisioning the New Court," *Review of Politics* 48 (1986): 463.

69. See the introduction above; Bollinger, *Tolerant Society;* and Meiklejohn, *Political Freedom.*

70. Cardozo, in *Palko v. Connecticut*, 302 U.S. 319 (1937).

71. See, e.g., Zachariah Chafee, Jr., *Free Speech in the United States* (Harvard University Press, 1941).

72. Brest and Vandenberg, "Anti-Pornography Movement," p. 659, emphases in original.

73. See, e.g., Dworkin, *Pornography;* Daly, *Gyn/Ecology.* For less ex-

treme examples of this view, see, e.g., Snitow, "Politics of the Antipornography Movement," p. 112; Mary Field Belenky, et al., *Women's Way of Knowing: The Development of Self, Voice, and Mind* (Basic Books, 1986), esp. intro.

74. This is one of the meanings that Dworkin and MacKinnon gave the hearings. See also Belenky, et. al., *Women's Way of Knowing*, intro. and ch. 1, on how women whose mentality is characterized by silence attempt to overcome this state.

75. Jenefsky, "Breaking the Silence," p. 78. On naming as power, see Dworkin, *Pornography*, pp. 17–18, 166–67.

76. MacKinnon, "Pornography, Civil Rights, and Speech," p. 42; *Feminism Unmodified*, p. 184. Women are also "survivors" in MacKinnon's universe. Eberts is quoted in June Callwood, "Feminist Debates and Civil Liberties," in *Women against Censorship*, ed. Burstyn, p. 122. I discuss these elements of the Skokie affair in *Nazis in Skokie*, esp. chs. 5 and 6.

77. Jean Bethke Elshtain, *Public Man/Private Women: Women in Social and Political Thought* (Princeton University Press, 1981), p. 205. See also Sennett, *Fall of Public Man*. Aristotle and Hannah Arendt also depict democratic politics in terms of trust, equal respect, and reciprocity. Arendt, *The Human Condition* (University of Chicago Press, 1958).

78. Matthew Stark interview.

79. Eric Hoffman, "Feminism, Pornography, and the Law," p. 506.

80. See Zurcher and Kirkpatrick, *Citizens for Decency*, p. 50: "Proporns" construe porn as existing only in the eye of the beholder. Harry Kalven, Jr., "The Metaphysics of the Law of Obscenity," *Supreme Court Review* (1960), p. 1.

81. Snitow, "Politics of the Antipornography Movement," pp. 112–13, 118. Many modern feminists extol agency and tolerance as means by which women can gain public power and contribute to democratic theory. The ordinance politics jeopardized these values.

82. See, e.g., Belenky, et al., *Women's Way of Knowing*. These authors discuss totally disempowered women who are characterized by "silence," but this category is only one among five that entail different degrees of power, knowledge, and confidence. Womens' experience is complex, consisting of more than simply absolute subordination. See also Elshtain, *Public Man/Private Woman*, esp. chs. 5, 6.

83. For a critique of this type of Manichean approach to feminist issues, see Grimshaw, *Philosophy and Feminist Thinking*, esp. ch. 5.

84. David Rubenstein, *City Pages*, "The Porn Law," 4 Jan. 1984.

85. Public Hearings on Ordinances to Add Pornography as Discrimination against Women, session II, p. 48. The 1986 commission also heard such testimony. See, e.g., testimony by "David," reported in Nobile and Nadler, *United State of America vs. Sex: How the Meese Commission Lied about Pornography* (Minotaur Press, 1986), pp. 37–39. For critiques of the therapeutic mentality's impact on public life, see Sennett, *Fall of Public Man;* and Philip Rieff, *The Triumph of the Therapeutic* (Harper, 1966).

86. Brest and Vandenberg, "Anti-Pornography Movement," p. 625.

87. Some writers have proposed that "relationships" and "responsibili-

ties" are more crucial to women than to men. Thus, pornography that leads to impersonal sex that engages merely our animal natures may be more disturbing to women than to men. Michelson points out that pornography disturbs many people precisely because it is essentially about our "animality." *The Aesthetics of Pornography.*

88. Testimony in Public Hearings, Session II, 12 Dec. 1983, pp. 61–64. Many women feel powerless and worthless in such situations, especially if they have not developed a strong sense of self before the problems begin. See Belenky, et al., *Women's Way of Knowing.*

89. Steve Cramer interview.

90. Dworkin, *Woman Hating*, p. 192; MacKinnon, *Feminism Unmodified*, p. 16. For critiques of the utopian strand in some feminist theory, see Elshtain, *Public Man/Private Woman*, ch. 5; Levin, *Feminism and Freedom*, ch. 1.

91. *Minneapolis Star and Tribune*, 31 Dec. 1983, p. 1A.

92. T. Stanton, "Fighting for Our Existence," in *New York Native*, 25 Feb. 1985. A number of interviewees mentioned Stanton's article. Dworkin and MacKinnon also define pornography and women's condition in terms of "terrorism." See MacKinnon, *Feminism Unmodified*, pp. 130, 140, 149–151, 183–38, 203. Dworkin, *Pornography*, pp. 15–17 and, generally, ch. 1.

93. Stanton, "Fighting for Our Existence." Similarly, MacKinnon dismisses non-radical feminists as non-feminists. See *Feminism Unmodified*, ch. 3.

94. "City Called Cynical in Antiporn Approach," *Minneapolis Star and Tribune*, 15 May 1984, p. 1B. See also Citizens against Pornography release, 22 July 1984; and Citizens against Pornography leaflets vilifying council members O'Brien, Carlson, Niemiec, Schulstad, and Rainville for opposing the ordinance. Similar critiques of liberal feminists are noted in Brest and Vandenberg, "Anti-Pornography Movement," pp. 655–56.

95. Interview with Pornography Resource Center staff, Minneapolis, August 1985.

96. Dworkin, *Pornography*. Freud also employed the method of illuminating the normal by unveiling and explaining the extreme or the abnormal (pathological), but he did not reduce the normal to the pathological, and he maintained a sense of irony and perspective.

97. MacKinnon, *Feminism Unmodified*, pp. 5, 15. Dworkin devotes several pages in *Pornography* to analogies between the historical treatment of women and Hitler's treatment of Jews; pp. 110, 139–47. This recalls the rhetoric of Anthony Comstock at the turn of the century; his accounts "revealed a country teetering on the brink of moral collapse. . . . He sometimes implies that the present generation will be the nation's last; that the sins of the fathers will simply annihilate their children." Kendrick, *Secret Museum*, pp. 138–41. Kendrick links the anti-pornography ordinance with Comstockian mentality: see ch. 8, "The Post-Pornographic Era." This link is also made by some feminists. See Kathleen Jones, "Eye of the Beholder," pp. 16, 28: "A discourse permeated by a language of control." See also June Callwood, "Feminist Debates and Civil Liberties," p. 129.

98. "Carlson Recalls Rape but Still Opposes Ord," *Minneapolis Star and Tribune,* 31 Dec. 1983; interview with Barbara Carlson, Minneapolis City Council, August 1985.

99. Barbara Carlson interview, her emphasis. For a critique of over-personalized politics and of the preoccupation of some feminists with victimization, see Jean Elshtain, *Public Man/Private Woman,* ch. 5; and "The Victim Syndrome," *The Progressive,* June 1982. See also Snitow, "Politics of the Antipornography Movement"; and Sennett, *Fall of Public Man.*

100. See Brest and Vandenberg, "Anti-Pornography Movement," p. 642.

101. Interview with Tony Scallon, Minneapolis City Council, May 1986.

102. Van White refused an interview; he is quoted in Brest and Vandenberg, "Anti-Pornography Movement," p. 633.

103. Interview with Walter Dziedzic, Minneapolis City Council, August 1985.

104. "Last Stand at City Hall," *Twin City Reader* 4 Jan 1984, p. 4; Matthew Stark interview, March 1986.

105. Steve Cramer interview; Charlee Hoyt interview; Transcript of Public Hearing.

106. David Bryden interview; also David Gross interview.

107. Kathy O'Brien and Barbara Carlson interviews. Rainville refused an interview.

108. Kathy O'Brien interview.

109. Callwood, "Feminist Debates and Civil Liberties," pp. 128–29.

110. Brest and Vandenberg, "Anti-Pornography Movement," p. 642.

111. Interview with Dennis Schulstadt, Minneapolis city council, May 1986, his emphasis.

112. One newspaper quoted Council President Rainville shouting "Cameras!" to television people during the December vote to ensure that they caught Hoyt's speech before her affirmative vote. David Rubenstein, *City Pages,* 4 Jan. 1984, p. 8. Indeed, the event was exactly the type of dramatic, bipolar conflict that attracts media attention—radical feminists vs. free speech; pornography and sin vs. the general welfare, etc. See Edward J. Epstein, *News from Nowhere: Television and the News* (Vintage, 1973), pp. 173, 241, 262–63. "Disorder" is also newsworthy. See Herbert J. Gans, *Deciding What's News* (Vintage, 1980), pp. 52–57.

113. Matthew Stark interview.

114. Kathy O'Brien interview, speaker's emphasis.

115. Naomi Scheman interview; Chartlee Hoyt interview; MacKinnon, "Pornography, Civil Rights, and Speech," pp. 9–10; Dworkin, *Pornography,* pp. 147–64. On the centrality of the racism analogy to many feminists, see Michael Levin, *Feminism and Freedom,* ch. 2.

116. Interview with Ron Edwards, president, Minneapolis Urban League, August 1985.

117. On disputes in the Office for Civil Rights over enforcement of Title IX governing women's rights as opposed to Titles VI and VII governing black rights, see Jeremy Rabkin, "Office for Civil Rights." See also Jo Freeman, *The*

Politics of Women's Liberation, pp. 40–43, on the inherent political conflicts between black and women's rights, which have black women caught in the crosscurrents.

118. Tim Campbell, quoted in Brest and Vandenberg, "Anti-Pornography Movement," p. 629. See also Campbell's testimony in the Public Hearings on Ordinances to Add Pornography as Discrimination against Women, session II, pp. 26–29. Campbell criticized MacKinnon's and Dworkin's radical premises. See Campbell, "Radical Feminism and the Anti-Porn Ordinance," *Hennepin Law* March-April 1984. In *Pornography,* Dworkin inveighs against male homosexuals for objectifying women as symbols in the same fashion as heterosexual men. See, e.g., p. 128.

119. David Gross interview, his emphasis.

120. Martha Allen, *Minneapolis Star and Tribune,* 2 March 1984, p. 1A. Allen was the leading reporter of the ordinance story in Minneapolis. See also David Bryden interview.

121. William Prock interview, his emphasis.

122. William Prock interview.

123. William Prock interview. Eric Hoffer, *The True Believer* (Harper and Row, 1951). See also Kathy O'Brien interview.

124. William Prock interview; interview with Jim Koplin, Pornography Resource Center, August 1985.

125. Brest and Vandenberg, "Anti-Pornography Movement," p. 621. The transcript of the hearings also reveals that MacKinnon and Dworkin (particularly MacKinnon) set the agenda, introduced speakers, and asked the key questions.

126. Public Hearing, session I, pp. 4–8; Brest and Vandenberg, "Anti-Pornography Movement," p. 621.

127. Brest and Vandenberg, "Anti-Pornography Movement," p. 624, Public Hearings.

128. Rist, "Polity, Politics, and Social Research: A Study in the Relationship of Federal Commissions and Social Science," in *The Pornography Controversy,* p. 248. About 80 percent of the 208 witnesses who testified before the 1986 commission in six cities supported more controls on pornography, and a majority of the commissioners were predisposed to controls. See Nobile and Nadler, *How the Meese Commission Lied,* pp. 27–28; Lynn, "New Developments in Pornography Regulation," pp. 42–48; *Final Report,* (1986), pp. 1845–61. After testimony by Nan Hunter, a leader of the Feminist Anti-Censorship Task Force in Chicago, MacKinnon testified and "the room fell silent. MacKinnon stirred the commissioners like no other witness": Nobile and Nadler, *How the Meese Commission Lied,* p. 61.

129. See MacKinnon, *Feminism Unmodified,* pp. 50–55, 190–91; for a critique of the strategy of turning all questions of knowledge into "social constructions," see Levin, *Feminism and Freedom,* chs. 3, 4.

130. Brest and Vandenberg, "Anti-Pornography Movement," p. 624.

131. Public Hearings, session I, pp. 45–60. Linda Lovelace and Michael McGrady, *Ordeal.*

132. Public Hearings, session II. See also Brest and Vandenberg, "Anti-Pornography Movement," pp. 630–31.

133. Brest and Vandenberg, p. 629, emphasis added.

134. *Wall Street Journal,* 27 Jan. 1984, editorial page.

135. A similar problem arose in the victim testimony before the 1986 commission. See Donald A. Downs, "The Attorney General's Commission and the New Politics of Pornography," *American Bar Foundation Research Journal* (1987), pp. 664–65. On the problems created by the ideology of victimization, see Elshtain, "Victimization Syndrome"; Barry, *Female Sexual Slavery,* pp. 43–49: "victimization . . . denies the woman the integrity of her humanity . . . victimization is an objectification" (p. 45).

136. William Prock interview, his emphases.

137. Matthew Stark interview.

138. Davis Gross interview, his emphasis. Kathy O'Brien characterized Donnerstein's testimony as naive. Other corroborating interviewees: Tony Scallon, Matthew Stark, William Prock, Barbara Carlson, Steve Cramer. See also the description of Donnerstein's testimony and the testimony of other "sex professors" before the 1986 commission in Nobile and Nadler, *How the Meese Commission Lied,* ch. 4: "The professor [Donnerstein] from Wisconsin seemed too content to be some things to all people" (p. 87). This view was shared by virtually all my informants in Minneapolis and Indianapolis as well.

139. Steve Cramer interview.

140. Dennis Schulstadt interview.

141. *Twin City Reader,* 14 Dec. 1983, p. 9.

142. Matthew Stark interview, his emphasis. See also "MCLU Protests City Pornography Tactics," *Minneapolis Star and Tribune,* 9 Feb 1984; "Porn Aftermath: MCLU Cries Foul," *Twin City Reader,* p. 1B. Corroborating interviewees: O'Brien, Carlson, Gross, Prock, Scallon, Schulstadt, Bryden.

143. See "Head of state MCLU asks Fraser to veto pornography law," *Minneapolis Star and Tribune,* 2 Jan. 1984.

144. Mathew Stark interview, his emphasis.

145. Matthew Stark interview. Ron Edwards of the Urban League maintained that this violation was symptomatic of the advocates' lack of concern for the ordinance's potential effect on black rights and other civil liberties. Ron Edwards interview.

146. William Prock interview.

147. Barbara Carlson interview, her emphases. Councilmember Slater died a few months after the issue wound down, before my interviews. See also "Council President Rainville angry at advocates' infiltration of Council Offices," *Twin City Reader,* 14 Dec. 1983, p. 9.

148. Matthew Stark interview. See also Martha S. Allen, "Dworkin, Stark clash again on smut, censorship views," *Minneapolis Tribune,* 20 May 1984, p. 24A: the story noted, "The two found no common ground at all yesterday in a debate, before 150 listeners sponsored by the Progressive Roundtable. The argument was heated."

149. Tony Scallon interview.

150. Steve Cramer interview; Matthew Stark interview. "Support for the old ordinance appears limited to a group of about 150 neighborhood, feminist, and lesbian activists," *Minneapolis Star and Tribune,* 27 May 1984, pp. 1A & 5A.

151. Interview with Cathy Forbes, NOW chapter leader. NOW is a more traditional, less radical women's group. See Freeman, *Politics of Women's Liberation*, ch. 3.

152. M. Berde and C. Berde, in *Minneapolis Star and Tribune*, 24 Dec. 1983, p. 7A.

153. William Prock interview.

154. Steve Cramer interview.

155. Charlee Hoyt interview.

156. Naomi Scheman interview, emphasis added. MacKinnon makes a similar statement about pornography's silencing effects in "Pornography, Civil Rights, and Speech," pp. 63–64. See also Susan Griffin, *Pornography and Silence: Culture's Revenge against Nature* (Harper, 1981).

157. Catharine MacKinnon, quoted in Brest and Vandenberg, "Anti-Pornography Movement," p. 628, emphasis added.

158. Tony Scallon interview.

159. See discussion in the introduction about the importance of political leaders' support for civil liberties.

160. Bryden, "Between the Two Constitutions: Feminism and Pornography." Bryden interview.

161. Like all civil rights law, however, feminist policy in seeking help from government has also contributed to the advance of bureaucracy, an ultimately conservative and self-serving force. See the discussion of this issue in Levin, *Feminism and Freedom*.

162. Ray Rist, on the 1970 commission, in "Polity, Politics and Social Research," in *The Pornography Controversy*, p. 265; Rist also cites Hannah Arendt on the importance of dialogue in public arenas. Frederick Schauer, who played an important role in formulating and recasting the 1986 commission report, also stated that the major intent of the report was to contribute to "public discourse" and "serious discussion and debate." *Final Report*, pp. 177–78, Schauer's personal statement. See also Hanson, *The Democratic Imagination in America*, which presents American history as a set of battles over the meaning of democracy.

163. Grossman, "The First Amendment and the New Anti-Pornography Statutes," *News for Teachers of Political Science*, Spring 1985, p. 19. In Laurence Tribe's scheme, this move pushed the ordinance from track two, in which speech is restricted because of concern about non-communicative consequences, to track one, in which strict scrutiny is needed because the restriction is based on communicative discrimination and concern. *American Constitutional Law*, 1st ed., ch. 12.

164. See, e.g., Tribe, *American Constitutional Law*, 2d ed. pp. 817–20. In the *Renton* zoning decision, for example, the Supreme Court considered motive, saying that "if 'a *motivating factor*' in enacting the ordinance was to restrict respondents' exercise of First Amendment rights the ordinance would be invalid, apparently no matter how small a part this motivating factor may have played in the City Council's decision." 106 S. Ct. 925 (1986), at 929 (quoting 748 F.2d at 537); emphasis in original.

165. See, e.g., Bollinger, *Tolerant Society*; Elshtain, *Public Main/Private Woman*; Sennett, *Fall of Public Man*.

227

166. Matthew Stark interview.

167. Kathleen Nichols interview, her emphases. Nichols also asserted that the tactics employed in Minneapolis would have backfired in Madison, a bulwark of adversary democracy. Dane County Supervisor Stuart Levitan told me the same thing (interview, June 1986), stressing Madison's historic commitment to adversary democracy as a substantive norm.

168. Sennett, *Fall of Public Man,* esp. ch. 13.

169. Steven Marcus' critique of "pornotopia" in *The Other Victorians* (Bantam Books, 1967), ch. 7, is the classic statement of this interpretation. Marcus also stresses the synecdochal structure of pornography. I will develop this logic in Chapter 5.

170. Cambridge Commission on the Status of Women, quoted in Brest and Vandenberg, "Anti-Pornography Movement," p. 659.

171. MacKinnon, *Feminism Unmodified,* p. 15. See also p. 7 and p. 233 n. 24, in which she compares womens' positions to the torture prisons of Latin America, citing Jacobo Timerman's *Prisoner without a Name, Cell without a Number* (Knopf, 1981), and the Amnesty International 1984 report, *Torture in the Eighties.*

172. Snitow, "Politics of the Antipornography Movement," p. 188.

173. See, e.g., Arendt, *The Human Condition;* Elshtain, *Public Man/ Private Woman,* esp. ch. 5. See also Glenn Tinder, *Community: Reflections of a Tragic Ideal* (Louisiana State University Press, 1980), which holds that democratic community requires inquiry, tolerance, and civility. In Mary Daly's gnostic words, however, women who remain within the historical world are reduced to being "fembots" or "mutants" who lack the attributes of authentic being. Mary Daly, *Gyn/Ecology.* See also Grimshaw, *Philosophy and Feminist Thinking,* pp. 124–27, for critiques of this way of thinking.

Chapter Four

1. "Indianapolis Enacts Anti-Pornography Bill: Feminists and Fundamentalists Team Up," *Gay Community News,* 19 May 1984, p. 1. Beulah Coughenour, the leading city-county council advocate of the ordinance in Indianapolis, told me, "They have a different climate up there [Minneapolis] about everything. They are more demonstrative, more active, etc. We don't have that here. . . . the Freeze Movement, the Hunger, whatever. We just don't have the kind of people here that do that. So there wasn't as much politicking about the ordinance as in Minneapolis." Interview with Beulah Coughenour, Indianapolis city-county council, March 1985.

2. Interview with John Sample, executive assistant to the mayor, Indianapolis, June 1985, emphasis added. See also C. James Owen and York Willbern, *Governing Metropolitan Indianapolis: The Politics of Unigov* (University of California Press, 1985), p. 22.

3. *State of the Community: Socio-Economic-Demographic Trends and Their Implications for the Central Indiana/Metropolitan Indianapolis Area* (Community Service Council, 1983), ch. 2. Hereafter called *State of the Community.*

4. Owen and Willbern, *Governing Metropolitan Indianapolis,* pp. 22–

23, quoting Friggens, "Without Federal Aid," *National Civic Review* 52 (1963): 274. The Ku Klux Klan also had influence in city politics until after the Second World War: Owen and Willbern, pp. 25–27, 44, 185. Indiana was a hotbed of Klan activity in the early twentieth century and is the only state to have had a Klansman as governor.

5. Owen and Willbern, pp. 7–8; chs. 7, 8. The Indianapolis Unigov structure, which combines many county and city functions, was modeled on Nashville's version and is the largest of its kind in the northern states. Some believe that schools were excluded because of the fear of desegregation orders that would apply county-wide. This is the view of Sam Jones, president of the Indianapolis Urban League, who was a vocal opponent of the anti-pornography ordinance. Nonetheless, the federal court in Indianapolis did issue a busing order in 1981 pursuant to a longstanding law suit. See "I.P.S. Busing: Breakthrough or Blight?" *Indianapolis Monthly,* August 1981, pp. 40–49. Jones also says that Unigov diluted the black vote—a charge that others have made against this form of government. Black leaders in Indianapolis (including Jones) have nonetheless largely supported Unigov because Republican leadership under it has pushed for civil rights more than previous governments. Some studies have shown that blacks in Indianapolis are less politically alienated than in other large cities; that is, they vote as frequently as other groups. Interview with Sam Jones, June 1985; Owen and Willbern, *Governing Metropolitan Indianapolis,* pp. 180–85. In the late 1970s, *Ebony* magazine named Indianapolis among the top ten cities in the U.S. for blacks: "Cities for Blacks," *Ebony,* February 1978, pp. 95–101.

6. Interview with Donald Miller, majority leader, Indianapolis City-County Council, July 1986.

7. Mark Dall, former Indianapolis City Attorney, now in private practice, March 1985.

8. Unigov also consolidated and integrated executive administrative functions under the mayor, including legal services, and similarly reorganized the legislative branch: "The reorganization of legislative functions had almost as significant an impact on the integration of local political control as it did in strengthening the mayor and the administrative agencies." Owen and Willbern, *Governing Metropolitan Indianapolis,* p. 144, also ch. 8.

9. Sam Jones interview.

10. Hudnut discusses this and other issues in his recent autobiography, *Minister/Mayor,* with Judy Keene (Westminster Press, 1987), pp. 151–58. He also discusses the anti-pornography ordinance issue, pp. 145–49. The U.S. Justice Department claimed that the Supreme Court precluded affirmative action in *Firefighters v. Stotts,* 467 U.S. 561 (1984); when the Supreme Court moved in the other direction in 1986, the Justice Department dropped its case against Indianapolis. See, *Sheet Metal Workers v. EEOC,* 106 S.Ct. 3019 (1986). According to Hudnut, "The Justice Department's action [in bringing suit] fanned the fires of racism in our community" (p. 155).

11. "Star of the Snowbelt, Indianapolis Thrives on Partnership of City, Business, and Philanthropy," *Wall Street Journal,* 14 July 1982, p. 1. See also "A Salute to American Cities: Indianapolis," *Nation's Business* 64 (1976), p. 46.

12. Fundamentalism is a much broader and more complex phenomenon than many observers and critics realize. Indeed, some groups like the Sojourners are conservative in doctrine but not at all in politics. Also, there is a distinction between conservatism and literalism; one can endorse fundamental principles without believing that sources of authority can be interpreted literally. On the complexity of the fundamentalist movement, see my colleague, R. Booth Fowler, *A New Engagement: Evangelical Political Thought.*

13. Hudnut, *Minister/Mayor,* esp. ch. 5, "Religion and Political Campaigning."

14. On crime, see *State of the Community,* ch. 9. Concerning population, Marion County lost 3.6% in the 1970s, whereas the seven contiguous counties had significant gains ranging from 17.9% to 50.4%, except for Shelby County to the southeast, which gained only 5.5%. *State of the Community,* ch. 2.

15. Interview with Larry Carroll, Department of Metropolitan Development, Division of Planning, March 1985; *Adult Entertainment Businesses in Indianapolis: An Analysis* (Indianapolis Dept. of Metropolitan Development, Div. of Planning, 1984), p. 1. The report defined "adult entertainment business" as "an establishment which primarily features sexually stimulating material or performances." Carroll helped develop this report.

16. Interview with the Rev. Greg Dixon, pastor, Baptist Temple, Indianapolis, March 1985. Dixon's ministerial office also recorded a tape made available to the public as part of his library of tapes on religious and social issues, entitled "Why Marion County Needs a New Prosecutor" (Temple Tape Ministry, 1979). See also, for example, "Naked Dancing in City Constitutional? It's 'Nudes' to Prosecutor Goldsmith," *Indianapolis Star,* 2 July 1981.

17. Interview with Richard Kammen, Indianapolis attorney with the firm McClure, McClure, and Kammen, June 1985.

18. "Police Arrest Clerks at Eight Adult Bookstores in Citywide Sweep," *Indianapolis Star,* 12 March 1983, p. 32.

19. See, for example, "Porno Bill, Not Yet Law, Faces Court Challenge," *Indianapolis Star,* 14 April 1983, p. 14.

20. Interview with Sergeant Thomas Rodgers, Indianapolis Police Dept., Vice and Child Abuse Unit, June 1985.

21. Interview with Dr. Philip Nine and Ron Hackler, executive committee, Central Indiana CDL, May 1985; Richard Kammen interview. The two cases were *4447 Corp. v. Goldsmith* (Goldsmith's name on this case is, according to sources, indicative of his desire to associate his name with the anti-pornography movement in Indianapolis) and *Saliba v. Indiana.* This situation illustrates the point made in Chapter 1 about reluctance to prosecute even in a conservative, anti-porn city.

22. Interview with Debbie Daniels, Assistant Marion County Prosecutor, June 1985; Richard Kammen interview. See also "New Effort to Open Porn Stores Quashed," *Indianapolis Star,* 22 Nov. 1983, and "Rackets Law Ruling Asked of High Court," *Indianapolis Star,* 11 May 1984.

23. Richard Kamman interview. See also *NYU Obscenity Project.*

24. *Adult Entertainment.* A previous "special exception" ordinance, which required prior zoning commission approval before an adult business

could be established, had been struck down by a local court on First Amendment grounds: Larry Carroll interview. A 1976 zoning ordinance that went into effect in 1978 prohibited adult entertainment businesses from operating within 500 feet of an area or location zoned for residences, libraries, schools, churches, historical preservation, parks, Market Square, universities, or community centers. A Johnson County judge (the case had a change of venue) declared the law unconstitutional because it "suppresses, censors and otherwise attempts to ban adult businesses from the city regardless (of) whether their stock in trade is protected under the freedoms of speech and of the press, which is tantamount to a prior restraint." See "Adult Bookstore Ordinance Judged Not Constitutional," *Indianapolis Star*, May 1981.

25. "Zoners to Curb Porno?" *Indianapolis News*, 15 May 1984.

26. *Indianapolis News*, 15 May 1984; Larry Carroll interview; City-County General Ordinance No. 44, 1984, MDC Docket #84-AO-4, Adopted 9 July 1984.

27. See, for example, George H. Nash, *The Conservative Intellectual Movement in America/Since 1945* (Basic Books, 1976).

28. Neuhaus, *The Naked Public Square*. Neuhaus interprets the naked public square partly as a religious vacuum. But this vacuum may also simply be a lack of substantive moral or community value, independent of religion.

29. Hoffman, "Feminism, Pornography, and the Law," p. 504.

30. Scruton, *Sexual Desire: A Moral Philosophy of the Erotic* (Free Press, 1986), esp. ch. 11. See also Robert C. Solomon, *The Passions: The Myth and Nature of Human Emotion* (University of Notre Dame Press, 1983), for a somewhat similar analysis of the rational ordering of the passions.

31. Hoffman, "Feminism, Pornography, and the Law," p. 505.

32. Ibid.

33. For representative conservative thought concerning the role of pornography in lessening shame and the importance of shame to a healthy society, see Waltler Berns, "Pornography vs. Democracy: The Case for Censorship," *The Public Interest* 22 (1971):13, which builds on Rousseau's classic treatment of shame in *Politics and the Arts* (ch. 7). For a view that links shame, modesty, and privacy, see Bruce Ritter, "Pornography and Privacy," in *Final Report*, the Attorney General's Commission on Pornography, pp. 115–34.

34. See, e.g., Irving Kristol, "Pornography, Obscenity, and the Case for Censorship," *New York Times Magazine*, 28 March 1971; Ernest van den Haag, "The Case for Censorship and Vice Versa," in *Perspectives on Pornography*, ed. Douglas A. Hughes, (St. Martin's, 1970), pp. 122–31.

35. Hoffman, "Feminism, Pornography, and the Law," p. 506.

36. Devlin, *The Enforcement of Morals* (Oxford University Press, 1965), pp. 9–10; 25.

37. Alan Crawford critiques the New Right from a conservative viewpoint for its lack of restraint in *Thunder on the Right*. He contrasts the conservative right and the "anticonservative right" and calls his last chapter "Rampageous Democracy." The last section of this chapter is headed "The Assault on Form."

38. See, e.g., Edmund Burke, *Reflections on the Revolution in France* (Bobbs-Merrill, 1955).

39. See Stephen L. Newman, *Liberalism at Wit's End: The Libertarian Revolt against the Modern State* (Cornell University Press, 1984). The tension between libertarianism and authority in conservative thought and politics is a major concern of such "neoconservative" thinkers as Irving Kristol: Kristol, *Reflections of a Neoconservative* (Basic Books, 1983).

40. Interview with June Beechler, Thirty-eighth and Shadeland Neighborhood Improvement Association, June 1985, her emphasis. Beechler was also a past president of Indianapolis CDL. Her point about neighborhood deterioration and property value depreciation was supported by the 1984 report, *Adult Entertainment Businesses in Indianapolis,* although that report found that values appreciated more slowly rather than declined. Also, it has been pointed out that in some cases neighborhood decline had set in before sex establishments arrived, the sex business being an effect rather than a cause; Richard Kammen interview.

41. Greg Dixon interview, his emphasis. In his autobiography, Hudnut saw a role for religion in politics but emphasized the need to keep religion in perspective. His views on the secular implications of religion are expressly Niebuhrian. Unlike Dixon, he disavows the role of agent of God. *Minister/Mayor,* pp. 52, 76, 81, 91–95, 101–4, 126, 141.

42. Interviews with Jack Lian, Ron Hackler, and Philip Nine, CDL of Central Indiana, May, June 1985. The use of demonstrations to assert community standards has become a major tactic for conservative groups, religiously based or not. See Jerry Kirk, *The Mind Polluters,* ch. 9, "An Individual Game Plan." Kirk is the leader of the anti-pornography movement in Cincinnati. The Supreme Court's 1987 decision in *Pope v. Illinois* may affect this strategy; see Chapter 1 above.

43. Jack Lian interview.

44. Lian's position on *Playboy* and similar material is echoed by other writers of repute. See, for example, John MacGregor's view that more pervasive sexual imagery is worse than hard-core pornography because it is premised on a view of sex as manipulative and objectified. MacGregor, "The Modern Machiavellians: The Pornography of Game Playing," in Ray C. Rist, *The Pornography Controversy.*

45. Ron Hackler interview, his emphasis. Hackler's line is the *Miller* line.

46. Philip Nine interview. Nine's views concerning pornography and religion are similar to those of Jerry Kirk, the Cincinnati minister and activist. See Kirk, *The Mind Polluters.* See also Rousas J. Rushdoony, *The Politics of Pornography* (Arlington House, 1974), who sees the politics of pornography as a struggle between religion and anti-religious world views. Zurcher and Kirkpatrick also found their "Con-porns" had stronger religious views than "Pro-porns." *Citizens for Decency,* pp. 241, 246, 255.

47. John Sample interview.

48. Hudnut interview. See also *Minister/Mayor,* pp. 145–49.

49. Interview with Sheila Kennedy, Indianapolis lawyer, former city counsel, June 1985. Kennedy stated, "The mayor is a close personal friend; I was part of his administration. He is a civil libertarian, and he really is concerned with the spread of pornography in our society. And somebody said to him, 'Oh, we have this nifty new tool.' And he went 'Oh, good!' After I talked

to him a while, he said 'That's not what I thought that ordinance meant at all.' And I said, 'Those people don't intend that result that you and I see.'" In *Minister/Mayor,* however, Hudnut still described MacKinnon as a "liberal feminist" (p. 147).

50. "Violent Porn Would Violate Indianapolis' Proposed Law," *Louisville Courier-Journal,* 10 April 1984. See also *U.S.A. Today,* 9 April 1984.

51. Interview with Debbie Daniels, Assistant Marion County Prosecutor, June 1985; interview with Mark Dall and Catherine Watson, assistant city attorneys, March 1985.

52. In Zurcher and Kirkpatrick's analysis of anti-porn movements in the 1960s, most of the activists were middle-aged or thereabouts: see *Citizens for Decency.* The anti-pornography ordinance, however, attracted younger as well as older advocates, especially in Minneapolis. The ordinance's roots in activist feminist movements help explain this difference. See Freeman, *The Politics of Women's Liberation,* ch. 2. In Indianapolis government younger women feminists like Daniels and Watson supported the ordinance for feminist reasons.

53. Interview with William Dowden, Indianapolis city-county council, July 1986.

54. Interview with Stephen West, Indianapolis city-county council, July 1986. Council President Beurt SerVaas expressed similar views in a telephone interview, March 1985. SerVaas was a co-sponsor with Beulah Coughenour of the ordinance.

55. Interview with David McGrath, member, Indianapolis city-county council, May 1985; his emphasis.

56. Interview with Beulah Coughenour, member, Indianapolis city-county council, March 1985.

57. Sheila Kennedy interview.

58. Beulah Coughenour interview, her emphasis.

59. Catherine Watson interview; Mark Dall concurred.

60. "Pornography Ordinance Gets Test Monday," *Indianapolis News,* 21 April 1984, p. 17. Charlee Hoyt, John Sample, Stephen West interviews. Hudnut was a former president of the National League of Cities and he saw championing the anti-pornography ordinance as a facet of Indianapolis's willingness to take risks on behalf of its own citizens and other cities. See *Minister/Mayor,* ch. 1: "An entrepreneurial city is willing to take risks" (p. 21); and pp. 145–49 (on the ordinance). Indianapolis was a leading plaintiff, with the National League of Cities, in the famous federalism case of the 1970s in which the Supreme Court ruled that Congress could not stipulate wages for local government employees: *National League of Cities v. Usery,* 426 U.S. 833 (1976).

61. Beulah Coughenour interview.

62. John Sample interview.

63. Beulah Coughenour interview. Many people have pointed out the sometimes stunning effect of some of the material that is available. Even libertarians may be shocked by what they see, and sometimes they change their views. Such exposure can amount to a conversion experience. See, e.g., Zurcher and Kirkpatrick, *Citizens for Decency,* pp. 129–33.

64. See *Indianapolis News,* 7 April 1984, on Coughenour meetings with legal dept. and prosecutor officers. Interview with Debbie Daniels, Assistant Prosecutor, Marion County, May 1985.

65. Mark Dall, Richard Kammen interviews. Early in the affair, according to Coughenour, Goldsmith met and talked with MacKinnon for four hours in San Francisco. Goldsmith discussed this conversation and its implications with Coughenour: Beulah Coughenour interview.

66. Catherine Watson, Mark Dall interviews. Martha S. Allen, "Indianapolis Ponders Minneapolis-type 'Porno' Law," *Minneapolis Star and Tribune,* 3 April 1984, p. 2B.

67. Catherine Watson interview.

68. Mark Dall interview, his emphasis.

69. "Mayor, Prosecutor Back Proposed Porno Law," *Indianapolis News,* 10 April 1984 (Tuesday), p. 1.

70. Beulah Coughenour interview.

71. Mark Dall interview.

72. Interview with John Ryan, Indianapolis City Attorney, August 1987.

73. The 1986 Attorney General's Commission also recommended that words be exempted from coverage. See *Final Report,* pp. 381–85.

74. Indianapolis council members David McGrath, Donald Miller, and Stephen West interviews.

75. Catherine Watson interview, her emphasis.

76. Mark Dall interview.

77. See Allen, "Indianapolis Ponders," *Minneapolis Star and Tribune,* 3 April 1984, p. 2B.

78. *Indianapolis News,* 10 April 1984, p. 1. Coughenour stressed this point with me in our interview, as well. Earlier she had told the press that she did not want to weaken the ordinance with too broad a definition of pornography. "I want to be able to know it when I see it. I can tell you when women are being penetrated by animals, or experiencing pain at being raped—in scenarios of torture. The others I'm not sure." Allen, *Minneapolis Star and Tribune,* 3 April 1984, p. 2B.

79. City-Council General Ordinance No. 24, 1984, amending Code of Indianapolis and Marion County, Chapter 16 (Human Relations and Equal Opportunity), Sec. 16-3, (g) (4)–(7).

80. General Ordinance No. 24, 1984, amending Code Chapter 16, Sec. 16-3, (v) (1)–(5)

81. *Indinapolis News,* 10 April 1984, p.1; interview with Michael Gradison ICLU Executive Director, March 1985.

82. Michael Gradison interview.

83. *Minister/Mayor,* p. 148.

84. Mark Dall, David McGrath interviews.

85. Administration Committee Notes, 16 April 1984, on Proposal No. 228, 1984.

86. "Antiporn Ordinance OK Sought," *Indianapolis News,* 17 April 1984, p.25; Administration Committee Notes, 16 April, p.1.

87. "Tougher Anti-pornography Law Advances," *Louisville Courier-Journal,* 17 April 1984, p.B8.

88. Administration Committee Notes, 16 April 1984, p.1.

89. Ibid, p.2.

90. Ibid.

91. "Antiporn Ordinance OK Sought," *Indianapolis News,* 17 April 1984, p. 25. Daniels also stressed this incident in her interview with me, as did Nine, Hackler, and Beechler of CDL. Interviews with Debbie Daniels, June Beechler, Phillip Nine, and Ron Hackler.

92. Statement of Bill Marsh, 16 April 1984, Indiana Civil Liberties Union printout, pp.1–3. Interview with Bill Marsh, Indiana University at Indianapolis Law School, June 1985. John Wood, "Statement on City-County Council Proposal 228," April 1984, pp. 1–6. Interview with Sam Jones, Indianapolis Urban League, June 1985. *Indianapolis News,* 17 April 1984, p. 17. Shelia Kennedy, "Memorandum to Members of the Administration Committee of City-County Council," 16 April 1984, pp. 1–2. Shelia Kennedy interview.

93. Interviews with Shelia Kennedy, Bill Marsh, Sam Jones, David McGrath.

94. Ron Hackler interview, his emphasis.

95. Administration Committee Notes, 16 April 1984, pp. 5–6.

96. David McGrath interview.

97. "Indianapolis Proposal Links Pornography, Discrimination," *Gary Post,* 17 April 1984, p. B9.

98. Sam Jones interview. Interview with Rozelle Boyd, Indianapolis City-Council Council, May 1985. Like leading blacks in Minneapolis (such as Ron Edwards), Boyd and Jones did not appreciate the civil rights logic of the ordinance, seeing it as feminist activists crowding out black civil rights.

99. "Board Sees Problems with Porno Duties," *Indianapolis News,* 20 April 1984, p. 30. Interview with Martha Bullock, chief officer, Indianapolis Equal Opportunity Advisory Board, June 1985. Bullock also mentioned that this type of oversight is not unheard of in legislative action.

100. "Board Sees Problems with Porno Duties," *Indianapolis News,* 20 April 1984, p. 30.

101. Beulah Coughenour interview.

102. Philip Nine, CDL Chairman, letter to council, 19 April 1984.

103. Beulah Coughenour interview.

104. "Exploitative Pornography," *Indianapolis News* editorial, 18 April 1984, p. 10; "A Step Too Far." Indianapolis Star editorial, 19 April 1984, p. 26. These two newspapers are conservative and are owned by Eugene C. Pulliam, who is considered one of the most influential men in Indiana; he is Vice President Dan Quayle's grandfather. Placating Pulliam was crucial to gaining public support of Unigov, for example. See Owen and Willbern, *Governing Metropolitan Indianapolis,* pp. 66–68. The *News* and the *Star* have supported anti-pornography efforts in the past, but they maintained skepticism toward the ordinance.

105. Interviews with Michael Gradison, Richard Kammen. Dall and

Watson told me that both of them were ambivalent about the product that did emerge—Dall more than Watson. Interviews with Dall and Watson, John Ryan.

106. *Indianapolis News,* 20 April 1984, p. 30

107. Interviews with David McGrath, Michael Gradison.

108. Rozelle Boyd interview, his emphasis.

109. David McGrath interview.

110. Interviews with Stephen West and Donald Miller, Republican Majority Leader. Hudnut, *Minister/Mayor,* p. 147. In *Feminism Unmodified,* MacKinnon devotes many pages to excoriating liberalism. See, e.g., p. 151: "If such gendered concepts are constructs of the male experience, imposed from the male standpoint on society as a whole, liberal morality expresses male supremacist politics."

111. David McGrath interview.

112. Mark Dall, Catherine Watson interviews. On the ordinance playing into the wrong hands, see Burstyn, ed., *Women against Censorship*; Jones, "The Eye of the Beholder."

113. William Marsh interview.

114. In "Panel Hears Debate on Porn," *Indianapolis Star,* 17 April 1984.

115. William Marsh interview. Marsh, who was present at the forum, was privy to his colleague Karlson's decision.

116. Beulah Coughenour interview.

117. Michael Gradison interview. Perhaps this is why NOW consistently refused to deal with my inquiries.

118. Sam Jones interview.

119. Mark Gradison, Beulah Coughenour, Mark Dall interviews. See also Hudnut's critique of ICLU on this issue in *Minister/Mayor,* p. 148.

120. "Pornography Ordinance Gets Test Monday," *Indianapolis News,* 21 April 1984, p. 17. This report included a section, "How They Stand." McGrath was listed as "firm" but, in actuality, he was not. Thus, firm support may have been overstated.

121. "Pornography Ordianance," *Indianapolis News,* 21 April 1984, p. 17. In Zurcher and Kirkpatrick, conservative "Con-porn" activists in "Southtown" also brought busloads of activists to a key anti-porn rally. *Citizens for Decency,* p. 156.

122. Ron Hackler interview.

123. See David McGrath and William Marsh interviews. MacKinnon also later presented as evidence a 10 Jan. 1984 telephone interview she conducted with Donnerstein: Administration Committee, Exhibit P, 4 June 1984; see pp. 8–10, on "normal males."

124. "Sex Films May Make Men More Accepting of Rape," *Indianapolis Star,* 24 April 1984, p. 6, and "Council OKs Pornography Ord.," *Indianapolis Star,* 24 April 1984, p. 1. City-County Council Meeting Notes, 23 April 1984. Coughenour, Miller, West, SerVaas interviews. Donnerstein got separate press treatment. Donnerstein himself felt uneasy about his testimony at Indianapolis and the motives of the council: Donnerstein interview.

125. Interviews with William Marsh (his emphasis), Sheila Kennedy, Sam Jones.

126. David McGrath interview.

127. Greg Dixon interview.

128. "New Porn Law to Gain National Attention," *Indianapolis News,* 24 April 1984, p. 1.

129. "Council OKs Pornography Ordinance," *Indianapolis Star,* 24 April 1984, p. 1.

130. David McGrath interview.

131. Michael Gradison interview, his emphasis. McGrath and Dowden confirmed Gradison's remark about McGrath's statement and position.

132. Mark Dall interview, his emphasis. My own interviews with leading council members confirmed Dall's comments about the lack of knowledge concerning the Ordinance. Among supporters, only McGrath, Dowden, and Coughenour seemed aware of its provisions and the First Amendment implications. The others spoke about it only in the most general terms. On the other side, one Democratic opponent I interviewed could not tell me what was bothersome about the ordinance.

133. William Marsh interview.

134. Jack Lian interview, his emphasis.

135. William Dowden interview.

136. *Indianapolis News,* 24 April 1984, p. 4; *Indianapolis Star,* 24 April 1984, p. 1.

137. Sheila Kennedy interview. Hudnut, *Minister/Mayor,* p. 138. See also Owen and Willbern, *Governing Metropolitan Indianapolis.*

138. Rozelle Boyd interview, his emphasis.

139. Donald Miller interview.

140. David McGrath interview.

141. Alienation from the political and legal order does tend to correlate with intensity in a political campaign. But in Zurcher and Kirkpatrick's study, the opposite was the case, as the more alienated "Con-porns" of "Southtown" engaged in a less hostile and intense campaign than the less aliented "Con-porns" of "Midville." *Citizens for Decency,* pp. 246–48.

142. Hudnut, *Minister/Mayor,* p. 64.

143. Shelia Kennedy interview.

144. See *Minister/Mayor,* p. 126. Hudnut couches this view in Niebuhrian terms. Hudnut interview.

145. Stephen West interview.

146. David McGrath interview.

147. Rozelle Boyd interview, his emphasis.

148. "Now for the Defense," *Indianapolis Star* editorial, 26 April 1984, p. 22, on the need for dispassionate judgement and the problem of a costly court battle; "Equal Opportunity Board Will Hear Porn Complaints," *Indianapolis News,* 25 April 1984, p. 45, on the problems of the OEB's role in enforcement; "Pornography Restriction Gets Mixed Reviews," *Indianapolis News,* 1 May 1984, p. 14, on variety of views among city elites.

149. "Lawsuit Filed Almost Immediately after Mayor Signs Anti-Porn

Law," *Indianapolis Star,* 2 May 1984, p. 1; "Anti-Porn Law Sponsor Welcomes Court Test," *Indianapolis News,* 2 May 1984, p. 17.

150. Whether or not the plaintiffs had standing in the case was an issue that Indianapolis attorneys raised in court and in interviews with me. See *American Booksellers Assoc. v. Hudnut,* U.S. Court of Appeals, 7th Cir. No. 84–3147, *Brief of Defendants-Appellants,* pp. 7–11. Mark Dall, Catherine Watson interviews. The Supreme Court has allowed an expanded doctrine of standing in First Amendment cases: individuals may litigate the rights of third parties if the law is vague or overbroad, even if a properly drawn law could legitimately apply to them. The idea is to prevent overbroad laws from chilling the inclination of third parties to engage in free speech. See Laurence Tribe, *American Constitutional Law,* 1st ed., pp. 711–12. Indianapolis lawyers claimed that the doctrine applied only to individuals whose speech is *not* protected by the First Amendment, who then stand in for third parties; they held that the plaintiffs in *Hudnut* lacked the requisite standing because they engage in expression clearly protected by the First Amendment. Parties to the suit were the Association of American Publishers, Council Periodical Distributors Association, Freedom to Read Foundation, International Periodical Distributors Association Inc., Koch News Co, National Association of College Stores, Inc., Omega Satellite Products Co., Video Shacks, Inc., Kelly Bentley.

151. *Indianapolis Star,* 2 May 1984, p. 1. Brief for Plaintiffs, American Booksellers Assoc. v. Hudnut, United States District Court for the Southern District of Indiana, Indianapolis Division, Cause No. IP 84–791 C.

152 "Censorship Is No One's Civil Right," *New York Times* editorial, 27 May 1984; "Civil Rights Law against Pornography Is Challenged," *New York Times,* 15 May 1984, p. A14.

153. *New York Times,* 15 May 1984, p. A14. John Ryan interview.

154. Mark Dall and Catherine Watson interview.

155. General Ord. No 35, 11 June 1984, amend. to Code of Indianapolis and Marion County, Indiana, Ch. 16 (1975), Sec. 16-1 (a) (2).

156. Beulah Coughenour interview.

157. Ind. Ord. 35, 11 June 1984, amend. to Code, Ch. 16, Sec. 16-3 (q) (6). Most commentary on the Indianapolis ordinance missed this crucial change at this point in the proceedings and treated the amended Sec. 16-3 (1) as if it were the original version. See, for example, Note, Anti-Pornography Laws and First Amendment Values," *Harvard Law Review* 98 (1984): 460, n. 2; Thomas A. McWatters III, "An Attempt to Regulate Pornography through Civil Rights Legislation: Is It Constitutional?" *Toledo Law Review* 16 (1984): 283–86; Marilyn J. Maag, "The Indianapolis Pornography Ordinance: Does the Right to Free Speech Outweigh Pornography's Harm to Women?" *Cincinnati Law Review* 54 (1985): 255–57.

158. Mark Dall, Catherine Watson interviews.

159. Catherine Watson interview, her emphasis. John Ryan reluctantly expressed a similar view.

160. Beulah Coughenour interview. This remark recalls Justice Stewart's remark about obscenity, "I know it when I see it." Of course, what one person knows in this area is not necessarily what another person knows.

161. Mark Dall interview, his emphasis.

162. The literature on cognitive dissonance perhaps may cast some light on this matter. Psychological ambivalence can be resolved by drawing distinctions which rationalize seeming inconsistency. See, for example, Roger Brown, *Social Psychology* (Free Press, 1965).

163. "Indianapolis Ordinance Tests Legal Claim of Discrimination," *Louisville Courier-Journal*, 27 July 1984, p. 1. In talking with me, Coughenour stressed Donnerstein's findings, but she also incorporated feminist arguments about "girlie" magazines: Beulah Coughenour interview. On the ordinance raising the spectre of "two constitutions," see David Bryden, "Between the Two Constitutions."

164. "Committee Amends New Porn Ordinance," *Indianapolis Star*, 5 June 1984, p. 25.

165. "Council Approves Anti-Porn Changes," *Indianapolis Washington Patriot*, 20 June 1984, p. 1.

166. *American Booksellers Ass'n Inc. v. Hudnut*, 598 F. Supp. 1316 (1984), at 1331–7. See also briefs cited in next note.

167. 598 F. Supp. at 1331, note 1. See also Defendants' Memorandum in Opposition to Plaintiff's Motion for Summary Judgment, p. 22.

168. 598 F. Supp. at 1331–2.

169. 458 U.S. 747 (1982).

170. 438 U.S. 726 (1976).

171. 427 U.S. 50 (1976).

172. 598 F. Supp. at 1332–5.

173. 598 F. Supp. at 1335. The notion of sociological or group rights is not entirely novel, however, as it has been the basis of much Fourteenth Amendment adjudication since the Second World War. See Gary McDowell, *Equity and the Constitution: The Supreme Court, Equitable Relief, and Public Policy* (University of Chicago Press, 1982); Horwitz, "The Jurisprudence of Brown"; Fiss, "Groups and the Equal Protection Clause."

174. 598 F. Supp. at 1336, 1337. Interestingly, Cass Sunstein, one promient legal scholar who advocates making "pornography" a new classification of unprotected expression, has also maintained that constitutional judicial review is predicated on protecting the integrity of the legislative process against "naked preferences"—those that are purely self-advantaging rather than public-advantaging. See Sunstein, "Naked Preferences and the Constitution." *Columbia Law Review* 84 (1984). The ordinance violated this principle, according to Barker. The political process that produced the ordinance corroborates this interpretation, and itself supports Barker's view.

175. 598 F. Supp. at 1337-41. Mark Dall and Catherine Watson interview. See also Randall D. B. Tigue, "Civil Rights and Censorship," pp. 88–90.

176. 598 F. Supp. at 1341-2. Barker did find that some of the trafficking and assault procedural requirements passed constitutional muster (under the *Freedman v. Maryland* test, 380 U.S. 51, 1965), but held that these sections were not severable from the more prominent defective parts: 598 F. Supp. at 1341.

177. "Attorneys for Anti-Porn Law Foes Submit Bill for $80,000," *Indianapolis Star*, 20 Feb. 1985.

178. "Officials Optimistic on Porn Ordinance," *Indianapolis News,* 8 June 1985.

179. *American Booksellers Ass'n. Inc. v. Hudnut,* 771 F. 2d 323 (1985), at 327-8.

180. 771F. 2d 323 (1985), at 328.

181. MacKinnon, of course, disagrees on both scores—neutral principles are a fiction (contra the "dominance approach" in *Feminism Unmodified,* and in "Pornography, Civil Rights, and Speech"). For the view that obscenity and pornography do constitute forms of political speech (or speech with political implications), see Richards, "Free Speech and Obscenity Law: Toward a Moral Theory of the First Amendment," *University of Pennsylvania Law Review* 123 (1974):45

182. William Dowden, Donald Miller interviews.

183. *American Booksellers Ass'n Inc. v. Hudnut,* 106 S. Ct. 1172, rehearing denied, -U.S.-, 106 S. Ct. 1664, 90 L. Ed. 2d 206 (1986).

184. William Dowden interview.

185. Donald Miller interview.

186. *American Booksellers Ass'n Inc. v. Hudnut,* 650 F. Supp. 324 (S.D. Ind. 1986).

187. 650 F. Supp. at 630, note 9.

188. William Dowden interview.

189. David McGrath telephone interview, July 1986.

190. Sheila Kennedy interview. In my own critique of the Skokie case, I develop an alternative "fighting words" approach applying direct-harms doctrine; this is consistent with liberal doctrine, although it takes greater account of content. See Downs, *Nazis in Skokie,* chaps. 1 and 8.

191. As Alexander Meiklejohn remarks, in *Political Freedom,* the First Amendment empowers "we, the people" to make the ultimate decisions. Critics charge that this theory posits a false unity in a society ridden with class and gender conflict. The Meiklejohn theory, however, does not deny such conflict but rather argues that a liberal doctrine of speech is essential to an open society that can confront these divisions.

192. 771 F. Supp. at 332–3.

193. This very burden is an important function, as it frustrates the desire to censor and to act without deliberation and restraint. See Bollinger, *Tolerant Society*; Cass Sunstein, "Naked Preferences and the First Amendment."

194. William Dowden interview; also McGrath, Gradison, Kennedy, Marsh, Boyd, and Jones interviews.

195. See Ronald Dworkin's distinction between "concepts" and "conceptions" in *Taking Rights Seriously,* pp. 134–36.

196. See the discussion of these issues in the Introduction.

197. Courts have not always come to the rescue of the First Amendment, as the liberal doctrine of speech has been accepted in only recent decades. Samuel Krislov's study of free speech cases from 1867 to 1958, for example, found that lower federal and state courts often ignored Supreme Court rulings. See Krislov, *The Supreme Court and Political Freedom* (Free Press, 1968).

198. This is a point that Bollinger does not adequately note in his oth-

erwise excellent book, *Tolerant Society.* While his emphasis on the value of restraint on the part of the state and the targets of unsettling speech is valuable, Bollinger undervalues the obligation of speakers to restrain their own passions at least minimally in the name of civility.

Chapter Five

1. Callwood, "Feminist Debates, Civil Liberties," p. 129.

2. See West, "Liberalism Rediscovered."

3. See, e.g., Hanna Pitkin, *The Concept of Representation* (University of California Press, 1972), ch. 9.

4. There has been an interesting reversal in the positions of newspapers and broadcast stations in local markets. Where numbers of newspapers once guaranteed diversity of expression, most cities are now one-paper monopolies, giving their publishers virtual control over what viewpoints will see print; where the limitations of the broadcast spectrum once justified governmental licensing and regulation, broadcasting outlets have now multiplied and the industry is now more competitive than are newspapers. For how social and economic change can alter the equations of power, see, e.g. Ithiel Poole, *Technologies of Freedom* (Harvard University Press, 1985).

5. At the end of his classic "Free Speech and Its Relation to Self-Government," Alexander Meiklejohn says that radio has failed to realize its potential to enrich the process of self-government. Television is even more guilty of such failure. Meiklejohn, *Political Freedom,* pp. 86–89. See also "Trash TV: From the Lurid to the Loud, Anything Goes," *Newsweek,* 14 Nov. 1988, p. 72.

6. See, e.g., Daniel Bell, *The Cultural Contradictions of Capitalism* (Basic Books, 1976); Michael Walzer, *Spheres of Justice: A Defense of Pluralism and Equality* (Basic Books, 1983).

7. Friedman, *Total Justice,* See also Lieberman, *Litigious Society,* on fiduciary and enviromental ethics in the modern liberal state; and Nonet and Selznick, *Law and Society in Transition: Toward Responsive Law* (Harper, 1978), on the movement away from a liberal notion of autonomous law toward responsive law.

8. See David M. Rabban, "The Emergence of Modern First Amendment Doctrine."

9. See, e.g., Callwood, "Feminist Debates and Civil Liberties."

10. See Unger, *Law in Modern Society,* ch. 3.

11. In Gramsci's sense, "cultural hegemony" prevails in any society. Tocqueville understood that cultural hegemony was specially important in democratic societies, as it is all that is left following the decline of traditional authority.

12. Andrea Dworkin, *Woman Hating,* p. 192. Camus, *The Rebel: An Essay on Man in Revolt,* trans. Bowers (Knopf, 1954), is a perceptive comment on the logical and psychological relation between utopianism and nihilism.

13. Bollinger, *Tolerant Society.* Accepting this doctrine does not entail tolerating all applications or exercises of this basic right. There can be dis-

agreement over the outer limits of a right at different levels and in different circumstances. Compare Bollinger to Downs, *Nazis in Skokie.*

14. See, e.g., John Milton's classic defense of free press in *Areopagitica:* "I cannot praise a fugitive and cloistered virtue, unexercised and unbreathed, that never sallies out and sees her adversary, but slinks out of the race where that immortal garland is to be run for, not without dust and heat." In *The Portable Milton,* ed. Douglas Bush (Penguin Books, 1976), p. 167.

15. Meiklejohn, *Political Freedom*; Bollinger, *Tolerant Society.* On how tolerance serves as a medium of self-understanding and dialogue, see also Glenn Tinder, *Tolerance: Toward a New Civility* (University of Massachusetts Press, 1974).

16. On manners and control of impulses and their relation to the responsible exercise of freedom, see Sennett, *Fall of Public Man;* Harvey C. Mansfield, Jr., "The Forms and Formalities of Liberty," *The Public Interest* (1983), p. 121.

17. There are tremendous forces in any organized society to deny dissent and the enthical status of non-conformists. Society is often less moral than individuals. See, e.g., Reinhold Niebuhr, *Moral Man, Immoral Society* (Scribner's, 1932). The same point applies to the state. See Thoreau, "Civil Disobedience," in *Civil Disobedience: Theory and Practice,* ed. H. Bedau (Pegasus, 1969). The sociological theory of the "group" (LaBon, Freud, etc.) is also relevant in this regard. See, e.g., Richard Sennett, ed., *The Psychology of Society* (Vintage, 1977), esp. pt. 1, sec. 2, "Collective Personality."

18. Tocqueville, *Democracy in America,* trans. Henry Reeves (Schocken, 1961), p. 1, esp. chs. 15, 16

19. See, e.g., Naomi Scheman interview; and Naomi Scheman, "Individualism and the Objects of Psychology"; Grimshaw, *Philosophy and Feminist Thinking,* chs. 6, 7.

20. Tigue, "Civil Rights and Censorship," p. 93. See also Joel Grossman, "The First Amendment and the New Anti-Pornography Statutes," p. 19. See also Tribe's distinction between "Track One" and "Track Two" restrictions: *American Constitutional Law,* 2d. ed., ch. 12.

21. 398 U.S. 58 (1970).

22. The equal protection doctrine with its distinction between invidious (purposeful) and non-invidious discrimination is analogous.

23. As we have seen, the Indianapolis ordinance came close to limiting its definition of pornography to these provisions but did not entirely succeed. The first version was largely limited to depictions of sexual violence; parts (ii), (iii), (iv), (vii), and (ix) as listed above were included. Before the court tests, however, the city added another provision that was, essentially, an amalgamation of all the Minneapolis sections originally left out: "Women are presented as sexual objects for domination, conquest, violation, exploitation, possession, or use, or through postures of servility of submission or display." This provision is clearly ideological and could apply to any text that depicted women in any negative fasion.

24. See, e.g., *Meritor Savings Bank v. Vinson,* 477 U.S. 57 (1986), at 63-9. See also Note, "Sexual Harassment Claims"; MacKinnon, *Sexual Harassment of Working Women,* p. 29.

25. See, e.g., *Cohen v. California,* 403 U.S. 15 (1971).

26. See Rabkin, "Office for Civil Rights"; White, "The Evolution of Reasoned Elaboration."

27. See, e.g., Kenneth Culp Davis, *Discretionary Justice: A Preliminary Inquiry* (University of Illinois Press, 1979).

28. Charlee Hoyt, Beulah Coughenour interviews.

29. See, e.g., *New York Times v. Sullivan,* 376 U.S. 376 U.S. 254 (1964). On the Blackstonian basis of early First Amendment understanding—in which free speech is the absence of prior restraints, not the absence of subsequent punishment or related action—see Leonard Levy, *Legacy of Suppression: Freedom of Speech and Press in Early American History* (Harvard University Press, 1960).

30. 380 U.S. 51 (1965); 420 U.S. 546 (1975).

31. Tigue, "Civil Rights and Censorship," pp. 115–16; *Freedman v. Maryland,* 380 U.S. at 58-60; *American Booksellers v. Hudnut,* 598 F. Supp., at 1340.

32. Tigue, "Civil Rights and Censorship," p. 117.

33. 598 F. Supp. at 1341.

34. Ibid.

35. *American Booksellers Ass'n. v. Hudnut,* 598 F. Supp., at 1330, emphasis added.

36. Tigue, "Civil Rights and Censorship," p. 105.

37. *Pinkus v. U.S.,* 436 U.S. 293 (1978). See also *Butler v. Michigan,* 352 U.S. 380 (1957).

38. See, e.g., *Olivia N. v. National Broadcasting Co.,* 126 Cal. App. 3d 488, 178 Cal Rptr. 888 (1981), cert. denied, 458 U.S. 1132: imitative acts following a violent sex scene in a television show (*Born Innocent*) are not a grounds for negligence action because of the chilling effect on First Amendment values and because it would be inconsistent with modern free speech doctrine; *Herceg v. Hustler,* 565 F. Supp. 802 (S.D. Tex. 1983): the decision rejected action for negligence and strict liability for speech claims of plaintiffs in a case involving death due to imitation by plaintiff's son and brother of a *Hustler* article on autoerotic asphyxiation. See also cases and issues discussed in Linz, Turner, Hesse, and Penrod, "Bases of Liability for Injuries Produced by Media Portrayals of Violent Pornography," in Malamuth and Donnerstein, *Pornography and Sexual Aggression,* ch. 11.

39. Schauer, "Causation Theory and the Causes of Sexual Violence."

40. Public libraries funded by city, state, or federal government, and private or public university or college libraries were exempted.

41. Baldwin, "Minneapolis Pornography Ordinance," p. 645.

42. See Nobile and Nadler, *How the Meese Commission Lied about Pornography,* pp. 95–96.

43. Jones, "Eye of the Beholder," p. 12. See also Foucault's analysis of Bentham's surveillance ideology in *Power/Knowledge,* p. 152.

44. See Walkowitz, "Male Vice and Female Virtue: Feminism and the Politics of Prostitution in Nineteenth Century Britain," in *Powers of Desire,* ed. A. Snitow, C. Stansell, and S. Thompson, pp. 419–38. See also Burstyn, "Political Precedents and Moral Crusades."

45. See Haiman, *Speech and Law in a Free Society,* chs. 10, 11.

46. Baldwin, "Minneapolis Pornography Ordinance," p. 644, emphasis added.

47. MCO, Title 7, ch. 139, Sec. 4, subd. (m), (2), i, iii, viii, x, xi.

48. MacKinnon, "Pornography, Civil Rights, and Speech," p. 37.

49. MCO, Title 7, op. cit., subd. (m), (1)

50. On reforms in rape law, see e.g., Tanford and Bocchino, "Rape Victim Shield Laws and the Sixth Amendment," *University of Pennsylvania Law Review* 128 (1980): 544. For treatment of cases involving womens' special vulnerability in instances involving self-defense against men, See ed. S. Kadish, S. Schulhofer, and M. Paulsen, *Criminal Law and Its Processes* (Little, Brown, 1983), pp. 721–50.

51. *Meritor Savings Bank v. Vinson,* 477 U.S. 57 (1986), at 68.

52. MacKinnon, "Pornography, Civil Rights, and Speech," p. 39.

53. *Final Report,* pp. 323–24.

54. See also, e.g., Note, "Anti-Pornography Laws and First Amendment Values."

55. Sunstein, "Pornography and the First Amendment," p. 592.

56. Ibid., pp. 592–93.

57. Ibid, pp. 603–44. See also Note, "Anti-Pornography Laws and First Amendment Values," pp. 469 ff.

58. See, e.g., David A. J. Richards, "Free Speech and Obscenity Law: Toward a Moral Theory of the First Amendment," *University of Pennsylvania Law Review* 123 (1974): 45.

59. Donnerstein, Linz, and Penrod, *The Question of Pornography.* I rely most strongly on this work, as it is the most recent. See also Malamuth and Donnerstein, eds., *Pornography and Sexual Aggression;* Nelson and Yaffe, eds., *The Influence of Pornography on Behavior;* Lynn, "New Restrictions on Pornography."

60. See, e.g., Lynn, "New Restricitions on Pornography"; Nobile and Nadler, *How the Meese Commission Lied about Pornography.*

61. Linz, Donnerstein, and Penrod now acknowledge that harm alone does not justify censorship. See "The Attorney General's Commission on Pornography." See also Schauer, "Causation Theory and the Causes of Sexual Violence."

62. See MacKinnon, "Pornography, Civil Rights, and Speech," pp. 32–38; *Final Report,* pp. 856–69; Sunstein, "Pornography and the First Amendment," pp. 595–97; Note, "Anti-Pornography Law and First Amendment Values;" and, of course, Linda Lovelace, *Ordeal.*

63. See, e.g., *Pittsburgh Press Co. v. Human Relations Comm'n.,* 413 U.S. 376 (1973); *Central Hudson Gas and Electric Corp. v. Public Service Comm.,* 447 U.S. 557 (1980).

64. I thank David Gross, the Minneapolis Assistant City Attorney, for this insight.

65. *Final Report,* p. 310; Sunstein, "Pornography and the First Amendment," p. 595.

66. Donnerstein, et al., *Question of Pornography,* pp. 100–102.

67. Ibid., p. 88, and, generally, ch. 5.

68. Those exposed to violent sex films in one study tended to blame victims for rape more than a control group did. See Linz, Donnerstein, and Penrod, "The Effects of Multiple Exposure to Filmed Violence against Women," *Journal of Communication* 34 (1984): 130.

69. See Donnerstein, et. al, *Question of Pornography,* chs. 5, 6.

70. N.M. Malamuth and J. V. P. Cheek, "The Effects of Mass Media Exposure on Acceptance of Violence against Women: A Field Experiment," *Journal of Research in Personality* 15 (1981): 436.

71. E. Donnerstein, L. Berkowitz, and D. Linz, "Role of Aggressive and Sexual Images in Violent Pornography," manuscript, University of Wisconsin at Madison, 1986. See Linz, Donnerstein, and Penrod, Attorney General's Commission on Pornography," p. 720.

72. Donnerstein, et al., *Question of Pornography,* p. 100.

73. Report of testimony, *Final Report,* pp. 773–80 In my interview with her, even Beulah Coughenour, sponsor of the ordinance in Indianapolis, criticized laws against rape in marriage because of her belief in the autonomy of the family. This position reveals the complexity of conflicting values in this area of social policy.

74. See Larry Baron and Murray A. Strauss, "Sexual Stratification, Pornography, and Rape in the United States," in Malamuth and Donnerstein, *Pornography and Sexual Aggression,* ch. 7; *Final Report;* Sunstein, "Pornography and the First Amendment," p. 599.

75. See Gray, "Exposure to Pornography and Aggression toward Women: The Case of the Angry Male," *Social Problems* 29 (1982): 394. Jessica Benjamin traces the roots of anger to the relation of the infant male to the mother: see "Master and Slave: The Fantasy of Erotic Domination." See also Martin Roth, "Pornography and Society: A Psychiatric View," in Yaffe and Nelson, *The Influence of Pornography on Behavior,* ch 1.

76. Linz, Donnerstein, and Penrod, "The Attorney General's Commission on Pornography," p. 722.

77. See, e.g., Zillman and Bryant, "Effects of Massive Exposure to Pornography," in Malamuth and Donnerstein, *Pornography and Sexual Aggression,* esp. pp. 135–36.

78. Donnerstein, et. al., *Question of Pornography,* p. 99. See N. Malamuth and J. Ceniti, "Repeated Exposure to Violent and Nonviolent Pornography: Likelihood of Raping Ratings and Laboratory Aggression against Women," *Aggressive Behavior* 12 (1986): 129.

79. Lynn, "New Restrictions on Pornography," p. 68.

80. Interview with Dan Linz, Madison, Wis., Sept. 1986.

81. Schauer, "Causation Theory and the Causes of Sexual Violence," pp. 742–45. In addition to discussing "deterministic" notions of causation, Schauer also discusses "attributive" causation, a pragmatic concept which limits the notion of causation to those domains within our practical control (pp. 747–49). Pornography is not causal in this sense, for aggressive sexual images are rampant in our society and the First Amendment closes large areas to attempts at control.

82. Ibid., p. 752. See also *Final Report,* pp. 306–20.

83. See, e.g., Larry Baron and Murray A. Straus, "Sexual Stratification,

Pornography and Rape in the United States," and John H. Court, "Sex and Violence: A Ripple Effect," both in Malamuth and Donnerstein, *Pornography and Sexual Aggression; Final Report,* pp. 939–52.

84. James Q. Wilson points out how it is difficult to control for simultaneous causal factors ("noise") in statistical studies of cause and effect pertaining to crime. See his discussion of the inherent limitations of statistical determinations of the deterrent value of criminal sanctions in *Thinking About Crime,* 2d. ed. (Basic Books, 1983), chs. 7–10.

85. See Hugo Adam Bedau, "A Philosopher's View," in Edwin M. Schur and Hugo Adam Bedau, *Victimless Crimes* (Prentice Hall, 1974); Ronald Dworkin, *Taking Rights Seriously.* These examples concern basic constitutional principles contained in the Bill of Rights. Questions surrounding issues such as the exclusionary rule and the *Miranda* warnings are different, as these involve policy rules designed by the Supreme Court to effectuate the principles contained in the Fourth, Fifth, and Sixth Amendments.

86. See Gubar, "Representing Pornography"; Michelson, *Aesthetics of Pornography,* says that pornorgraphy represents "moral anarchy" which is a "touchstone for a modern imagination disgusted with the blind and mechanical (or electronic) optimism of rich and powerful societies" (p. 18).

87. *Forgive Me—I Have Sinned,* in *Final Report,* pp. 1668–93. The movie was found obscene in *U.S. v. Sovereign News Co., General Video of America, et. al.,* No. CR84–00149-L(A) (W.D. Ky.).

88. Sunstein, "Pornography and the First Amendment," p. 593.

89. See, e.g., Susan Rubin Suleiman's analysis of the relation between pornography and artistic experimentation in "Pornography, Transgression, and the Avant-Garde: Bataille's *Story of the Eye,*" in *The Poetics of Gender,* ed. Nancy K. Miller (New York, 1986), pp. 117–36. This approach is in accord with Susan Sontag's "The Pornographic Imagination." See also Ortega, "The Dehumanization of Art," in *The Dehumanization of Art and Other Essays on Art, Culture, and Literature* (Princeton University Press, 1968).

90. Sabato, *On Heroes and Tombs,* trans. Helen Lane (Godine, 1981).

91. William Gass, "A Case of Sincerity and Obsession," *New Republic,* 23 Sept. 1981, pp. 27–28.

92. Sontag, "The Pornographic Imagination," pp. 152–57. See also Suleiman, "Pornography, Transgression, and the Avant-Garde."

93. George P. Elliot, "Against Pornography, pp. 89–92. Miller, *Tropic of Cancer* (Grove Press, 1961). *Tropic* was the subject of sensational court cases across America: see Charles Rembar, *The End of Obscenity,* pp. 163–211. Rembar was the defense lawyer in the case. The Supreme Court case is *Grove Press v. Gerstein,* 378 U.S. 577.

94. Camus, *The Rebel.*

95. Nietzsche, for example, understood the rage against the tragic basis of reality to be the ultimate form of nihilism. Nietzsche's doctrine of the eternal recurrence of the same is predicated on a primary Nietzchean value: *amor fati.* See, e.g., *Ecce Homo,* trans. Walter Kaufman (Vintage, 1967).

96. I argue here for recognizing the *manifest* artistic content of some violent pornography. As we saw above, there may also be *latent* or secondary

functional effects that resemble art. See the discussions of the remissive value of pornography in Chapter 1 and below of Peckham's *Art and Pornography*.

97. See, e.g., *United States v. One Reel of Film,* 481 F. 2d 206 (1st Cir. 1973): *Deep Throat* was held lacking in serious social value.

98. See Steinem, *Outrageous Acts and Everyday Rebellions.*

99. As I mentioned, Michelson's aesthetic interpretation of pornography is predicated on pornography's representation of animality. Michelson downplays the other side of the dialectic, however. *The Aesthetics of Pornography.* For a sensitive ethological treatment of the links between animality and humanity, see Mary Midgely, *Beast and Man.*

100. Peckham, *Art and Pornography,* pp. 104–20

101. See Scruton, *Sexual Desire;* Hoffman, "Feminism, Pornography, and the Law."

102. Marcus, *The Other Victorians,* ch. 7, "Conclusion: Pornotopia," pp. 270–80. This account comports with those of several conservative theorists discussed in chapter 4. Some feminist theorists also see pornography as a symptom of deep-seated rage against the mother or the natural order. See Benjamin, "Master and Slave: The Fantasy of Erotic Domination"; Griffin, *Pornography and Silence: Culture's Revenge against Nature.*

103. In Freud's analysis of the stages of psycho-sexual development in *Three Essays on the Theory of Sexuality* (Basic Books, 1963), all human sexuality and personality exhibit twists and turns (perversions used as a neutral term), but there is also a psychologically normative goal of genitality which involves sublimation of primitive desire (libido) into love for mature objects. Marcus's book on the culture of psychoanalysis explores the fascinating dialectic of perversion and normality: *Freud and the Culture of Psychoanalysis: Studies in the Transition from Victorian Humanism to Modernity* (George Allen & Unwin, 1984), ch.2.

104. Hence MacKinnon's absolutist reduction of sexuality to its social origins is an act of certitude that is inherently suspect. Leaders of the Pornography Resource Center in Minneapolis made a similar claim in talking with me.

105. For Sartre, such "capturing' or "possessing" is part of a futile quest to deny the contingency and indeterminacy of consciousness and the ravages of time. (Pornography is the target of similar charges, as we will see). Blake commented on a comparable quest; paradoxically, one loses the sense of the eternal by attempting to make it last eternally: "He who binds himself to a joy/Does the winged life destroy;/But he who kisses the joy as it flies/Lives in eternity's sun rise." William Blake, "Eternity," in *Selected Poetry and Prose of Blake,* ed. Northrop Frye (Modern Library, Random House, 1953), p. 63.

106. Scruton, *Sexual Desire,* pp. 120–25. See Sartre, *Being and Nothingness.* For a feminist depiction of *The Story of O* that accords with this understanding, see Kaja Silverman, "*Histoire d 'O:* The Construction of a Female Subject."

107. Marcus, *The Other Victorians,* p. 151–61. This raises a Marxist perspective that sees pornography as a representation of class relations and as

247

a pathological form of compensation for the alienation of desire in capitalism. Marcus does not, however, depict pornography as compensation in this sense. See, e.g., Alan Soble, *Pornography: Marxism, Feminism, and the Future of Sexuality,* esp. ch. 4.

108. Bollinger, *Tolerant Society.*

109. See Steinem, "Erotica vs. Pornography"; Grimshaw, *Philosophy and Feminist Thinking,* pp. 215–26, "On Caring."

110. See Ernest Becker's discussion of fetishism and perversions in *The Denial of Death* (Free Press, 1973), pp. 223, 234–44; and *The Structure of Evil* (Free Press, 1968), pp. 179–85, 245–46. I will discuss how pornography paradoxically can constitute both a denial of and an obsession with death. On how the commoditization of women's body parts is a capitalistic form of sexual consciousness, see Alan Soble, *Pornography,* ch. 4.

111. See Kristol, "Pornography, Obscenity, and the Case for Censorship"; Scruton, *Sexual Desire,* pp. 317–20. Such complete control and domination satisfies an infantile desire to maintain absolute dominion over the mother and the breast (the futile attempt to put eternity into a bottle, qua Blake). The inevitable failure of this quest is said to result in a rage that it is the project of maturation to surmount. Erik Erikson, *Childhood and Society* (Norton, 1963), pp. 78–80, suggests that the "Fall" occurs when the infant loses dominion over the breast at weaning. This loss gives birth to rage, and pornography could be a compensation.

112. Scruton, *Sexual Desire,* p. 140.

113. Ibid., p. 295. Sartre depicts racism in similar terms: it provides an object of hatred which allows the racist to escape the anxiety of uncertainty and self-knowledge. "Portrait of an Antisemite," in *Existentialism from Dostoyevsky to Sartre,* ed. W. Kaufman (New American Library, 1975). Hence, it is no psychological accident that much pornography includes racist depictions and appeals. The ultimate object is the manipulation of the object of desire, at least in fantasy. Of course, this fantasy can also be remissive.

114. Scruton, *Sexual Desire,* pp. 317–19.

115. See Nietzsche, *The Birth of Tragedy,* trans. Francis Golffing (Doubleday, 1956).

116. This is the ideal of psychoanalysis, and it is the goal of the *Three Essays on Sexuality.*

117. Freud's pessimism concerning the ability of civilization to adequately accommodate the conflicting demands of culture and desire is expressed in *Civilization and Its Discontents,* trans. James Strachey (Norton, 1961). Peckham's defense of pornography is based on his understanding of its functional role of providing remissive relief to the inescapable frustrations engendered by any social order: *Art and Pornography.*

118. At one point in his writing, Nietzsche discussed the proper relation between the Apollonian and the Dionysian. A healthy being balances and synthesizes these two forces rather than giving vent to only one. The prevalence of sheer pornography (and pornographic art with intellectual value) could signify the sundering of this balance. Nietzsche surely would have considered pornography decadent and unacceptable, especially because it represents a weak will to power.

119. See, e.g., Freud, *Jokes and Their Relation to the Unconscious,* vol. 8, standard ed. (1960). Herman Hesse, *Steppenwolf,* trans. Basil Creighton (Holt, Rinehart, and Winston, 1963).

120. Interestingly, Marcus applauds precisely this logic in his excellent book on Freud, *Freud and the Culture of Psychoanalysis.* In chapter 2, "Freud's *Three Essays on the Theory of Sexuality,*" Marcus describes how Freud's concept of sexuality turns on the struggle between the normative ideal and the constant threat from the libido. Perversions represent tentative yet precarious resolutions of this struggle, as do neuroses.

121. Psychoanalysis is, of course, also predicated on this form of interplay. It offers a path to internal tolerance and restraint.

122. Augustine, *The Confessions of Saint Augustine,* trans. Rex Warner (New American Library, 1963). See also Nietzsche's Zarathustra: "Everything is ensnared, entangled, enamored." *Thus Spoke Zarathustra,* in *The Portable Nietzsche,* ed. and trans. Kaufman (Viking, 1968).

123. C. G. Jung, "Aion: Phenomenology of the Self"; "The Shadow," in *The Portable Jung,* pp. 139–63. Jung depicts the shadow as a problem but also as a wellspring of creativity. Lev Shestov portrays Dostoyevsky's art in a similar manner. Dostoyevsky's greatest passion emerges in his portrayals of his most demonic characters, who also serve as vehicles for redemption. Les Shestov, *Dostoevsky, Tolstoy and Nietzsche* (Ohio University Press, 1969), ch. 2. In this regard, *The Brothers Karamozov* is the culmination of Dostoyevsky's vision.

124. Scruton, *Sexual Desire,* pp. 146–47. See also Reinhold Niebuhr, *The Nature and Destiny of Man,* vol. 1, *Human Nature* (Scribner's, 1964): he sees human nature as torn between aspirations for transcendence and the inescapably corruptive aspects of the self (and the quest for transcendence is also a source of great evil). On the relation between embodiment and notions of sin and defilement, see Paul Ricour, *The Symbolism of Evil* (Beacon Press, 1967), pt. 1

125. Jose Ortega y Gasset, *Meditations on Hunting,* Howard B. Wescott, trans. (Scribner's, 1985), p. 91. For Ortega's theory comparing love and sexual desire to hunting in certain respects, see *On Love,* trans. T. Talbot (Meridian, 1976).

126. Ortega, *On Hunting,* pp. 94, 97.

127. Marcus, *The Other Victorians,* p. 280. See also Stanley Rosen on language, desire, and nihilism: "Nature furnishes man with desire, but it also furnishes him with speech, or the means of satisfying desire in such a way as to threaten it constantly with extinction. Man is that paradoxical being, unique so far as we know, who strives for a perfection which, if attained would altogether deprive him of his nature"; Rosen, *Nihilism: A Philosophical Essay* (Yale University Press, 1969), p. 214.

128. Hence, true desire can only be consumated by those who are the most successful at living, who have integrated the forces of the self, and achieved a measure of control or restraint over the impulses of the self without smothering their life-enhancing power. See Erik Erikson, *Insight and Responsibility: Lectures on the Ethical Implications of Psychoanalytic Insight* (Norton, 1964), ch. 4.

129. Freud, *Beyond the Pleasure Principle,* trans. J. Strachey (Bantam, 1969).

130. On the social roots of sexuality and language, see MacKinnon, *Feminism Unmodified,* ch. 3, "Desire and Power." For an interesting treatment of the personal, subjective meaning of words—especially those pertaining to sexuality, the body, the soul, and the self, see Milan Kundera's novel, *The Unbearable Lightness of Being,* trans. Michael Henry Heim (Harper & Row, 1985), pt. 3, "Words Misunderstood." On the need to preserve the tension between the communal and the individual and the injustices that occur if either side of this tension is eliminated, see Roberto Unger, *Knowledge and Politics.* See also *Passion: An Essay on Personality* (Free Press, 1984), pp. 53–57, where Unger's analysis of the social "hero" as an embodiment of the dialectic between the socially accepted and the socially transcendent illustrates the point under discussion. Unger maintains that the hero's quest ultimately fails to resolve the incompletion and alienation inherent in personality and social existence. But this does not discredit the hero's efforts; no social agenda can be absolutely successful. The classic sympathetic treatment of the "hero" is Joseph Campbell's *The Hero with a Thousand Faces* (Princeton University Press, 1949). Campbell's psychological approach is similar the approach I take in this chapter.

131. Peckham, *Art and Pornography,* pp. 189–91. See also Ortega, *On Love,* on the lure of the escape from the tensions of consciousness as a retreat from responsibility.

132. Peckham, *Art and Pornography.* p. 216. Peckham calls *The Story of O* "the most remarkably and psychologically subtle of such works, for it is precisely its point that to achieve a perfect will to submission is to achieve a great triumph, as great as the achievement of the perfect will to challenge" (p. 218).

133. *Sexual Desire,* pp. 298, 301. Scruton's argument builds on Hegel's notion of the master-slave relationship. See Hegel, *The Phenomenoloy of Mind,* trans. J. B. Baillie (Harper, 1967), pp. 229–33.

134. See D. Zillman, J. B. Weaver, N. Mundorf, and C. F. Aust, "Effects of an Opposite-Gender Companion's Affect to Horror on Distress, Delight, and Attraction," *Journal of Personality and Social Psychology* 51 (1986): 586, discussed in Linz, Donnerstein, and Penrod, "The Attorney General's Commission on Pornography," pp. 735–36.

135. The nature/nurture conflict regarding sexuality rests on a false dichotomy. Both aspects are involved and so both ethological and sociological perspectives on the structure of desire and sexuality are useful. On the interplay of these factors in human nature, see Mary Midgley, *Beast and Man: The Roots of Human Nature.* Midgley is an open-minded ethologist.

136. See, e.g., Gay Talese, *Thy Neighbor's Wife* (Doubleday, 1980), which confers a religiosity upon sex. See also the conservative critique of pornography as a diabolical substitute for religion in Rousas J. Rushdoony, *Politics of Pornography,* ch. 2, "Pornography as a Religious Expression."

137. On the decline of sublimation and adequate substitute objects of desire in the modern "disenchanted" world, see Geza Roheim's little-noted but

perceptive book, *The Origin and Function of Culture* (Nervous and Mental Monograph no. 69, 1969).

138. See, e.g., *Winters v. New York,* 333 U.S. 507 (1948).

139. Gubar, "Representing Pornography"; Michelson, *Aesthetics of Pornography.*

140. Donnerstein, et al., *Question of Pornography,* p. 111, their emphasis. The study is by Malamuth, Check, and Briere, "Sexual Arousal in Response to Aggression: Ideological, Aggressive, and Sexual Correlates," *Journal of Personality and Social Psychology* 50 (1986): 330.

141. Donnerstein interview. The Malamuth study is the one referred to in n. 140 above.

142. Donnerstein, et. al., *Question of Pornography,* pp. 109–10. See also Malamuth and Check, "Rape Fantasies as a Function of Exposure to Violent Sexual Stimuli," *Archives of Sexual Behavior* 10 (1981): 33.

143. Donnerstein, et. al., *Question of Pornography,* p. 110. See also E. Donnerstein, L. Berkowitz, and D. Linz, *Role of Aggressive and Sexual Images in Violent Pornography.* Unpublished manuscript, University of Wisconsin at Madison, 1986.

144. See, e.g., National Commission on the Causes and Prevention of Violence, *Report* (U.S. Government Printing Office, 1969); Surgeon General's Scientific Advisory Committee on Televison and Social Behavior, "Television and Growing Up: The Impact of Televised Violence" (U.S. Government Printing Office, 1972); National Institute of Mental Health *Report on Television and Violence* (1982).

145. Donnerstein, et al., *Question of Pornography,* pp. 112–23.

146. Ibid., p. 107.

147. Peter Michelson, "The Pleasures of Commodity, or How to Make the World Safe for Pornography," in *Pornography Controversy,* ed. Rist, pp. 140ff., 149. See also Soble, *Pornography,* ch. 4.

148. Activists in Zurcher and Kirkpatrick's cities seemed to be content with largely symbolic victories over porography: *Citizens for Decency,* p. 219. See also Stephen B. Wasby, "Public Law, Politics, and the Local Court: Obscene Literature in Portland," *Journal of Public Law* 14 (1965): 105.

149. See *New York University Obscenity Project.*

150. Donnerstein interview.

151. The recommendations for private action are discussed in the *Final Report,* pt. 2. ch. 8. pp. 419–32.

152. On the superiority of social control mechanisms (including moral consensus) over law as a means of controling crime, see James Q. Wilson, "Crime and American Culture," *The Public Interest* (1982), p. 22.

153. See, e.g., John C. Cleary, "Telephone Pornography: First Amendment Constraints on Shielding Children from Dial-A-Porn," *Harvard Journal on Legislation* 22 (1985): 503, note.

154. The distinction between "assimilationist" and "pluralist" conceptions of law is discussed in Post, "Cultural Heterogeneity and the Law."

155. Schauer, for example, endorses a similar approach to implementation in "Causation Theory and the Causes of Sexual Violence," pp. 769–70.

251

156. 413 U.S., at 25.

157. Schauer, *Law of Obscenity,* pp. 111–12.

158. See, e.g., *Final Report,* pt. 4, ch. 5, "The History of the Regulation of Pornography."

159. For a discussion of the effects on readers' imaginations of sexual romance novels, see Janice A. Radway, *Reading the Romance* (University of North Carolina Press, 1984).

160. *Final Report,* p. 383.

161. Shiffrin, "The First Amendment and Economic Regulation," p. 1283, his emphasis.

162. See Ronald Dworkin, *Taking Rights Seriously* and "Liberalism." See also West, "Liberalism Rediscovered."

163. For example, the Fifth and Fourteenth Amendments provide that liberty can be abridged by due process of law.

164. See Meiklejohn's distinction between the major right of public speech and other, lower-status private liberties in *Political Freedom.* Meiklejohn extends this analysis to speech itself. Speech about public issues and with social value merits high-level First Amendment protection, whereas other forms of speech merit only the lower-level protection of the due process clauses. This approach is consistent with the two-level approach to speech adjudication in *Chaplinsky* as well as with *Miller v. California.* The understanding of what constitutes public speech has, however, expanded in recent decades.

INDEX

Adams, Henry, 51
Adjudication of legislator's motives, 91
Affirmative action and free speech, 5
Alexander family, 53–54
Alexander v. City of Minneapolis, 55
American Booksellers' Association, 131
American Booksellers Ass'n v. Hudnut:
District Court decision, 135–37; initiated, 131; U.S. Court of Appeals decision, 137–39. *See also* Barker, Judge Sara Evans; Easterbrook, Judge Frank; Indianapolis anti-pornography ordinance
American Civil Liberties Union, xvii–xviii. *See also* Indiana Civil Liberties Union; Minnesota Civil Liberties Union
An American Tragedy, 12. See also *Commonwealth v. Friede*
Anderson, Liz, 54, 55
Anti-pornography ordinances: administrative procedures, 156–57; "assault" provision, 157–58; basic content and background, xi-xii; civil emphasis as censorship, 156; "coercion" provision, 160–61; conflation of speech and action, 159; deviations from obscenity standards, 155; disregard for artistic value, 172; disrespect for intellectual freedom or value, xxi, 155; "forcing" provision, 161; lack of perspective, 149–50; new political alliances, xiii;

opposition to individual responsibility, 5, 46, 158–59; play into conservative hands, 148; as pragmatic or progressive liberalism, 8; as substantive equality, 7; "trafficking" provision, 158–60; as violation of modern doctrine of speech, 152–62. *See also* Indianapolis anti-pornography ordinance; Minneapolis anti-pornography ordinance; New anti-pornography movement
Anti-viewpoint discrimination principle, xvi, 7, 153–54. *See also* Content neutrality doctrine; Modern doctrine of speech
Arendt, Hannah, 228n. 173
Areopagitica, xxii, 144, 242n. 14. *See also* Milton, John
Attorney General's Commission on Pornography (1986): basic conclusions, 1–2; concept of multiple causation, 41, 170–71; differences from 1970 Commission on Obscenity and Pornography, 1–2; format of hearings compared to Minneapolis, 82; lack of imagination, 173; on the nature of violent pornography, 162–63; policy on the printed word, 196; synthesis of new anti-pornography viewpoints, 2
Augustine, Saint, 182
Autonomous law, 147

261

263

DATE DUE

MAY 05 2011			
GAYLORD			PRINTED IN U.S.A.

Political science/Law

Fresh empirical evidence of pornography's negative effects and the resurgence of feminist and conservative critiques have caused local, state, and federal officials to reassess the pornography issue. In *The New Politics of Pornography*, Donald Alexander Downs explores the contemporary antipornography movement and addresses difficult questions about the limits of free speech. Drawing on official transcripts and extensive interviews, Downs recreates and analyzes landmark cases in Minneapolis and Indianapolis. He argues persuasively that both conservative and liberal camps are often characterized by extreme intolerance which hampers open policy debate and may ultimately threaten our modern doctrine of free speech. Downs concludes with a balanced and nuanced discussion of what First Amendment protections pornography should be afforded. This provocative and interdisciplinary work will interest students of political science, women's studies, civil liberties, and constitutional law.

"The feminist critique of pornography poses a profound challenge to the traditional theory of free expression. . . . Downs offers an original, thorough, and insightful analysis of this challenge and places the issue in historical, political, and theoretical perspective."
—Geoffrey R. Stone, Dean, University of Chicago Law School

"The hallmarks of this careful study are reason, empathy, and moderation. It is a welcome antidote to the blinkered ideologies that have dominated discussions of pornography. Downs gives both sides of the pornography debate a fair hearing, while patiently exposing the weaknesses of absolutist positions. This is the voice of a true scholar."
—David P. Bryden, Co-editor, *Constitutional Commentary*

"The pornography controversy is turning white-hot, and systematic study is much needed. . . . The empirical research underlying *The New Politics of Pornography* is original, timely, and valuable."
—Robert C. Post, University of California at Berkeley

DONALD ALEXANDER DOWNS is associate professor of political science at the University of Wisconsin at Madison. He is the author of *Nazis in Skokie: Freedom, Community, and the First Amendment*.

THE UNIVERSITY OF CHICAGO

ISBN 0-226-16163-